Volume Eleven

American Tribal Religions

a monograph series,
published by the
University of Nebraska Press

Karl W. Luckert, General Editor

Department of Religious Studies
Southwest Missouri State University

American Tribal Religions

Published in Collaboration with Lufa-type
and the Museum of Northern Arizona

MAASAW: PROFILE OF A HOPI GOD

Ekkehart Malotki
Michael Lomatuway'ma

Drawings by
Petra Roeckerath

University of Nebraska Press

Lincoln and London

The paper in this book meets the minimum requirements of
American National Standard of Information Sciences —
Permanence of Paper for Printed Library Materials, ANSI
z39.48 – 1984

Library of Congress Cataloging-in-Publication Data
Malotki, Ekkehart.
  Maasaw : profile of a Hopi god.
  (American tribal religions ; v. 11)
  1. Hopi Indians — Religion and mythology. 2. Indians of
North America — Arizona — Religion and mythology.
I. Lomatuway'ma, Michael. II. Title. III. Series.
E99.H7M344 1987   299'.78   87 – 163
ISBN 0-8032-3118-0 (alk. paper)
ISBN 0-8032-8148-X (pbk. : alk. paper)

Contents

Preface and Acknowledgments

for "American Tribal Religions"
Volumes Ten and Eleven

Maasaw is probably the most intriguing and multifaceted divine personage in Hopi mythology. As an omnipresent deity who embraces the whole spectrum of Hopi reality, from anthropogeny to apocalypse, he has left a deep imprint on the Hopi psyche. His pervasiveness is reflected in the multitude of folk beliefs associated with him as a god, as well as in the numerous tales in which he acts as the protagonist. The present volumes, *Stories of Maasaw — a Hopi God* and *Maasaw — Profile of a Hopi God,* though comprehensive in scope, can capture only part of the vast amount of lore that surrounds this god in Hopi oral tradition and religion.

While *Stories of Maasaw — a Hopi God* (Volume 10 in the American Tribal Religions [ATR] series) presents the god as a story character, the sequel, *Maasaw — Profile of a Hopi God* (ATR 11) rounds out the deity's image with ethnographic commentary. All of the Hopi stories and texts, with the exception of Stories 11 and 12, are published here for the first time. (The exceptions cited were published earlier in *Gullible Coyote/Una'ihu* and *Hopitutuwutsi/Hopi Tales.*) A special feature of these volumes is their bilingual presentation, on one hand to help preserve the Hopi language for posterity and to ensure, on the other hand, a maximum of cultural authenticity for the printed message. Nevertheless, a number of English passages had to be included to fill some of the gaps in the larger literary Maasaw mosaic.

All of the narratives, and the majority of texts, were collected by me in the field. During 1984 and 1985 this work was made possible with support from the Organized Research Committee at Northern Arizona University. I acknowledge this help with deep appreciation.

Michael Lomatuway'ma, my long-time Hopi consultant and co-worker, has greatly helped in the transcribing, translating, and editing of the recorded materials. He formulated many of the entries in the Glossary, and he told Stories 1, 9, and 11. For all his valuable contributions he is named, deservedly, as co-author of the two Maasaw volumes.

Stories 7, 14, and 16 were remembered by his wife Lorena. Her late brother, Sidney Namingha Junior, who was endowed just like his sister with a phenomenal memory, told stories 3, 6, 13, and 15. Story 4 was recorded from Franklin Suhu, and Story 12 from Herschel Talashoma. While all of the aforementioned narrators were affiliated with the Third Mesa village of Hotvela, the four remaining stories are of Second Mesa provenience. Thus, numbers 5 and 8 were given to me by the late Leslie Koyawena of Supawlavi. Stories 2 and 10 were shared by a man from Songoopavi who wishes to remain unnamed. To each and all of the above I am deeply indebted, not only for having given me permission to record their tales on tape, but also for endorsing my intention to commit them to print.

I am equally grateful to the many Hopi consultants who have volunteered their recollections concerning the traditions of Maasaw. In this regard I must mention once again the late Sidney Namingha Junior, an initiate of the Kwan society, for his highly reliable information. The same recognition applies to his sister Lorena and his mother Rebecca who always have shared their knowledge with great enthusiasm. Valuable insights also have come from the late Percy Lomaquahu who was affiliated with the Al society. I also thank Emory Sekaquaptewa, my Hopi colleague at the University of Arizona. All the remaining contributors, among them a member of the nearly extinct Maasaw clan, have preferred to remain anonymous. Their reason for requesting anonymity has generally been attributed to the sensitive nature of all matters related to Maasaw and the sphere of death.

Text materials that were collected outside the Third Mesa villages were adjusted phonologically to the standardized writing system used throughout these volumes. This system is based on the Hopi majority dialect that is spoken in the Third Mesa area. All Hopi words in passages quoted from the secondary literature, including village names, were adjusted to conform to the same standards of orthography.

Petra Roeckerath—"Meisterschüler" of a German academy of arts, and holding a M.Ed. in American Indian Education—has created the black and white illustrations. These reflect her fine empathy for indigenous cultures and Indian art styles of the Southwest. Her artistic talent has added much to both Maasaw volumes. I am forever grateful to her for her contributions. I also thank Henry Hooper, Associate Vice President for Academic Affairs, Research, and Graduate Studies—at NAU—for subsidising the illustrations for these volumes.

My colleague, Anna-Marie Aldaz, made some fine stylistic observations concerning *Maasaw—Profile of a Hopi God*. My friend Ken "Puhuyamtiwa" Gary, from San Diego, greatly improved the readability of the narratives in English, as well as the ethnographic passages. The staff of the NAU Ralph M. Bilby Research Center, under Evelyn Wong's supervision, eased the enormous task of typing and retyping the manuscript at various stages.

Paula Gussio, media specialist at NAU's "University News and Publications," helped develop and print my photographs. Dorothy House, Don Weaver, and Elaine Hughes from the Museum of Northern Arizona, as well as Mary Graham from the Heard Museum, were instrumental in the acquisition of additional photographs. Peter "Yaahanma" Pilles, a man with a keen archaeological eye, found the physical evidence which confirmed that, indeed, I had rediscovered Maasaw's cave in the Salt Canyon. Jerry "Masihonaw" West provided an "aerial high" which I will never forget—I thank him for having returned me safely to the realm of those who still walk on the surface of the earth. To each of the above goes a warm word of appreciation.

Finally, my special thanks go to Karl W. Luckert. His rounds of critical comments were truly helpful in putting my writings in a more balanced perspective. I am most grateful to him for incorporating my findings on Maasaw in his American Tribal Religions monograph series. His daughter Heidi, who did a great job typesetting the bilingual work, also deserves a big thank you.

A few portions of the Glossary appeared first in *Hopi Coyote Tales/ Istutuwutsi* and *Gullible Coyote/Una'ihu*. I thank both the University of Nebraska Press and the University of Arizona Press for permission to reprint these passages. The same applies to the essay on the Hopi Alphabet which originally was published in *Hopi Coyote Tales/Istutuwutsi*.

Ekkehart Malotki

MAASAW: PROFILE OF A HOPI GOD

Naat itam it qataymataq qatuuqat maasawuy
tutavoyat hapi ang hinwisa.

We still go by the instructions of Maasaw,
who lives unseen.

Maasaw and the Realm of Death

In the entire pantheon of Hopi mythological figures none is more important than the god Maasaw. His complexity and wealth of associations within the Hopi scheme of the world is immense. Moreover, no other deity has undergone such drastic changes as Maasaw. Although he apparently began his career in Hopi history at a rather low level as a trickster and prankster, still traceable in a few surviving stories, his phenomenal rise to the status of a near-monotheistic divinity is well documented. While regarded as the god of death and ruler of the underworld, he is also believed to be the aboriginal proprietor of the earth, the owner of fire and crops, and the maker of all things animal and vegetal.

Furthermore, he is venerated as the giver and caretaker of life, the defender of Hopi ways, and as a powerful war deity. In his actions, he can be benevolent as well as malevolent, and in his appearance he may horrify as a monstrous bogeyman or appeal in the shape of a handsome youth. Endowed also with the makings of a culture hero, the god has, in recent times, gained apocalyptic stature by being revered as a savior or destroyer of humankind on the last day of this world. Today, the god is regarded as either Satan or Great Spirit within Hopi society.

The subject matter of this first chapter divides naturally into two sections. After a thorough exploration of the semantic scope of the name "Maasaw," the god himself can be introduced as a mythological figure whose primary focus rests in his lively relationship with the realm of death.[1]

"MAASAW" IN HOPI SEMANTICS

The Hopi word *maasaw* represents something like an "animate conceptualization of death." Its basic meaning is thus best rendered as "dead person." In this sense the word can be used, for example, in such sentences as *maasawuy aw yori* "he looked at a dead person," or *maasawuy hakim tumaltote'* "when people tend to a dead person." The word can not be employed, however, to convey the meaning "dead body." This notion would be translated by *mokpu*,[2] a derived nominal from the verb *mooki* "to die." On the basis of the animate ingredient inherent in *maasaw*, the term may also be rendered "death spirit." Thus, while Cushing's choice "corpse demon" (1923:165) can still be regarded as a somewhat justifiable rendition of the word on the grounds that "demon"

---

[1] In light of the enormous range of ideas linked with the god, an etymological analysis of the god's name should reveal some clues to its semantic kernel. Linguistically, the word *maasaw* is an animate nominal. In utterance-final situations the noun may attach the strong and weak pausal suffixes -'u or -u typically available to this noun class, hence *maasaw'u* or *maasawu*. The nominal can be dualized and pluralized. With *maasaw-t* "two Maasaws" as dual form, the plural is attested in two shapes, *ma-msa-m* and *maa-mas-t*. Both show the feature of reduplication which, in conjunction with the animate plural markers -m or -t, brings about the meaning "more than two Maasaws." The respective singular, dual, and plural objective case forms are *maasawuy*, *maasawtuy*, and *mamsamuy* or *maamastuy*.

[2] The plural form of *mokpu* is *so'pum*, derived from *so'a*, the suppletive plural of the verb *mooki* "to die." With the animate plural marker -m, *so'pum* translates as "dead ones" but never takes on the meaning of "death spirits."

has a strong animate association, "skeleton," Voth's preference for the term in most of his writings, (1905a:12, 13, 18), is a mistranslation. The Hopi word for "skeleton" is *maslakvu*. Signifying literally something like "dried up dead person," it can also denote "mummified corpse."

The interpretation of *maasaw* as a "death spirit" is manifest in a variety of sources. Many of the narratives compiled in the preceding companion volume, "American Tribal Religions" Volume Ten (ATR 10), demonstrate the term with this meaning. As a death spirit a *maasaw* can enjoy all of the kin relationships that typically occur in Hopi society. Conceived as *mamsam* or *maamast*, the plural form of *maasaw*, the "living dead" are believed to visit their respective home villages during the night of *Astotokya*. [3]

Additional confirmation for this meaning of *maasaw* comes from the Hopi custom of drawing four parallel cornmeal lines between the village and a new grave to prevent the "deceased person" from returning to the living. This practice, which is termed *maasawuy uuta* "to close out the death spirit," is mistakenly interpreted by Stephen as "closing the door against Maasaw" (1936:824). The above saying has nothing to do with the god.

Further proof for *maasaw* to denote "death spirit" can be gleaned from an ancient warrior initiation rite. To qualify as a *pas qaleetaqa* or "real warrior," (literally "a very courageous strongman"), a Hopi man formerly had to kill and scalp an enemy. The actual trophy, according to Titiev's sources, was referred to by the scalp taker as *ti'at* "his son." Toward the end of his initiation into the warrior society of the *momtsit*, the neophyte was taken to a shrine from which he had to circle the village. In the course of this circuit the candidate was expected to look over his shoulder four times to see if "his son," that is, his victim, was coming after him in the form of a spirit. "If the slayer was lucky, no Maasaw would follow" (1944:159-60). Thus, again we find the word *maasaw* used in the sense of a "living death spirit."

According to one recorded tradition, possibly tinted by Christianity, Maasaw as god of death is actually supposed to have been merely an ordinary *maasaw* at one point in his career. Or he is a spirit of the dead who, somehow, came to life again and in this way got his name. Apparently, the god was punished for some transgression and hurled into the *koysö*, the "fiery ground pit," reserved for all the wicked in the Hopi

[3]For additional information on Astotokya and the visit of the dead see Chapter 12.

nether world. He survived the ordeal and returned to the upper world (Yava 1978:107).[4]

The interpretation of Maasaw's genesis, as an ordinary death spirit, is not shared by Waters. According to his sources the god already had an important role in the underworld. He "had been appointed head care-taker of the Third World, but, becoming a little self-important, he had lost his humility before the Creator. Being a spirit, he could not die, so Tay'owa took his appointment away from him and made him the deity of death and the underworld. Then when the Third World was destroyed, Tay'owa decided to give him another chance, as he had the people, and appointed him to guard and protect this Fourth World as its caretaker" (1963:21).

When used as a proper name, Maasaw signifies "death personage" or simply "death." In keeping with his ceremonial status Maasaw can, therefore, be termed the "god of death." Maasaw as "personified death" is consequently not applicable to the concept of "biological death." This notion is once again derived from the verb *mooki* "to die." Featuring the nominalizing suffix -*w*(*u*), the form *mokiw*(*u*) is exemplified in the following sentence:

TEXT 1

Qá hak as yep mokiwuy aw suu-   Nobody wishes to die (literally, is
taq'ewniqw itam pangsoqsa hoyta.   willing to accept death) although
                                      that is our destiny.

Morphologically, the word *maasaw* can be "decomposed" into the root *maas*- "dead" and the nominalizer -*w*, whose underlying form is -*wu*, as is evident from the pausal suffixes mentioned above. In attaching the nominalizer, the linking vowel *a* is inserted to facilitate pronunciation. Compound lexemes, involving the constituent *maasaw*, are relatively rare. When they occur as the second element of a compound, the long stem vowel is retained. Examples are *loma*-, *nukus*-, and *wuko-maasaw* (good, evil, and big Maasaw), and the neologism *pahan-maasaw* "White man's Maasaw," which stands for the Anglo concept of

---

[4] A recollection from one of Courlander's Third Mesa informants corroborates this mythological fate of Maasaw: "Maasaw had already been thrown out by some spirit, like Satan in the Bible, thrown out and burned up. But he had a strong spirit or power. He was thrown into a place where stuff was burned, but he survived" (1982:100).

"devil." With the exception of the derived forms *maasawniwti* "to become
a death spirit" and *maasawuy'taqa* "one [tale] which deals with the god
Maasaw or a death spirit," instances featuring *maasaw* as initial or
intermediary element typically shorten the long root vowel. Thus,
masaw-katsina designates "the kachina embodying the essence of Maasaw
as the god of death." *Masaw-süki* "Maasaw farted at him" is attributed
to the breaking of a taboo and implies for the target person "to get a cold
sore." The reduplicated compound verbs *ma-masaw-u* and *ma-masaw-
lawu* refer to the ceremonial practice of "impersonating the god."

All other compound forms incorporating the semantic notions
inherent in the term *maasaw* display the root *maas-* in its vowel-shortened
shape *mas-*. This morphophonemic observation rules out any etymological connection with the color term *maasi* "gray." The latter consistently draws on the compound base *masi-*, for instance, *masi-lelwi* "to
paint it gray," *masi-lelent* "members of the Gray Flute society," *masi-
tsu'a* "gray rattlesnake," etc. Whether Hopi *mas-* is related in any way to
the reconstructed Uto-Aztecan proto element **mas-*, denoting "deer," is
not clear at this point. The examples listed by Miller are exclusively
attested in southern Uto-Aztecan languages: *máaso* in Mayo and Yaqui,
masat in Aztec, *mwasá* in Cora, and *máza* in Huichol (1967:28).

Compounds with the modifier stem *mas-* may be grouped on the
basis of the semantic value most prominent in them. Many of them
center around the content "dead person," primarily in conjunction
with Hopi burial rites. *Mas-himu* is a "thing belonging to the dead."[5]
Mas-saqa is "the grave ladder" which permits the spirit of the deceased
person to emerge from the grave on the fourth day following the interment. *Mas-nakwayto* refers to the custom of "taking food to the dead at
the grave site" on the third day of this four day span. After handling a
corpse, purification from contagion with death is necessary. *Mas-
navahoma* alludes to this cleansing rite of "bathing oneself in juniper
smoke." The bowl used for this purpose is called *mas-navahompi*. *Mas-
vakna* means "to affect someone's basket weaving materials with atrophy." The highly specific verb is generally used by a basket weaver who
is concerned that the dyes might not stick to her weaving materials. This
is thought to happen if a person who recently had contact with a dead
person, for example in conjunction with a funeral, should approach the
weaver in the course of the crucial dyeing process. For this reason the
woman will normally carry out this task in a secluded area. *Maski* is the

---

[5]Compare Glossary in "American Tribal Religions," Volume 10 (ATR 10), under
"Things Belonging to the Dead." All subsequent references to "Glossary" refer to that
same volume.

"home of the dead" in the underworld. *Mas-yahanta* means "to be digging up the dead" and has not been coined in reference to white archaeologists. According to the Hopi, both dogs and *popwaqt* "sorcerers," engage in this practice. The expression *mas-huyiy'ta* "he has sold a corpse" may have originated in the days when the Hopi first saw mummies displayed in museums. The term is used when one is envious of or has no clue to another person's sudden gain of profit. *Mas-qötö* denotes a "skull," *mas-tama* a "tooth from a dead person," and *mas-'öqa* are "bones of the dead."[6] *Mas-tsöqya* are the "brains of a dead person," offered as food in a story dealing with witchcraft. The stative verb *mas-vekyewta* is said of "a body which is in the state of putrefaction." *Mas-lakvu*, as was already stated above, denotes "skeleton" or "mummy." The imperfective verb *mas-kukta* implies "the state when a limb is asleep or dead," that is, "without sensation." Perfective *mas-kuyti* refers to the onset of this feeling.

A second group of examples with the modifier *mas-* points directly to Maasaw, the god of death. *Mas-wikkatsintawi*, for example, is "a song chanted by the kachinas who fetch Maasaw" during the Nevenwehekiw ritual. *Mas-ki*, in addition to "home of the dead," is also "the shrine belonging to Maasaw." *Mas-wungwa* is "a member of the Maasaw clan." The corresponding plural form is *mas-ngyam*. The *mas-wimi* or "Maasaw society" consists of all former ceremonial impersonators of the god, who in turn are referred to as *mas-wiwimkyam* or "Maasaw initiates."[7] *Mas-kwakwant* is a slightly derogatory label for the "members of the Kwan society who consider Maasaw as their spiritual father." For this reason also the *kwankiva* or "kiva of the Kwan society" is frequently called *mas-kiva*, "Maasaw's kiva." *Mas-vaklawu* or *mas-vakmumuya* are both verbs denoting "to cry like Maasaw." *Mas-o'okiw* means "being poor like Maasaw."[8] Perfective *mas-'asi* or imperfective *mas-'a'asi* are verbs which occur in a taboo warning against washing one's hair at night because one would "wash one's hair with Maasaw or the dead."[9] The plural verb *mas-hintsatskya*, "they are doing something related to Maasaw," alludes to the performing of a ceremony pertaining to the god. *Mas-hinta* means "to be afflicted with a disease caused by Maasaw," for example

---

[6]Compare the Glossary under "Maasaw Initiates."

[7]Compare the Glossary under "Maasaw Initiates."

[8]Compare the Glossary under "Poor as Maasaw."

[9]Compare the Glossary under "Washing One's Hair with the Dead."

mas-lakiwta when "one's body is withered like that of a dead person."[10]
Mas-tuwutsi is a story featuring the real Maasaw or other spirits of the
dead as protagonists.[11] *Mas-mana,* "dead girl," in this context, usually
implies a "demon girl."[12] *Mas-yuwsina* refers to "the dressing of the
impersonator in the guise of the god." It may also imply that a particular
part of a costume or a garment "is put on in a fashion opposite from the
proper Hopi way." *Mas-torikiwta,* in this sense, directly points at "having
something slung over the wrong shoulder, such as the left shoulder
instead of the right, like Maasaw." *Mas-'uwiwita* is "the flickering fire of
Maasaw," stemming from the god's torch and seen occasionally at night.
Causative *mas-huruutapna,* "he made him stop dead in his tracks,"
designates the petrifying effect Maasaw has on a mortal when he con-
fronts him. *Mas-huruuti,* an intransitive verb, refers to "a night-mare
triggered specifically by an embrace from Maasaw or other dead spirit."
In addition, this state can be triggered in a situation in which a person
becomes extremely frightened. In *mas-hohomtima,* "going along with the
feeling that a dead spirit-creature is behind one," the Maasaw reference
is no longer as overriding as in the ones cited above. The same is true
for *mas-kyelemtinuma,* "to go about guarding something at night,
accompanied by a spirit."

The semantic motivation for using *mas-* in connection with the
botanical terms *mas-kiisi,* "mushroom" (literally, death-shade/um-
brella), and *mas-tutsaya,* "death-yucca sifter," a flower identified as
Melacothrix sonchoides by Voth (no date)[13] is not clear to Hopi informants. *Mas-totovi,* a fly for which I can offer no English name, is
described by Titiev as "a greenish blue bottlefly which lays its eggs in
dead animals or decaying matter of some sort." In addition, the fly is
sometimes "linked to witches and other creatures of evil. It is often
thought that their arrival may portend the coming of such calamities as
the death of relatives" (1972:217-18). In its non-reduplicated form,
mas-totovi is part of the kachina name *mas-topkatsina.* Again, I can
supply no clue as to its connection with death. The verb *mas-vuhikna,*
finally, is used in the sense of "to make a mistake." Specifically, it denotes

[10]For additional information on the diseases attributed to Maasaw see Chapter 8.

[11]Such a story is also referred to as *maasawuy'taqa* "one which has a Maasaw or
death spirit." The respective plural form for this concept is *maasawuy'yungqa.*

[12]For a story featuring a *masmana* or "demon girl" see Malotki (1978: 137-49).

[13]The English term of this spring annual is Yellow Saucer (Arthur Phillips: Personal
communication 1985).

the situation when a person delivering a speech "does not know what to say next." The latter meaning may somehow relate to the effect of "speechlessness" which Maasaw produces in a person when he reveals himself to him. The derived noun *mas-vuhikni*, correspondingly, implies "mistake."

Personal names with the element *mas-* are unattested — only the full form Maasaw and the diminutive Masaw-hoya "Little Maasaw" occur in the onomastic domain. There exists, however, a host of topographical appellations incorporating the morpheme. Without repeating the gloss for *mas-* "Maasaw/death" in the subsequent examples in each case, *Mas-tukwi* refers to "a butte," *Mas-tanga* to "a hole in the ground," *Mas-tupatsa* to "an upper story," conceived of as a small mesa-like feature sitting on top of another mesa, *Mas-tupqa* to "a canyon" or "gulch," *mas-tsomo* to "a hill," *Mas-tuwi* to "a ledge," *Mas-tuyqa* to "an outside corner" or "something jutting out like a promontory," *mas-tuupela* to "a cliff," *Mas-vösö* to "an inside corner," *mas-voksö* to "a hole in the wall," *Mas-qantupha*, generally used in its abbreviated form *Qantupha*, to "a flat area." The place name *Mas-qötö* "head of Maasaw/skull," also attested as *Mas-qötnamuri* "ridge of skulls," refers to a location where Awat'ovi captives were slaughtered by the Hopi after the destruction of their village. *Maasaw* itself, in its full shape, designates a place in the vicinity of Munqapi. *Wuko-maasaw* "big Maasaw" occurs as a location name near Orayvi.

Both meanings of *maasaw*, that of "spirit/god of death" and that of "dead person/death spirit," are amply documented in the Hopi folk texts presented in this book as well as in the literature. The demarcation line between the two meanings is not always easy to draw. For this reason the term *maasaw* will be left untranslated throughout this work. In a number of my narratives the Maasaw portrayed has, at first, all the makings of a death spirit, only to be tinged with the characteristics of the real god later on. In Story 14 (ATR 10), for instance, a Maasaw youth is initially portrayed as just one individual dead person among the many *maamast* or "dead" who reside at Mastanga. Toward the end of the story, however, after completing his courtship successfully, the youth assumes the traditional guardianship of the land, one of the roles performed only by the real god.

With the semantic evidence here presented, it has become obvious that the essence of Maasaw is contained in his connection with death.

MAASAW AS GOD AND MYTHIC FIGURE

As god of death Maasaw is generally feared by the Hopi. Titiev reports of a sick man who, after hearing someone trying the knob of the entrance door, "was very badly frightened, as he suspected that it might be Maasaw, coming to fetch him to the land of the dead" (1972:269). Catching sight of the god is believed to spell death for the beholder himself or for one of his relatives, as is attested by Talayesva: "As we passed Maasaw's shrine, the Warrior warned me not to look back, for I might see the terrible god of Death on our trail, a sign that I or one of my relatives would die shortly" (1942:245). Maasaw is also the master of death and has charge of the underworld. He "represents death, for he controls the fate of the deserted spirit in Maski, the underworld" (Nequatewa 1936:126). The following statement also confirms this belief.

TEXT 2

Pay pi antsa pangqaqwangwuniqw pam maasaw pi pay mokpu. Niiqe oovi pay pi itaanavotiniqw pam so'pumuy himuy'taqe oovi pam son pumuy amuupa qa tunatyawnumngwu. Qa hak pumuy yuuyuynaniqw oovi pam tuwat pang tuutu'amit ang mihikqw waynumngwu. Pu' hiituwat tu'amqölpa hom'o'oytinumyaqw paasat pam pay ephaqam piw pumuy amumum angningwuqat pay kitotangwu.

It is commonly held that Maasaw represents a demised being. Thus it is Hopi belief that he is in charge of the dead, and for this reason he goes about them in a watchful manner. So that no one will molest the dead, he makes nightly visits among the graveyards. Some members of religious societies go about these burial sites depositing prayer feathers along with sacred cornmeal, and Hopi knowledge states that on some of these occasions the god goes along accompanying them.

In one segment of an emergence myth, which I was able to record, Maasaw defines his own role as god of death as follows:

TEXT 3

"Antsa nu' it tuuwaqatsit himuy'-kyangw pu' nu' piw it qatsit aw tunatyawtay. Pu' mokqa atkyami ikiy aw sinotimantaniqat put nu' pep piw aw tunatyawtay," yaw pam put aw kita. "Nu' hapi qa himu nukpana. Niikyangw nu' it mo-kiwuy piw himuy'taqw oovi himuwa qa hiita akw hinkyangw mookye' inumimantaniy. Inuminiqw pu' nu' put paas tavikyangw pu' nu' yangqw put kivaytsiwat aw wiikye' pu' nu' pangso atkyami piw sukwat qatsit aw put tavimantaniy. Yan hapi nu' yaapiy umuy yep tumalay'-taniy," yaw pam kita.

"I truly own this place and also take care of life. Furthermore, I make sure that whoever dies comes to reside in my home down below," Maasaw revealed. "I'm no evil being, however. I'm simply the keeper of death. This means that anyone who dies with a pure heart will come to me. As soon as he does, I'll welcome him and take him to the opening of a kiva from where I send him down to the underworld to another life. Hence-forth I'll tend to you in this man-ner," he explained.

As the following prayer indicates, Maasaw is actually implored by the Hopi to lead the soul safely to its home in the netherworld. The god is asked to act in the role of a psychopomp.

TEXT 4

Pay himuwa naamahin mokq hakim pay put piw maasawuy aw engem naanawaknangwu. "Ta'ay, um itana maasaw'uy. I' yep antsa itamuy maatavi. Um put haqami itam maskimiq sasqayaqw pangsoq-haqami um put paas wiikiy'mani." Yanhaqam itam put maasawuy aw naanawaknat pu' hakim put tavi-yangwu.

Even though a person has passed away, a prayer is still spoken to Maasaw in behalf of the deceased. "Now, our father Maasaw, this one has really left us. Lead him with care to the land of death in the underworld where we travel after our demise." After some such prayer to Maasaw the dead person is laid to rest.

There are sporadic indications that Maasaw is actually believed to have introduced death to this world. Cushing, in his emergence version, tells of a homely girl who was jealous of another, more attractive girl. So, out of jealousy, "(with the aid of Corpse Demon) she caused her death.

Now this was the first death" (1923:166). In another emergence episode, which credits Maasaw with the creation of daylight, the god himself suggested the introduction of death as a means of guaranteeing the rotation of the sun.

TEXT 5

"Antsa'ay," yaw kita. "Itam hapi su'an yukuy," yaw kita. "Oovi nu' uumi pangqawni: I' hapi ura sinot hiikyay'tani. I' sinot hapi wihuyat akw uwiwitaqe oovi pam a'ni mukiitikyangw pu' pam piw a'ni talniy'tay. Yaniqw oovi yaapiy son himuwa hapi qa mokmantani... Pu' pam himuwa pante' pam hapi pay inumi sinotimantani. Pu' pam tuwat yep inumum qa talpuva hinnummantanikyangw pam pi pay umungem put taawat warikniy'tamantani. Oovi pay himuwa pantiqw pay uma qa pas hin aw wuuwantotamantaniy."

"Well," Maasaw continued, "we were successful in our undertakings. So let me explain the following to you now: keeping the sun going will be possible only at the expense of human life. Only by flaming with human grease can the sun burn with such heat that it will produce enough light. For this reason people will have to die from now on... At the time of his death the deceased person then becomes one of my people and joins me roaming about in darkness while he keeps the sun going. So don't be troubled when someone passes away." This is what Maasaw revealed to the people's leader.

Surprisingly enough, Hopi folklore does not provide a great deal of insight into Maasaw's role in the underworld, nor are Hopi informants very familiar with this aspect of the god. Stephen mentions the grave as Maasaw's house and entrance to the world below. "Maasaw has a two-story house.... The graveyard is Maasaw's kiva.... The surface we see is the roof of the second story, we will not see the interior until we die.... The grave is the entrance to Maski, the dead go to the lower stage or story where the houses are as those we live in" (1936:150-51).

Talayesva, in his autobiography, recalls a dream in which he journeyed to Maski, the "home of the dead," and actually encountered the god (1942:126). The dream, as it turns out, is based in many of its essential details on the numerous folk stories which draw on the motif of a living person traveling to the underworld to explore it, and returning again to the world of the living. An episode similar to the one related by Talayesva also occurs in one of the Maski narratives collected by me:

TEXT 6

Paasat pu' yaw oovi puma pangqw oomiq ahoy pisoq'iwma. Yaw oovi puma aqw haykyalaqw yaw himu amungk suqlalayku. Pu' yaw pam ahoy yori. Noq angqw yaw amungk himu warikiwta. Pay yaw as taa-qa'eway, wupakukuy'ta yaw himu. Pu' yaw suqömhokyay'ta, pu' yaw ungwqötöy'ta. Pu' yaw hiita piw puuyawta. Pay yaw himu sakwa-pösaala'eway. Pu' yaw piw hitta yawkyangw, son pi qa maawikiy. Yaw pumuy sungwkiy'ma.

Pu' yaw puma oomiq pituqw pu' yaw kwaaniy'taqa put aw pang-qawu, "Pam hapi maasaw pangqw itamungk wupto. Pam hapi ung ngu'e' ung ahoy wikni. Paasat pu' um son ahoy uutokoy aqw pituni. Um oovi kyaktaytini. Yupay," aw yaw kita.

Thereupon they hastened to retreat to the top. As they neared their destination, something came behind them producing a clacking noise. Now the youth looked over his shoulder and spotted a creature loping along. It appeared to be a man with enormous feet. His legs were dark-hued and his head was covered with blood. There was also something floating behind him, resembling an indigo-colored blanket. In his hand he held an object, surely his club. This being was quickly gaining ground on the two.

As they reached the crest, the Kwan man said to him, "That's Maasaw coming after us. If he catches you, he'll take you back. Then you won't be able to return to your body. So hurry up. Run on!" he encouraged him.

In the light of the relatively little information available on Maasaw's role in Maski, Bradfield's suggestion, that the god may have been en-trusted with his charge of the underworld by mistake, has a ring of plausibility. "Due, I think, to a false association between Maasaw, death, the fire pits, darkness, and the after-life as a place of punishment (a notion alien to Hopi thinking, except in the single case of witches), Maasaw has mistakenly been invested with control of the underworld — and has even come to be regarded *primarily* as the deity having charge over death and the after-life, whereas *primarily* (and aboriginally) *he is the deity in control of the earth and of crops*, as his association with the Above witnesses" (1973:258).

Obviously, Maasaw's bond with Maski cannot be explained away as easily as Bradfield would like to. There is definite evidence of this bond in Hopi tradition, yet it is admittedly weak compared to the strong link the god maintains with *tuuwaqatsi*, "the land of the living." In this

sense Maasaw is a god of the "center" along the nadir-zenith axis of Hopi cosmography, as Geertz has concluded (1985:227).

In conjunction with the notion, that death is the reverse of life, Maasaw as the supreme deity of death is endowed with many behavioral traits which are contrary to those of the living. The Hopi are quite aware of this fact.

TEXT 7

Pay pi itam naat taayungqam hin hiita hintotingwuniqw pam maasaw tuwat qa itamun hiita hintit pam tuwat ahoywat pantingwu. Noq itam pi suyan taalat ep yakta- kyangw pu' piw pantaqat ep hiita tuway'numyangwuniqw pam qa panta. Pam tuwat qa talpuva waynumkyangw piw hiita suyan tuway'numngwu.

Hopi hin hiita hintingwuniqw pam maasaw pi pay put qa an hiita hintingwu. Pam put hiita hin- tsakpiy nahoyngwaniy'ta. Pam oovi kivamiq pakye' pam tuwat saaqat teevenge'wat aw atkyami hawngwu. Pu' hopi pi saaqat hopkye'wat pangso hawngwu. Pu' maasaw hiita tuwat putvoqwat torikiwtaqw pu' hopi suyvoqwat hiita torikiw- tangwu. Hak oovi hiita putvoqwat torikiwtaqw haqawat nanaptaqam pangqaqwangwu, "Pam put mastorikiwta."

Maasaw does things in a manner which runs directly counter to the way we mortals live and act. While we go about and see in broad daylight, he does not. He roams the land in the darkness of the night and can see quite clearly then.

Whatever the Hopi does, Maasaw reverses. For instance, upon enter- ing the kiva, Maasaw will descend to the lower floor portion by going around the west side of the entrance ladder. A Hopi, on the other hand, goes around the east side of the ladder to reach this level. By the same token, Maasaw drapes things over his left shoulder, while a Hopi slings them over the right. Thus, when people see a person with something slung over his left shoulder, they comment, "He has it draped over his shoulder in the fashion of Maasaw."

This reversal of things also holds for Maski, "the land of the dead." It is a land of opposites. Thus, when it is daytime on earth, darkness reigns in the below; summer in the upper world corresponds to winter in the lower world. The inhabitants of Maski, too, act in reverse to what the living customarily do. In tales featuring the motif of a Hopi's journey to the afterworld,[14] the spirits of the dead think of themselves as alive, while the visitor is regarded as a *maasaw* or "dead person." Being weightless souls, the dead can climb ladders made of sunflower stalks. Food is never consumed physically by them, only the steam and aroma are inhaled. When going on a rabbit hunt, the dead stalk grasshoppers and crickets instead of cottontails and jack rabbits.

Finally, Maasaw's undisputed connection with death can also be seen in the fact that he is believed to have an abode in the vicinity of Sipaapuni, the former emergence hole through which now the spirit of a dead person enters the afterworld. This link is evident from a tale transmitted by Titiev: "Soon the older Twin came to the home of the Nukpana (Maasaw), who is the head chief of the canyon and who dwelt there long before Pöqangwhoya's arrival. Of him the Twin asked as a favor that he help whatever Hopi should pass that way in the future and Maasaw agreed to do so" (1937:258).

---

[14]Compare Voth (1905a: 116-19) and Courlander (1972: 121-31).

Appearance and Physique

Maasaw's fundamental dualism, as god of death and life, is also reflected in his physical appearance. He is depicted both as a grotesque, repulsive looking, and as an attractive being in the guise of a handsome youth. Although, overall, the god's ghastly features are described in much greater detail, his image of a beautiful young man is equally well established. The main traits that render Maasaw's appearance appealing can be gathered from Texts 8 and 9.

TEXT 8

Noq pay pi peetu lavaytangwuniqw pam yaw hak maasaw pas suhimu-tiyoniikyangw yaw angaapuyaw-tangwu. Pam pay naat kya pi hak tiyoniikyangw yang itamuy tuma-lay'ta. Pu' pam yaw moohot akw qötösom'iwkyangw pu' piw yalaa-kwilawtangwu. Noq pam pay sutsep pantangwu, naamahin kwatsvakiwte'. Pu' piw tukwap-ngöntangwu. Pu' yaw pam sa-kwanapnat naavankyangw pu' sakwavitkunat pitkuntangwu. Pu' pam qa kwatsvakiwte' yan yuwsiy'-tangwu.

Some say that Maasaw is a handsome young man with long cascading hair. In spite of his youthful age he tends to our needs in this world. Around his head he wears strands of split yucca leaves,[1] and from his nose downward a strip of black hematite streaks to each of his cheeks. He is always made up in this manner even when hidden under his mask. Around his neck hangs a strand of turquoise beads,[2] and he wears an indigo-hued poncho-like shirt, as well as a breech clout of the same color.

TEXT 9

Pam yaw hak maasaw qa kwaatsiy ang pakiwte' suhimutaqaningwu. Pu' yaw pam piw lomayuwsiy'-tangwu. Niikyangw pam yaw suqömtaqaniikyangw yaw yalaa-kwilawtangwu. Pankyangw pu' yaw pam piw lomatukwapngön-tangwu. Panhaqam yuwsiy'taqat kya pi piw aw yortota. Niikyangw pam ephaqam put hiita nuu-tsel'ewakw kwaatsit ang pakiw-tangwu.

The god Maasaw is claimed to be very handsome when not wearing his mask. He is also supposed to be clothed very nicely. His skin is dark and he has a streak of black hematite running from the bridge of his nose downward to each cheek. He also wears a beautiful strand of turquoise beads about his neck. People have seen him garbed in this way. At certain times, however, he is under a grotesque mask.

[1]Compare the Glossary under "Yucca Headband."

[2]These details are basically confirmed in one of the myths collected by Voth. The avian messenger sent by the people in the underworld, to explore the surface of the earth, encounters the god as "a very handsome man. He had four strands of turquoise around his neck and very large turquoise ear pendants. On his face he had two black lines running from the upper part of his nose to his cheeks, and made with specular iron" (1905a: 12).

Exposure to the god's "death" aspect, as a rule, has terrible consequences for a mortal. Petrified by feelings of terror and panic, a mortal instantly loses his consciousness. This transformation into a death-like state may, however, be only temporary. Texts 10 and 11 shed light on this matter from a Hopi point of view.

TEXT 10

Pay pi peetu pangqaqwangwuniqw hak pas maasawuy aw pituqw hakiy yaw ang hintingwu, hak mokngwu. Niikyangw pay hak qa pas pas mokngwü. Noq pay hak ahoy yan unangwte' pay aapiy piw qa hintangwu. Pu' pay pam piw hakiy qa hintsanngwu. Pam pi pay qa nukpananingwuniiqe oovi qa panwat piw putakw tuuhintsaatsanngwu.

According to some, a person's encounter with the true Maasaw usually has negative consequences, often death. One does not really die, however. After regaining consciousness a person lives on quite normally. The god does not simply harm people. He is not an evil being and consequently does not injure anybody with his ability to deaden a person's senses.

TEXT 11

Pu' maasaw yaw hakiy aw pituqw hak yaw son put wuuyavo aw taytat pay hak mokngwu. Niikyangw pay hak qa pas pas mokngwu, pay hak mashuruutingwu. Pay panwat hak mokngwu. Ason pas pam aapiy-niqw pu' pay hak piw ahoy yan unangwtingwu.

In an encounter with Maasaw, a human being cannot look upon the god for long before losing consciousness as if dead. But it is not actually death in the true meaning of the word that the person experiences; rather, he can be described as being petrified and stunned from fright. It is in this sense that one dies, so to speak. Upon the god's departure, the person so affected by the encounter comes to again.

Petrification from fright coupled with the loss of speech are the immediate results of catching a glimpse of the god. This reaction to Maasaw, linguistically conceptualized as *mashuruuti*, "to become solid from Maasaw," is said to occur both in humans and dogs.

TEXT 12

Maasaw a'ni lay'tangwuniqw oovi yan tis nu'an hopinen son put qa mamqasi. Meh, pay himuwa yaavaqwniikyangw kya pi put tuwe' pu' pam pay mashuruute' pu' as töqtinikyangw haktonsa pantingwu. Son pam tönay yamaknani. Pu' oovi kur pam mihikqw waynumniniqw pu' pooko haqam as wahahaykunikyangw son pam wahakiy piw yamaknani.

Since Maasaw is an extremely potent being, a mere mortal is of necessity afraid of him. For example, the instant one spots the god one becomes petrified from fright, even though one is still at a distance from him. One tries to scream, but one's voice will not come out. The same is true if Maasaw is about at night and a dog should try to bark; he, too, will be unable to do so.

The device which permits Maasaw to undergo an instant metamorphosis from beautiful to ugly, and vice versa, is his mask. An episode from a myth preserved by Stephen illustrates the god's change from a hideous creature "covered with blood and loathsomeness," to a being with an attractive face: "Maasaw then took his own head off; he began at the chin and turned his head back, and lifted it off, and placing it upon the ground he sat upon it, and behold! Maasaw had become a handsome youth" (1939:204).

A Hopi testimonial in regard to this use of Maasaw's mask is contained in Text 13.

TEXT 13

I' hak maasaw pay as piw qa pas pas pan soniwa. Pam pay put tuvikuy'ta. Niiqe pam pay put kwaatsiy'taqe oovi pay ephaqamsa put ang pakingwu. Pam pay imuy katsinmuy amun kwatsvakiwtangwu. Pam pay as piw yan itamun hopiniiqe pam oovi pay put panis kwaatsiy'ta.

Maasaw's mask is only a facade and doesn't represent his actual appearance. He slips his mask on only once in a while. He is masked similar to the kachinas and, except for this mask, is a human being just like us.

The mask, which can be donned and doffed at will by the god, is described as "very ugly, with large open eye-holes and a large mouth" (Voth 1905a:12). The fact that the hideous mask is often equated with the head of Maasaw is evident from a First Mesa legend. In this legend the god is portrayed as coming among the people "looking like a horrible skeleton, and his bones rattling dreadfully. He menaced them with awful gestures, and lifted off his fleshless head and thrust it into their faces" (Mindeleff 1886:18).

A vivid depiction of Maasaw's head, including the eyes, is given in Text 14.

TEXT 14

I' maasaw yaw susukwhömiy'-tangwuniiqe yaw oovi talqötöningwu. Pu' pam pay mihikqwsa tuwat waynumngwuniiqe oovi pangsa tuwat postalaningwunii-kyangw pu' pam piw it qööhit himuy'ta. Niiqe pam haqam pi pas tuwat qööhiy aw qatungwu. Niiqe pam yaw sutsep put aw tsoylantangwuniqw oovi yaw put qööhiyat angqw aw a'ni kokhalngwu. Noq yaw put qööhiyat angqw as a'ni kokhalngwuniqw put taywa'at qa taqtingwu. Noq pu' pam yaw piw pas maakya. Pu' yaw pam oovi sowit niine' pu' yaw pam put ungwayat tuwat qötömi wuutangwu. Noq pu' pam ungwa naanatsva kwasiwmangwuniiqe oovi pam suytsepngwat pööngal'iw-mangwuniqw putakw put qötö'at wuuyoq'iwma. Pu' yaw pam kya pi pang paas taqtikyangw pu' pööngal'iwtaqw oovi put taywayat aqw qa pitungwu, pam koosöw.

Maasaw is said to be almost bald, having only a few strands of hair on his head. Since he only travels about at night, his vision is clearest then. He is also the owner of fire. Maasaw sits at an unknown place and constantly stokes his fire, causing a wave of searing heat to be emitted from it. In spite of this intense heat radiation, his face never gets burned. This is because the god, who is reputed to be a very capable hunter, makes it a habit to pour the blood[3] of his prey on his head whenever he slays a jack rabbit. As layer upon layer of this blood is baked by the fire and builds up in thickness, his head grows larger and larger. These layers of encrusted blood are so dense that the heat from the fire cannot penetrate them and thus does not reach his face. Con-

---

[3]Tyler suggests that "it is impossible to use the word blood without thinking of 'life's blood.' Beyond that generality there are specific relations between blood and fertility, notably menses in the human female" (1964: 20). Compare also Chapter 6.

Niiqe pam pay yaw oovi put koo-
söwuy qa nanvotngwu.

Noq pu' yaw pam oovi piw mihikqw waynumninik pu' pam yaw
tuwat poosiynit pu' mo'amiq töövut
panangwu. Pankyangw pu' pam
mihikqw waynume warikiwnumqw
pu' pangsoq hukvaqw pu' yaw
pangqw sumawuy akw kootalngwu.
Putakw yaw pam tuwat tutskwat
tuway'kyangw mihikqw waynumngwu. Paniqw oovi peetu hopiit
pangqaqwangwu, "Maasaw qööhit
taytay," kitotangwu.

sequently, he is not even aware of
the heat.

Also, each time Maasaw intends to
go about during the night, he
places hot embers into his eyes and
mouth. Whenever he moves about
in this fashion, air blows into his
eyes, causing them to glow. In this
way he manages to see the ground
at night. Thus some Hopis say,
"Maasaw has fire for eyes."

The individual features which account for the god's terrifying ugliness
are once more summarized in the subsequent statement:

TEXT 15

People say that Maasaw is a repulsive being. His head is so
enormous and so bloody that it
shines a little when light falls on it.
His mouth is round and his eyes
are hollow. Furthermore, his forehead bulges out in a large ridge.

Noq pay puma pangqaqwangwuniqw yaw pam himu nuutsel'ewayningwu. Wukoqötöy'tangwu yaw
pam himu. U'ngwasat yaw qötöy'-
tangwuniqw oovi pay yaw put
angqw hihin talqaqsalngwu. Niikyangw pu' yaw pam piw supongmo'ay'kyangw pu' piw kori'voy'-
tangwu. Pankyangw pu' yaw qalkyaqe pam wukonamuruy'tangwu.

Figure 1

Figure 2

Figure 3

Figure 4

Maasaw petroglyphs at Tutuventiwngwu (Willow Springs, AZ). Two basic configurations portray the god: the frontal view with eyes and mouth (Figures 1 and 4) and the "pac-man" type profile emphasizing the god's bulging forehead (Figures 2, 3, and 4). The petroglyphs shown here, and below in Figures 7-9 and 14, were engraved into the oxidized layer of the rock surface by a participant in a Hopi salt expedition on its way to the Grand Canyon. Photographs by E. Malotki.

As a rule, Maasaw is already endowed with his bloody visage when the Hopi first encounter the god after their emergence from the underworld. An etiological story-fragment explaining how Maasaw acquired his terrible features is available from Courlander: "He was thrown into the fire down in Maski, but he didn't die. He crawled out of the fire. He was burnt pretty bad, all over his skin, and his skin was all burned off. He was pretty terrible looking, with a red head and blood all over him" (1982:101).

Parsons, in a peculiar note, reports that Maasaw is also called "Kwapqöhikpu, Broken Neck, because he fell off the cliff and broke his neck" (Stephen 1936:995). None of my informants were able to confirm this epithet nor can I find any other allusion to this bodily disformation of the god in the literature.

Voth, however, has preserved a tale concerning the genesis of the god's bloody features which locates this event in a time frame that is definitely post-emergence. Since the story is one of the few for which the original Hopi version is available, on which Voth based his published translation,[4] both the Hopi and the English versions are cited here in full as Text 16.[5]

---

[4]Voth's version titled "Mas-tuwuchi (Skeleton Myth)" is contained in Folder No. 81 of his materials stored at the Mennonite Library and Archives Information and Research Center in North Newton, Kansas. His translation is available in (1905a: 123).

[5]Voth's original provides the Hopi linguist with the unique opportunity of appraising the famous missionary's grasp of the Hopi language. Note that his orthographic notation has here been adjusted to the standardized writing system used throughout this book. Where appropriate, grammatical mistakes, oversights such as missing particles, postpositions and erroneous word compositions, were corrected. The many pausal endings which occur throughout his rendition indicate that the text was taken from dictation. These pausal endings are omitted in our version since they would not surface in natural speech flow. With the exceptions of certain mistranslations, which were ironed out, the English version is given verbatim. Most striking about the story format are its staccato style and terseness. In this respect the text resembles more a story capsule or story abstract than a narrative designed to entertain. Once again, I attribute this succinctness, which is not compatible with Hopi story telling, to the circumstances under which the tale had to be recorded. Obviously, a tape recorder would have permitted the story teller to indulge much more in the details of a tale's plot.

TEXT 16

Aliksa'i. Yaw piw hanokiveq yee-
siwa. Noq tömö' a'ni nuvayokva.
A'ni yaw nuvati. Pu' yaw haanom
maqwisa. Kiy ayo' kwiniwi yaw
maqwisa, taawat kiiyat awi'. Pu'
yaw puma pep maqlalwa nuvava'a,
taataptuy. Yaw niitoti taataptuy.
Niitotit angqw ninma, naat piw
yaw maktiwisa.

Noq walpiy kwiningya, puhuvave,
pep yaw kur maasaw maqqatu.
Mihikqw kur yaw tuwat pam
maqnumngwu. Pam yaw taalawvaqw teevep pam puwngwu. Yaw
kur taataptuy niiti. Naat yaw
puwqw pay kur haanom yaw aw
öki. Pas yaw wuwuko'wat ep yaw
pam maasaw kiy'ta. Pu' yaw
haanom aw ökiqw taavo wari. Pu'
yaw ngööngöya. "Hawa! Hawa!"
yaw kitota.

Pu' yaw put maasawuy puwqat
su'aqw tso'o, pam taavo. Pu'
haanom yaw tuwat aqw tsotso'ya;
a'ni yaw mowawatota. Kur yaw
pam maasaw owat atpip tuunimuy
a'ni oyiy'ta. Pu' yaw pam maasaw
suqtuptut pu' waaya. Kur yaw
owat tsukuy'taqat aqw ongo. Pu'
yaw sutsivo warikt piw ongo.
Qötö'at yaw poro. Pantsaknuma,
yaw ongtinuma. Pu' yaw qötö'at
poromtiqw a'ni yaw ang ungwa
mumunya. Yaw pam hisat as
qöötsat qötöy'tangwu, noq pu' yaw
haanomuy amutsviy ungwawsat

Aliksa'i. In Hano the people were
living. In the winter it snowed very
much and there was much snow,
and the Hano went hunting. North
of the village they were hunting
towards the Sun shrine, and they
were hunting rabbits there in the
snow. They killed a great many
rabbits. When they had killed a
great many they went home, but
still hunting.

North of Walpi, at Puhu Spring,
Maasaw happened to be camping
to hunt. He normally hunts at
night and goes to bed as the day
breaks. There were a great many
rabbits. Maasaw was still asleep
when the Hano arrived. He was
resting among some huge boulders.
When the Hano came, a cottontail was running and they followed
him. "Hawa! Hawa!" they said, and
pursued him.

The rabbit jumped down just
where the Maasaw was sleeping.
The Hano also jumped down,
making a great deal of noise. The
Maasaw had a great deal of game
under the rock. Now the Maasaw
jumped up quickly and ran. He
ran against a point in the rock,
then he ran in a different direction
and again ran against the rock.
He had thus perforated his head.
In that way he again ran against
the rock from place to place. When
his head was full of holes the blood
was streaming down. A long time
ago he used to have a white head,
but on account of the Hano now he

qötöy'ta. Pu' yaw tuunimuyatuy naahuyva. Pangqw pu' yaw puma naanamangw'iwa. Pay yaw as oovi haanom qa pangqe' yaktaqw maasaw yaw naat qöötsat qötöy'tani. Yaasava.

always has a bloody head. Now they distributed his game and then carried their heavy loads home. Had the Hano not been going around there, the Maasaw would still have a white head. This long is the story.

In addition to his monstrous head, the god's gigantic feet are marked as extraordinary. "His feet are shaped like a man's but are about the length of the forearm" (Stephen 1936:150). Text 17 is in agreement with Stephen's statement and others in the literature, which ascribe to the god the dimensions of a veritable "big-foot."

TEXT 17

Pay pi pangqaqwangwuniqw yaw maasaw wukokukuy'tangwu. Pam yaw antsa wupakukuy'tangwuqat pay ima put kukyat aw yortotaqam yan lavaytangwu.

There is a general consensus that Maasaw possesses enormous feet. Those who have seen his tracks relate that his feet are very long indeed.

According to traditions of the Walpi Snake clan, Maasaw's footprints, when first discovered, were seen to go "in a series of six concentric circles around the mesa" (Stephen 1936:637). Rendered elsewhere by Stephen with four concentric circles (1939:203), this symbol, termed *potaveni* or "coiled plaque design" in Hopi, is found in rock art sites throughout the Southwest. Hopis, however, generally interpret the concentric circles to symbolize their migrations on this continent.

Somewhat contradictory to the clear prints left by the god is the shuffling mode in which he is supposed to move along.

TEXT 18

Itamuy hopiituyniqw i' maasaw tuwat tsipipitinumngwu. Pay pi peetu aw yortotaqam pangqaq-

According to Hopi lore, Maasaw walks about shuffling his feet. A few who have seen him insist that

wangwu. Noq pam yaw pay pas
sutsep pansa waynuma. Niiqe pam
oovi pay kya qa hisat pas suusus
waynuma. Pay ura hak hoohut
pookyaqw pam tutskwavanen pay
ephaqamsa pang tongtimangwu-
niqw pan himu tsipipitinumngwu.
Noq it maasawuy kuku'at pan
tutskwava hintsakmangwu.

this is so. He always walks in this
manner. His pace is never slow.
Maasaw's peculiar way of moving
may be likened to the flight of an
arrow. As the arrow is released,
it zooms along, every once in a
while touching the surface of the
ground. The noise produced in the
process is the same one Maasaw's
feet generate as he travels across
the land.

As related by one of my informants, the overall color impressions of
Maasaw's body are gray. Stephen, on the other hand, reports it as "always
black, shining black" (1936:150).

TEXT 19

Ima peetu sinom put maasawuy aw
yortotaqam pangqaqwangwuniqw
pam yaw soosoy masiplangpuni-
ngwu.

The few people who have seen
Maasaw agree that his entire body
is one gray mass.

A further physical monstrosity attributed to Maasaw is a tail.
Stephen, who is the only one to mention this detail, points to the similar-
ity of this trait with the white man's devil. "In the long ago the Hopi
Maasaw, like the Pahanmaasaw, the White Maasaw, had a tail that
dragged in the sand, and Maasaw used to carry it, held the bight of it in
his hand. This tail was offensive to children, they dreaded it and used to
weep and fall into fits of terror at it, so Maasaw cut off the tail, chopped
it in little bits and flung them in the sea, for this occurred in the far west,
where the great water is, beyond Kalipooni [California]. The chopped
bits of the tail became the fish (paakiw) that are now in the great water"
(1936:150).

Highly distinctive in Maasaw's appearance is the woman's dress which forms part of his apparel.[6] Since Maasaw as god of death is the antithesis to life, he typically does things by opposites. This is also shown in the way he wears the dress.

TEXT 20

Pu' pam maasaw kwatsvakiwte' pam kanelsakwitsa yuwsiy'tangwu. Niikyangw pu' pam piw ahoywatsa hiita yuwsiy'tangwu. Ispi pam pi pay maasawniiqe piw pay mokpuniiqe qa hopit an qatuuqe oovi qa an yuwsiy'tangwu. Niikyangw pam put kanelsakwit qa pitkuntangwu, pam put torikiwtangwu. Niiqe oovi pam put torikiwtaqw put putngaqwwat sukyaktsi'at maataqningwu. Noq oovi hakiy hiita pan torikiwtaqw hakiy aw pangqaqwangwu, "Um mastorikiwta."

When Maasaw is hidden under his mask, he is dressed in a tattered woman's dress. However, he wears everything contrary to the Hopi norm. He does so because he is Maasaw, a being who is dead and who does not live like the Hopi. Thus, he wears the ragged woman's dress not as a kilt but slung over the left shoulder and fastened just below the right armpit, baring his right shoulder. To a person wearing a piece of clothing in this fashion people say, "You've got it draped over your shoulders like Maasaw."

Maasaw's dress basically constitutes a death shroud and must be obtained directly from the dead. The process of acquiring the proper dress is the same for the god as for his impersonator.[7]

TEXT 21

Pu' pangqaqwangwuniqw pam mamasawniqa yaw mit pas tuu-'amit angqw hiitawat kanelkwasayat nasimokyaatangwu. Pu' yaw

People say that the Maasaw impersonator always borrows a Hopi woman's dress directly from a gravesite. When the day before the

[6]Tyler surmises that the dress may "indicate an attempt to combine a female with a male element in the same fertility spirit" (1964: 21).

[7]Compare Story 15 (ATR 10) and Chapter 6.

oovi maswikkatsintotokmi haykyal-
tiqw pu' yaw pam tuutu'amit ang
put tunglay'numngwu. Pu' yaw
himuwa qa maqaninik put huur
nguy'tangwu. Pu' pay himuwa put
ookwatuwe' pay put suumaqangwu.
Maqaqw pu' pam pas put yuwsingwu. Hisat pi kanelkwasit akw
hiitawat mokqat mokyaatotangwu.
Mit pi pay tiposhoyat, qa wimkyat
mokq put pay qa amyangwu. Put
pay paysoq siisikpumiq tsurukna-
yat pu' angk owat akw uutayangwu. Noq i' pas maasaw pay put
mamasawqat amum sunan yuwsiy'-
tangwu. Ispi pam mamasawqa pay
put pas maasawuy tututskyayna-
ngwuniiqe oovi son put qa an yuwsiy'tani.

climax of the Maswik kachina
ceremony approaches, he wanders
about the graves pleading with the
dead for this piece of clothing. If
one is unwilling to give her garment up, she will tenaciously
cling to it. One who sympathizes
with the impersonator, however,
will readily surrender it to him.
This dress is then used as part of
the impersonator's costume. In the
past it was customary to wrap a
woman's corpse in her dress before
her interment. Uninitiated
children, on the other hand, were
not buried but rather stuffed into a
crevice, which in turn was sealed
with rocks. The real Maasaw
dresses in exactly the same manner
as the person who portrays him in
the ceremony. Since the impersonator mimics Maasaw, he must of
necessity wear the same apparel.

The terrible odor Maasaw exudes is related, among other factors, to
the smelly grave clothes he dons. This information may be gleaned from
Text 22 which I obtained. This olfactorily offensive characteristic
ascribed to Maasaw is also confirmed by Wallis: "He emits a horrible
stench" (1936:6).

TEXT 22

Noq pu' piw pangqaqwangwuniqw
yaw maasaw a'ni hovaqtungwu, ispi
pam mi' peekyewtaqa ungwa
qötöyat aw wuutsiwtangwuniqw
oovi. Noq pam pi pay it pas qa
atsat maasawuy qötöyat ang hisat-
ngahaqaqw pantaqe oovi paas
peekyewta. Pu' pam pi pay piw

Maasaw is reputed to exude a
horrendous stench; this stench
results from the fact that he normally pours rotten blood over his
head. Because this blood has been
covering the god's head since time
immemorial, it is completely
putrified. By the same token,

mokpuniiqe pay peekyewtangwu-
niiqe oovi a'ni kya pi hovaqtungwu.
Niikyangw pay qa qötö'atsa. It
maasawuy hapi pay yuwsi'at paas
peekyet akw qarokiwtangwuniiqe
oovi pan a'ni hovaqtuqat hova-
langwuy'tangwu.

Maasaw is a dead and decomposed
being; this explains why he stinks
so awfully. But it is not only his
head which is so putrid. His garb,
too, is so encrusted with pus that it
emanates a terribly offensive odor.

Maasaw's shoes, probably in the form of sandals as they have been
excavated in many prehistoric Pueblo sites, are said to be fashioned
from yucca.

TEXT 23

Pu' antsa pam maasaw yaw moo-
totsta. Moohot angqw tootsi'at
yukiwta. Pam mooho kya pi a'ni
huruningwu. Pu' yaw pam moohot
piw maasomkyangw pu' piw ho-
kyaasomtangwu.

It is true also that Maasaw wears
shoes fashioned from yucca fibers.
These fibers are extremely tough.
Yucca leaves are also tied about his
wrists and just below his knees.

This plant material, commonly termed *mooho* in Hopi, stems from
the narrow-leaved and not from the broad-leaved yucca variety, which is
known as *samowa*. Yucca, which was already mentioned in Text 8 in
conjunction with the god's headband, is also decoratively tied around
his arms and legs. The special relationship that exists between Maasaw
and the plant is underlined by a taboo mentioned in Text 24.

TEXT 24

Hak yaw moohot akw qa naapa
somlawngwu. Pam hapi maasawuy
yuwsi'atniqw oovi hak qa moohot
akw naapa somlawngwu. Hak yaw
pantiqw i' maasaw yaw hakiy

One should not tie yucca leaves to
one's body. Yucca is part of Maasaw's dress, and consequently one
does not attach it to oneself. The
person who does so anyway, will
become so desirable to Maasaw
that as a result he will become

kwangway'qw hak masna'pal-
ngwuqat kitotangwu.

afflicted with the disease *masna'paliwta*. [8]

Besides the *kopitsoki* or "cedar bark torch" associated with Maasaw (see Chapter 5), the god is said to carry a cylindrical club. Supposedly filled with all sorts of seeds (see Chapter 6), it serves the god as a weapon.

TEXT 25

Pam hapi maasaw tuwat maawikit
sutsep yawnumngwunen pam hakiy
putakw niinangwu. Niikyangw pay
qa pas pi pas antsa hakiy niinangwu. Pay panis hakiy sawitok-
nangwu. Niikyangw pam piw
suyngaqw put yawnumngwuniiqe
suyngaqw hakiy wuvaatangwu, qa
putngaqw.

Maasaw always carries a drumstick-
shaped club around with him to
kill people. Actually, he does not
really slay them but rather knocks
them unconscious. Again, contrary
to the norm, he carries the club in
his left hand and strikes with that
hand instead of with his right.

Maasaw is believed to utter a very distinctive wail. The auditory impression of this wail is frequently likened to the very deep drawn-out howl of a dog.[9] According to Stephen the god "long ago prohibited anyone from making the peculiar bu-hu'-ing call after dark, he alone has that call and whenever it is heard people know Maasaw is near" (1936:152).

TEXT 26

Pay pi peetu put aw tuqayiy'yungqam pangqaqwangwuniqw pay yaw
pam maasaw tuwat pas naap
sutskye' paklawngwu, pay pas qa

The few who have heard Maasaw
relate that he has a very distinctive
howl, quite different from anything
else. He lets out his cry in a very

---

[8]For details concerning this disease, reputedly brought on by Maasaw, see Chapter 8.

[9]Compare Titiev (1972: 81 and 91).

Figure 5.—Pictographic signatures from a petition drafted in March 1894 requesting clarification of Hopi land claims. One of the signers' clan totem depicts the god Maasaw holding his *maawiki* or ''club.'' National Archive: RG 75, 1884—14830L, p.4. See also Dockstader, Frederick J. ''Hopi History, 1850—1940.'' In *Southwest,* edited by A. Ortiz. Vol. 9 *Handbook of the American Indians,* Washington: Smithsonian Institution, 1979, p.528.

hiita ani'. Niikyangw i' maasaw yaw paklawe' pam yaw pas wuukoq ang pantingwu. Pu' yaw pam piw töötökiy pas wiisilangwu. "Anoo," pay yaw pam yanhaqam paklawngwu.

Noq ephaqam pi pooko pay piw pan wukovaklawe' pay pas wiisilangwu. Pan pi pooko paklawe' masvakmumuyngwuniiqat kitotangwu. Niikyangw pam pay qa maasawuy an paklawngwu. Noq pay qa soosoyam sinom put maasawuy hin töqtingwuniqw navotiy'-yungwa. Niikyangw pay pam pooko

deep, drawn-out, wailing voice. "Anoo," roughly approximates the sound of his cry.

Occasionally, a dog will howl out in that same low, drawn-out tone. When a dog does this, people say he is barking in the fashion of Maasaw, even though the dog's howl does not really resemble Maasaw's cry. Not everyone is aware of the manner in which Maasaw lets out his cry. But it is at times when a dog bellows out

ephaqam nuutsel'ewakw paklaw-
ngwuniqw oovi sinom pangqaqwangwu, "Pooko masvakmumuya."

Pu' piw yaw pooko pan pakmumuye' pay yaw tu'alangw'iwte' pan
hingqawlawngwuniiqat it piw
hopiit kitotangwu. Pu' pay peetu
pangqaqwangwuniqw yaw himu
pay tu'alangw'eway pangso kiimi
pituqw pu' yaw himuwa pooko
navote' pu' yaw piw pan masvak-
mumuyngwu. Niikyangw qa
maasawuy awi'. It pas qa atsat
maasawuy waynumqw puma pay
put qa aw wahahatotangwu.

such an eerie sound that people
declare, "The dog is crying like
Maasaw."

The Hopi also say that a dog
producing sounds of this nature is
possessed by a demon. Some claim
that when an evil spirit approaches
the village and a dog senses this, he
will howl in the fashion of Maasaw.
He does not really howl at Maasaw,
however. When the real Maasaw
is going about, dogs never bark at
him.

Maasaw in Emergence Mythology

As a subsequently discovered ruler of the upper world, Maasaw played a central role in the emergence of mankind from the underworld. The narrative corpus[1] on this important event in Hopi mythology shows the deity in a multitude of situations which, chronologically, comprise the entire range from a pre-emergence to a post-emergence phase.

---

[1]For a summary of emergence materials, portraying the event from a Third Mesa perspective, see Geertz (1985: 238). As Geertz points out, "not a single published version (and that includes all the versions from the other Mesas) contains the original Hopi text" (1985: 219). He identifies the chief informant for each emergence myth and offers critical comments on different versions, including his own still unpublished recordings.

In First Mesa emergence versions Maasaw actively intervened on behalf of the people confined in the lower world. He assisted them in their efforts to reach the present world which, in some traditions, is believed to constitute the fourth in a series of worlds, cosmo-architecturally situated on top of each other. In a myth transmitted by Stephen, the germination god Muy'ingwa was troubled by certain subterranean noises. "Maasaw was pleased when he heard this and he determined to rescue, from the wrath of the other gods, all of those confined people who would live in his land and furnish him with occasional nourishment. In those days the gods had the power of discerning the thoughts of others. Thus it became known to them that Maasaw was about to search for the noises. He had said in council that these cries came from people, not beasts, and he wished to befriend them, but the other gods wished to kill them. The gods knew Maasaw to be in earnest and thought if he discovered and befriended the strange people, he would grow more powerful than any of them and would rule the whole land and leave no place for them" (1929:52).

The preceding passage clearly characterizes Maasaw as already a caring friend of Hopikind early in its mythological history. In accordance with his benevolent attitude, Maasaw later also lent a helping hand at the Sipaapuni,[2] the actual place of emergence. "Maasaw stood astride of the orifice, and, as each Hopi made his appearance, Maasaw linked his arm in that of the Hopi, helping him up to the surface and greeting him with welcome" (Stephen 1936:137).

Third Mesa emergence myths depict Maasaw in a more passive role. Upon hearing footsteps in the upper world, a group of steadfast Hopi enmeshed in a medley of corruption, strife, and total disregard for values, decided to leave this state of koyaanisqatsi or "crazy life" behind. For this purpose they sent avian emissaries to explore the unknown above. The shrike finally succeeded in reaching the hole in the sky and was the first to discover Maasaw.

---

[2]Waters thinks that sipaapuni is etymologically "derived from the two words for 'navel' and 'path from,' thus denoting 'the umbilical cord leading from Mother Earth' and symbolizing 'the path of man's Emergence from the previous underworld' " (1963: 129). This interpretation is linguistically not provable. While no morphological unit in the place name can be identified to reflect the notion "path from," the terms sipna "navel" and siihu "navel cord," at least share the initial portion with the word. Possibly also related to the first syllable si- are the forms süpaq "at the crotch" and süpaqw "from the crotch." Unlike this body part, which in Hopi only occurs in locational case forms, tipkya, the term for "womb," constitutes a true noun. Its sound structure, however, is etymologically quite unlinkable with the emergence-place designation, Sipaapuni.

TEXT 27

Pu' yaw pam pas naasungwnat pu' yaw pam pangqw nakwsu. Pay pi yaw qa pas suyan tala. Yaw mihikiwtaqat pan yaw taala. Noq piw yaw haqam qööhiwta. Pu' yaw pam put tuwaaqe pu' yaw put qööhit su'aqwa'.

Noq yaw paahusa. Qa haqam yaw himu tutskwa. Soosovik yaw i' paahu. Panmakyangw pu' yaw pam aqw oomiqhaqami pituqw piw yaw hak pep qatuqw pep yaw tutskwa maatsiwta. Pu' pay yaw pep qa pas wuuyaq tutskwaniqw aqlavaqe yaw soosovik paahu. Noq pep yaw hak qööhiy aw qatuqw yaw pam put aw pitu.

Pu' yaw pam pay paas navotiy'ta yaw pam hak hisat wupniqatniqw pay yaw pam oovi kur put nuutaytakyangw hisat hapininiqw pam yaw qa suyan navotiy'ta. Pu' yaw aw pituuqe pay yaw pam put naat qa aw hingqawqw pay pam put yaw qatu'a'awna. "Qatu'uy, um hak waynumay," yaw aw kita.

"Owiy," yaw kita.

"Ta'ay, yangqw nöösa'ay," yaw pam kitaaqe yaw put tunös'a'aw-·naqw pu' yaw puma hiita nösniniqw put yaw pam aw hoyokna. Noq pam yaw tsöngmokiwtaqe yaw pam oovi nösqw pu' yaw pam put tuuvingta, "Ta'ay, son pi um qa

It was only after the shrike had rested and caught his breath that he continued on. Complete darkness reigned, black as night. But then, much to his surprise he saw light which radiated from a fire. Upon spotting the fire he headed directly towards it.

There was water everywhere; solid land did not exist. The entire earth was covered with water. As the bird flew along, he finally reached higher ground and, much to his amazement, caught sight of someone sitting where the land appeared visible. It was not a very large piece of land and it, too, was completely surrounded by water. When the shrike reached the person, he noticed that he sat there facing the fire.

This person knew very well that one day someone would climb up from the underworld so he sat there waiting for his arrival, although he was not sure when exactly he would show up. When the shrike approached him he was asked to sit down before he had uttered a sound. "Have a seat, stranger," the man said to him.

"Yes," the shrike replied.

"Come on, join me in my meal," the man invited the bird, nudging towards his visitor some food. Since the shrike was famished, he helped himself to the food until the man by the fire suggested, "Now then,

pas hiita oovi waynumay," yaw aw kita. Yaw pam aw kitat paasat pu' yaw pam maasawniiqey aw pangqawu. Pam yaw yep it tutskwat aw tunatyawta.

"Haw owi?" yaw kita.

"Owi, pay nu' yangqw umumi taytangwuniiqe pay nu' paas navotiy'ta. Noq nu' umumi navotiy'taqe pas nu' qa haalaytiy," yaw kita. "Pay puye'em uma sonqa naat yantotini. Noq pay nu' kya qa nakwhaniy," yaw kita. "Pay nu' yaasaqsa tutskway'taqe nu' it kyaakyawnay," yaw aw kita. "Taq uma hapi naato piw a'ni tunatyawyungqw pay nu' oovi kya son umuy pew nöngakniqat naawaknaniy," yaw kitaaqe yaw qa nakwha.

"Noq pi itam pep atkya pas huru'pokkyangw itam yan nukushintotiqe itam kur haqami watqaniqe pu' itam oovi yan haqami piw sukwat tutskwat hepwisay," yaw kita.

"Owi asaa', pay nu' umumi paas navotiy'tay," yaw maasaw kita. "Pay nu' kya son oovi nakwhaniy," yaw kita.

"Kur antsa'ay, pay pi nu' pan pumuy aa'awnaniy," yaw motsni kitaaqe pu' yaw pam pangqw ahoy.

Noq pu' yaw puma hakim pep tsovawtaqam put motsnit ayay'yungqam yaw put nuutayyungwa. Noq pu' yaw pam pituuqe yaw yanhaqam amumi lavayti. Yaw pam

there must be some reason for your being about." With that he divulged to his visitor that he was Maasaw, the caretaker of this world.

"Oh yes?" replied the bird.

"Indeed, I've been observing all of you from this place and am fully aware of the events down below. I know everything about you and I'm grieved," he continued. "This was bound to happen to you. I may, therefore, not grant you your wishes. I only have this much land and treasure it dearly. Also, you still have great ambitions; hence, I don't think I would want you to make your emergence to this upper world," the man by the fire said, thereby refusing to give them permission.

"But down below we are very crowded," the shrike protested, "and we have reached such a state of corruption that we don't know where to go. That's why we're searching for another world."

"Yes, that may be so, but I know you very well," Maasaw asserted. "I don't think I'll allow you to come."

"I understand. I'll tell them what your response was," the shrike declared and then flew back.

Down in the underworld the people who had delegated this task to the shrike were still gathered awaiting his return. Finally, the bird reappeared and told them that he

antsa pep put hakiy aw pitu. Noq
pay yaw as pep antsa piw suukya
tutskwaniqw pam yaw hak maasaw
pep qatuuqa pay qa nakwha
pumuy pangso nöngaknaniqey.
Yan yaw pam tuu'awvaqe pay yaw
antsa kur qa lomanavota.

had met a stranger. He explained
that there was, indeed, another
world up there, but that Maasaw,
the person who dwelled there had
refused to grant them permission to
enter. This was the news the shrike
had brought back. No doubt, it
was not very heartening.

As it turned out, omniscient Maasaw, who was quite aware of people's plight in the world underground, initially declined to deliver them
from their life of chaos. A renewed appeal to the god, however, proved
successful when it was accompanied by a gift of prayer feathers.

TEXT 28

Noq pu' yaw puma pep atkya-
yaqam it paahot tumaltotat pu'
yaw puma pangqaqwa, "Ta'ay, um
pu' it itaatumalay yankyangw aw
ahoyniy," yaw puma kitota. "Put
um aw pituuqey put um it aw
oyani. Put hapi itam engem it
paahot tumaltota. Put um aw
pangqawqw okiw as itamuy ookwatuwe' itamuy tangataniy," yaw
puma put aw kitota. "Nu' hapi as
imuy itimuy kyaakyawnaqw oovi
as itamuy pangso yayvanaqw pu'
paasat pi pay imawat yep hinwat
naayukunayani. Pay pi ima son pi
pas wuuyavo yesniy," yaw pam
mongwi'am paasat pu' kita.

Noq pu' yaw pay aapiy pas qavongvaqw pu' yaw pam motsni pumuy
tumalayamuy yankyangw pu' piw
aw oomi. Paasat pay yaw pam
navotiy'ta haqe' pangso oomi
hötsiniqw pay yaw pam oovi suu-
pangsohaqami. Pu' yaw pam

The people down below now set to
fashioning prayer feathers. Upon
finishing them they commanded
the shrike, "Now, take the product
of our labor and return once more
to the upper world. Give these
prayer feathers to the man you
met. We made them specifically
for him. Tell Maasaw to have pity
on us and permit us to enter his
world." And the leader added,
"My children here are really dear
to me. Should he let us go up
there, the rest here can do whatever they wish to each other. They
cannot live on like this for a great
length of time anymore."

The following morning the shrike
took their prayer feathers and once
again winged skyward. This time
he knew where the opening into the
upper world was located and
headed straight toward it. Climbing higher and higher until he

pangso wupkyangw pu' yaw pam
piw aw pituqw pay yaw naat piw
pam ep qööhiy aw qatuwta. Pu'
yaw pam motsni put aw piw
pituuqe pu' yaw pam put engem
paahot kivaaqey yaw aw pangqawu. Niiqe pu' yaw pam put aw
oyat pu' yaw pam put aw hiita
tuu'awvaqey put yaw aw lalvaya.

Pu' yaw maasaw pumuy tumalayamuy kwusunakyangw pu' yaw put
aw pangqawu, "Kwakwhay, kur
antsa'ay. Pay pi nu' as ura qa
nakwhaqw pay kya pi uma son
tuutuqayyaniqe oovi kur it yanhaqam tumaltotay. Noq pay kya
pi nu' oovi son nawus umuy qa
hu'wanani. Niikyangw nu' oovi son
nawus uumi qa pangqawniy," yaw
kita. "Pay hapi uma naat a'ni
hiita tunatyawyungwa. Niikyangw
pu' uma hapi angqwyanikyangw
uma it umuunukpanay pep o'yaniy," yaw kita. "Uma hapi put pay
qa enang yankyaakyangw pewyani.
Uma hapi haqaapiy naat nuy qa
kyaptsitotaniy," yaw kita. "Noq
kur umungaqw haqawa put enang
yankyangw angqw pewniqw nu'
hapi pay paasat umuy maatapniy,"
kita yaw maasawniiqe pu' yaw pam
pumuy pay hu'wanaqw pu' pam
motsni pangqw ahoy piw yanwat
tuu'awma.

reached his destination, he once
again came to Maasaw, who as
before was still seated in front of
his fire. The shrike told him that
he had brought some prayer
feathers for him. He handed them
over to him and gave him the
message from the people.

Maasaw accepted their gift and
said to the bird, "Thank you,
indeed. As you recall, I declined
your request to come here but you
seem to be very persistent. These
prayer feathers prove that point.
So I suppose I'll have to agree to
your wishes. I must
mention one thing to you, though,"
he added. "You're still filled with
great plans and expectations, for
the future. This time, however,
when you're ready to come, I want
you to leave your evil ways behind.
By all means, don't bring them
along. There will still come a time
when you won't show any respect
toward me anymore. Hence, if one
of you should come along with
wickedness, I'll abandon you
immediately." Thus the god
Maasaw spoke and thereby granted
them permission to come. Thereupon the shrike flew back to relate
this different news.

A simple reed, magically raised to such a height that it could pierce
the sky, eventually became the device through which mankind climbed to
the surface world. Concerned that the wicked, too, might attempt to
invade the new world, the leader of the escapees finally pulled up the
reed "so that a great many people that were still on it dropped back"
(Voth 1905a:19).

The following emergence excerpt differs from all other published versions in that Maasaw is indirectly blamed for the existence of evil on this earth. While personally supervising the exodus from the below, he got momentarily sidetracked and, as a result of this carelessness, an evil person emerged to the paradisiacal world above. The instant the god realized his oversight, he severed the reed.[3]

TEXT 29

Pu' yaw puma sinom pay qa pas maamanguy'yat yaw paaqavit ang nööngankyangw pu' pew yayva. Pu' yaw pam maasaw, pam yep it tutskwat himuy'taqa, yaw pumuy amumi tunatyawta. Pu' yaw pam pumuy amumi pangqawu hak himuwungwanen yaw haqamiwat- mantani. Naanan'i'vo yaw pam pumuy oo'oya. Niiqe pam yaw pumuy ngyamuy pan paas naa- nan'i'vo oo'oyqe yaw pumuy sinmuy amumi hihin qa tunatyaltiqw pay yaw kur pam suukya powaqa put aqle' yamakqw pam yaw qa navota. Pay pi puma popwaqt a'ni tutuhist- niqw pay yaw pam oovi son put qa tuwiy akw hin maasawuy aqle' yamakqw pam yaw qa navota.

Pu' yaw pam navotqe pu', "Haakiy, haakiy!" yaw kitat pu' yaw pam aw

Without a trace of fatigue the people worked their way through the inner portion of the reed and finally climbed out into this world. Maasaw, the proprietor of this earth, kept a close eye on them and assigned every clan group to a certain location. But, while he was busy placing all the people of each lineage into the various sites, he relaxed his watchfulness and failed to notice that a witch slipped by him. Witches, as is well known, possess magical powers. One of them must have utilized these powers for she succeeded in sneak- ing past Maasaw without being detected.

The moment Maasaw became aware of his oversight, he shouted,

[3]Powell, whose 1870 recording of the Orayvi emergence version is the oldest in existence, apparently confused Maasaw with Matsito. Evidence for this misunderstanding is provided in his suggestion that Matsito, generally considered to be the mythic founder of Orayvi, is "probably an ancestral god" (1972: 24).

Instead of a reed, it is in Powell's version a tree whose branches are "thrust through the crevice in the lower-world sky. Then the people climbed up, in one long stream; still up they came until all the good were there. Ma-chi-ta [read: Maasaw], standing on the brink of the crevice, looked down, and saw the tree filled with the bad, who were following; then he caught the growing ladder by the upper boughs, twisted it from its foundation in the soil beneath, and threw it over, and the wicked fell down in a pile of mangled, groaning, cursing humanity" (1972: 26).

wari. "Pay paasa'niy," yaw pam
kita. "I' hapi nukpana pay paapu
as qa yep umumumniqat nu' naa-
waknaqw pay hapi suukyawa
umumum yama. Pay pi nu' kur
hin piw it pas aqw ahoy nu'an
tuuvaniqw pay pi nawus yep
qatuni. Niikyangw pay nu' hin
lavaytiqw pay i' hapi pan pu' yep
qatuni. Noq pay pi'iy," yaw kita.

Yanhaqam yaw puma hakim
pangqw nöngakkyangw pay yaw
puma kur piw put nukpanat enang
wikkyaakyangwyaqw pu' yaw pam
maasaw pay paasat pang put
paaqavit tuku. Pu' yaw pam put
sipaapunit aqw ahoy uuta. Pangqw
pu' yaw pumayakyangw pu' yaw
puma pep haqam tsomoy'taqw pep
yaw puma mooti yesva. Pep pu'
yaw puma oovi yeskyaakyangw put
pas maasawuy amum yeese. Noq
pep yaw pam maasaw a'ni uuyiy'ta.
Yaw hiihiita samit, morit, kawayvatngat, meloonit, pösövit, sipalat
pep uuyiy'ta. Pas yaw qa hiita pam
hak pep qa uuyiy'ta.

"Wait, wait!" and rushed towards
the emergence hole. "That's
enough now," he commanded. "No
evil being was supposed to come
with you, yet one managed to get
by me. That can't be helped now.
Since she's here, she'll have to stay.
Still, she'll have to live according to
the rules I laid down for you. Well,
what's done is done," Maasaw
lamented.

In this fashion the people made
their entrance into this upper
world. But since they had brought
one evil person along, Maasaw
severed the reed through which
they were emerging. Thereupon he
sealed shut the site of the emergence, commonly called Sipaapuni.
The people now left the Sipaapuni
and established their first settle-
ment at a place marked by a hill.
While they dwelled there, they
actually lived with Maasaw. At
this site Maasaw owned a field
abundant with a variety of crops.
Among them were corn, beans,
watermelons, muskmelons, cotton,
and peaches. He had all the crops
that could possibly be grown.

According to the tradition transmitted by Powell, Maasaw's first
order of business was raising the ceiling of the sky. "'When the people
had spread out through this world, they found the ceiling, or sky, so low
that they could not walk without stooping, and they murmured. Then
Ma-chi-ta [correctly Maasaw who is being confused with Matsito],
standing in the very center of this story, placed his shoulder against the
sky, and lifted it to where it is now" (1972:26).

    The subsequent episode from a Second Mesa version of the emer-
gence tale represents a detailed account of the Hopis' first face to face

encounter with Maasaw. In it the god, wearing his bloody mask, identified himself as the owner of the land, caretaker of life, and keeper of
death. The Hopi, in turn, assured the god of their willingness to accept
him as their leader and promised to live their lives remembering him in
their prayers.

TEXT 30

Pu' puma yaw pew nöngakqw yaw
yep qa taala. Noq pu' yaw puma
pay haqam nöngakqey naat pay
pepyaqw yaw amukwningyahaqam
qööhit angqw kootala. Qa taala pi
yaw pepniqw oovi yaw pephaqam
susmataq qööhi uwiwita. Pu' yaw
pumuy mongwi'am pangqawu,
"Pay kur hak yep mooti qatu."
Pu' yaw puma naatuvinglalwa,
"Sen hak pephaqam qööhiy'ta?
Sen pi pam hak it tutskwat himuy'taqa. Sen pam hak himu'u?"
yaw puma ii'it naatuvinglalwa.

Niikyangw yaw puma qa suutaq'ewya awyaniqe. Niiqe pu' yaw
puma oovi pay pas aapiy wuuyavo-
tiqw pu' yaw aw kuyvawisni. Noq
pu' yaw oovi pam mongwi imuy
hohongvituy amumi pangqawu yaw
awyaniqat. Pu' yaw puma oovi
haqam qööhiniqw pangso yaw
pumaya. Niiqe puma yaw as awyaqw yaw qa hak haqam. Niikyangw pay yaw kur as hak ep
qööhiy'taqw yaw oovi put qööhit
qötsvi'at epe'. Pu' yaw puma ang
pannumyakyangw pay panis yaw
hakiy kukyatsa tutwa. Noq yaw
pam hak pep waynumqa yaw kur
wupakukuy'ta. Qa hisat yaw puma
haqam paasavat hakiy kukyat aw

When the people finally entered
this upper world, they were en-
gulfed in darkness. They were still
at their site of emergence, when
they noticed to the north of them
a light shining forth from a fire.
Since it was utterly dark, the
flaming of the fire was very distinct. The people's leader said,
"It looks as if someone lives here
already." They all asked themselves, "Who on earth could have
a fire going? Maybe he's the owner
of this land. Who can that be?"

No one was willing to venture up
to the place of the fire. After some
time had passed, it was finally
decided to go and explore. The
leader, therefore, ordered several
of his strongmen to move toward
the location. They did as bidden
and advanced towards the fire.
Yet, upon reaching their destination, there was no soul in sight.
From all the evidence, however, it
was clear that someone had kept a
fire going there, for there were still
the remaining ashes. The only
other thing the men discovered as
they went about the site were
footprints which, evidently, belonged to a person with enormous
feet. Never before had the men

yorikya. Pas kya yaw pam oovi
himu hak pas wukotaqa. Yanhaqam yaw puma hohongvit put
mongwiy aw ahoy tuu'awvaya.

Noq pu' yaw pam mongwi'am
pangqawu, "Pas kya pay pam hak
himu pay pavanniiqa. Pu' sen pi
pay pam piw hak himu nukpana,"
yaw pam mongwi'am kitaaqe qa
haalayti.

Niiqe pu' yaw pam pumuy mongsungwmuy tsovalaqe pu' amumi
pangqawu, "Ura antsa ima hohongvit pangso qööhit awyat yaw
qa hiita tutwaqey yan ahoy tuu'awvayay. Yaw qa himu qööhi epnii-
kyangw pay yaw hak as kur ep
waynuma. Niikyangw yaw hak
wupakukuy'ta. Hak yaw sumataq
wukotaqaniiqe oovi paasavathaqam
kuukuy'ta. Noq nu' it aw wuu-
wantaqe oovi umuy tsovala. Itam
pu' yep pahoyesve' put yukuyaqw
pu' ason put haqawat kiwiskyaa-
kyangw piw awyani. Pam hak kya
pep it tutskwat himuy'te' sen
itamuy hintsanni. Paniqw oovi
itam it paahot hintsaktivaye'
yukuyaqw pu' haqawat itamungaqw pangso put aw kiwisniy,"
yaw pam pumuy amumi kita.

Pu' yaw oovi puma sungwamat
pay put su'an unangwtotiqe pu'
yaw aw pangqaqwa, "Kur antsa'ay," yaw kitota. "Pay pi son
hak qa pas pavan himuniiqe oovi
yephaqam qatuy," yaw kitota. "Pi
as qa hak haqam'eway'oy. Noq pay
antsa itam putsa qööhitsa tutwa-
ngwuniqw pay pi itam antsa pan-
totiniy," yaw puma kitota, sung-

come across human tracks of such
size. Hence, they concluded that
the keeper of the fire had to be a
giant. These findings the strongmen reported to their leader.

Their leader declared, "This being,
whoever he is, must be one endowed with great powers. He may
also be someone evil." Stating this
the leader grew disheartened.

He then gathered his fellow leaders
and said to them, "As you recall,
these brave ones went to the camp-
fire and reported that they did
not find anyone. The fire was out,
but someone had obviously been
walking about there, a creature
with enormous footprints. He
appears to be a giant by the looks
of his tracks. I've mulled all of this
over and decided to call this as-
sembly. Today we shall make
prayer feathers here and when
we're finished, some of us must
take them to that being. He may
very well be the owner of this
world and intend to do us harm. So
let's start working on these prayer
feathers. When they're finished,
some from our group will take
them there for us."

The leader's associates agreed and
replied, "Yes, indeed, that person
must have magical powers to be
living here. Although nobody seems
to be there, we keep seeing a fire.
So let's do what we decided to do."

wamat. Pu' yaw puma oovi put
pahotmalat pep aw tumalay'yungwa.

Pantsakkyaakyangw pu' yaw puma
yukuya. Paas yaw puma put yukuyat pu' yaw puma put tumalay
aw naanawakna. Pu' yaw piw tsoo-
tsongya put paahot awi'. Niiqe yan
yaw puma wuuwankyaakyangw put
pahotmalay aw unangwvaasiy
hooyintota. "Antsa um hak yep
qatuuqat ungem hapi itam it
yukuyay. Noq um itaatumalay
itamuy ömaatoyne' pu' putakw
tuwat mongvasniy," yaw puma
yanhaqam put tumalay aw naana-
waknakyangw tsootsonglalwa.

Noq pu' yaw i' mongwi'am pangqawu, "Ta'ay," yaw kita, "hak hapi
it aw kimaniy," yaw kita. "Hak pay
itamungaqw pavanniiqa it pangso
kimaniy," yaw kita.

Noq pu' yaw puma as put naa-
tuvinglalwaqw pay yaw qa hak
hingqawu. Hisatniqw pu' yaw
hakim naalöyöm tootim naa'o'ya.
"Pay itamyaniy. Pay itam put aw
kiwisniy," yaw puma kitota.

Noq pu' yaw pam mongwi'am
tsuyakqe yaw pangqawu, "Kwakwhay," yaw kita. "Antsa uma it
aw kiwisniy," yaw kita. "Ta'ay,
yep'ey. Uma it aw kiwise' uma put
hakiy aw pangqaqwani, 'Ta'ay,
itam yep it ungem yanvayay,' uma
aw kitotani."

Yanhaqam yaw pam pumuy
amumi tutaptat pu' put paahot
hiita aw paas mokyaatat pu' yaw
pam pumuy tootimuy amumi put

With that they set to work on the
prayer feathers.

Eventually, their task was completed. The men, next, prayed and
smoked over the feathers. As they
blew the smoke over the feathers,
they instilled into them their most
heartfelt concerns: "We truly made
these prayer things for you who
inhabit this place. Accept the
product of our labor and benefit
from it." In this manner the men
prayed as they smoked over their
work.

Thereupon the people's leader said,
"Now then, someone has to carry
the feathers over to that being. It
must be one who is strong and
stalwart."

The men kept asking one another
but they all remained silent.
Finally, after a good length of time
had elapsed, four young men
volunteered. "We'll do it. We'll
take the feathers over," they exclaimed.

"Thank you," the leader cried in
appreciation. "Yes, by all means,
take these things over. Here they
are. When you deliver them to him
just say, 'All right, we brought
these here for you.' That's all I
want you to say."

Following these instructions the
leader carefully wrapped up the
prayer feathers and then handed
them to the young men. "Now,

pahomokit tavi. "Ta'ay, yantaniy,"
yaw kita. "It uma aw yaawisni."

Pangqw pu' yaw puma oovi nankwusaqe pu' yaw put pangso qööhit
piw awya. Niiqe pu' yaw puma put
qööhit aw ökiwisqw yaw put angqw
kootala. Noq pam yaw hak qööhit
aw qatuuqa pay yaw put qööhit
aqwwat taykyangw yaw huur
moto'ta. Pay yaw pam hin soniwqw
pay yaw puma put yoyrikya. Noq
pas yaw pam hak nuutsel'ewayniqw
pay yaw puma paasat tsaatsawnaqe
pay yaw puma mashuruutotiqe pay
yaw put qa aw o'yat pay yaw puma
hisatniqw ahoy yan unangwtotiqe
pu' yaw pangqw ahoy watqa.
Watqaqe pu' yaw puma yanhaqam
put kikmongwit aw tuu'awvaya.

Noq pu' yaw pam pumuy amumi
pangqawu, "Is ohiy," yaw kita,
"pay uma son nawus qa piw awyani. Niikyangw uma paapu hapi
pas aw ökiniy. Pay pi as umuy qa
hintsanqw uma soq tsaatsawnaqe
oovi watqay. Pay kya as hak tuw-
qanen son umuy haqawat as qa
mu'ani. Umuy hintsannikyangw
umuy qa hintsanay," yaw pam kita.
"Uma oovi son nawus qa piw
awyani."

Pu' yaw oovi pam kikmongwi ep
piw paahot tumalay'ta. Noq pu'
yaw pam yukuuqe pu' yaw pam piw
pumuy aw hoona. "Ta'ay, uma
awye' uma paapu it aw o'yani.
Uma hakiy pas aw ökiniy," yaw
pam kita.

Pu' yaw puma oovi ep piw awya.
Niiqe puma yaw piw aw ökiwisqw
pay yaw piw ep qööhiwta. Nii-

this is it," he said. "Take them to
that person."

With that the men set out once
again and headed in the direction
of the fire. As they neared their
goal, the glow emitted from the fire
was quite distinct. Some being
hunkered in front of the fire
facing the flames. His head was
bent forward, pressing against his
chest. Now the men's eyes fell on
the creature's face. What hideous
looks! The men became so frightened at this point that they froze in
their tracks, unable to present their
offerings. The instant they re-
covered from their shock again
they took to their heels. Having
fled they related to their leader
what they had seen.

The leader exclaimed, "Too bad,
you'll have to go back. But this
time make sure you walk up to the
man. He did you no harm, yet you
cowards ran away out of fear. Had
he been an enemy, he would surely
have shot one of you. He could
have destroyed you but he didn't.
Therefore you have no choice but
to return."

Once more the leader engaged in
making prayer feathers. After completing his task, he sent the four
young men off for a second time.
"Now, when you get to him this
time, be sure to give these prayer
feathers to him. You must face
him," he commanded the men.

The men did as bidden. Once
again, as they were nearing their
destination, they found a fire burn-

kyangw pay yaw qa hak ep'eway.
Pu' yaw puma pas aw ökikyangw
pu' yaw put hakiy tutwa. Yaw hak
piw naat qööhiy aw qatuwta.
Niikyangw yaw hak pas wukoqötöy'kyangw yaw hak suplangput
qötöy'ta. Yaw hak himu wukoqötö-
niqw pay yaw puma piw tsaatsawnaqe pu' yaw naatuvinglalwa
sen pi yaw puma awyaniqey. Pu'
yaw puma tsaatsawnaqe yaw kur
hintotini. Is uti, pi yaw hak qa
soniwa. Nuutsel'ewakw yaw hak
pitsangway'ta.

Hisatniqw pu' yaw puma maqasne-
veq aw hoytiwiskyangw pu' yaw
nawis'ewtiqw pay naat tsawiniw-
kyaakyangw yaw aw öki. Noq yaw
antsa puma awyaqw pay yaw pam
hak piw an qööhit aqwwat tayta.
Niikyangw yaw qötö'at yaasayoq-
niqw yaw puma yansa paasat
yoyrikya. Pu' yaw puma aw pangqaqwa, "Ya um hak'iy?" yaw puma
aw kitota. Noq pay yaw pam hak
qa amumi hingqawu.

Pu' yaw puma piwya. "Ya um
hak'iy?" yaw aw kitota. Piw yaw
qa amumi hingqawu.

Pu' yaw paasat piwya. "Haw, ya
um hak'iy?" yaw puma aw kitota.

Piw yaw qa amumi hingqawqw pu'
yaw paasat suus peeti. Pay pi hopi
naalössa aqw hiita tuwaniy'tangwuniqw pu' yaw puma oovi piw tuu-
vingtota, "Ta'ay, ya um hak'iy?"
yaw kitota.

Pu' yaw pam paasat pumuy amumi
pangqawu, "Owiy," yaw kita, "pay
nuu'uy," yaw kita. Pangqawt pu'

ing. Yet, no one appeared to be
there. Not until they were close to
the fire did they discover the
stranger. As on the previous
occasion he sat there facing the
flames. His head was enormous and
distinctly red. So huge was the size
of his head that fear once again
struck the hearts of the men. They
inquired of one another as to
whether or not they should ad-
vance. They were so terrified that
they did not know what to do.
What a horrible sight the stranger
presented! His facial features were
simply grotesque.

Eventually, the four men began
moving again, apprehensively, to
be sure. Finally, after much time
had gone by, and still scared out of
their wits, they stepped up to the
figure. As before, he sat there
staring at the fire. The immense
size of his head was the only thing
the men were able to distinguish
at this time. Then they addressed
him. "Who are you?" they inquired. But the man did not reply.

The men repeated their question.
"Who are you?" But again there
was no reply.

They repeated their question a
third time. "Once more, who are
you?" they demanded.

But the man remained silent. Now
only one more time was left, as
things are done in fours by the
Hopi. So they queried for the last
time, "Come on, who are you?"

At this point the man finally
answered. "Yes," he uttered, "it's

yaw pam pumuy amumi namtö.
Noq yaw is uti. Pay yaw pam hak
pas kur antsa nuutsel'ewakw pitsangway'ta. Pas yaw himu nu'an
wukoqötöy'kyangw pu' yaw piw
talqötö. Pankyangw pu' yaw piw
ungwvukuwta. Niikyangw yaw pam
kur kwatsvakiwtaqw puma yaw qa
navotiy'yungwa. Noq pam hapi
yaw kur put hiita ang pakiwkyangw
yaw pumuy amumi naamaatakna.
Is uti, yaw hiita nuutsel'ewakw ang
pakiwta. Pu' yaw pam amumi
pangqawu, "Ta'ay, yeese'ey," yaw
kita. "Pay nu' as hisat umuy nuutaytaqw pas uma nuy qa poo-
tayay," yaw pam amumi kita. "Pay
nu' tuwat yep it tutskwat himuy'-
taqe oovi nu' paniqw yep yantay,"
yaw pam kita. "Noq uma antsa
pew inumi nönga. Noq nu' hapi
yep nalqatqe oovi haalayti. Nu' as
hakiy haqniy'ta. Noq tsangaw uma
ökiy. Niikyangw nu' hapi maasaw'uy," yaw kita. "Nu' hapi
maasaw."

Pu' yaw puma tootim put aw
pangqaqwa, "Haw owi? Ta'ay,
yep'ey," yaw kitota. "It puma pep
itaamomngwit ungem tumaltotat
angqw pew itamuy hoonayaqw oovi
itam yep it ungem yanvayay," yaw
puma put aw kitotaqe pu' yaw put
pahomokit aw taviya.

Pu' yaw pam maasaw put tsawik-
naqe yaw himu pep mookiwtaqw
maamatsqe yaw haalayti. "Is kwakwhay," yaw kita, "kwakwhay, Kur
pu'haqam hak yep it inungem
yukuniy," yaw kita. "Uma hapi
ahoy umuumongwiy awye' uma
aw pangqaqwaqwaqw angqw naap-

me." With this response he turned
around to face the men. What a
dreadful sight to behold, this
stranger with his ghastly looks!
Not only was his head massive, it
was also hairless. In addition, his
face was caked with blood. What
the men did not know, was that he
was wearing a mask when he
showed himself to them. It was
horrible, this repulsive mask which
covered his face. But now he spoke
to the men. "All right, sit down,"
he invited. "For ages I've been
awaiting your arrival but you never
came to call on me. I'm the owner
of this world; that's the reason
I'm here. Now that you've made
your emergence into this world and
come to me, I'm glad because I
live here all alone. I've been in
need of company and consider it
fortunate that you've arrived. I'm
known by the name of Maasaw,"
the figure declared. "I'm Maasaw."

The young men replied, "Is that
so? Very well then, accept these
things our leaders prepared for
you. They sent us here to bring
them to you." With that they
presented the wrapped prayer
feathers to him.

Maasaw unwrapped the bundle
and when he realized what was
contained within, he grew de-
lighted. "Thanks a lot," he exclaimed. "Thank you! To this day
I had to wait for someone to make
such a gift for me. When you
return to your leader, tell him to
call on me. Once he appears in

niqat'ay," yaw kita. "Angqw naap-
niqw pu' nu' yep put aw hin tutaptani. Hin nu' aw lavaytiniy," yaw
kita.

"Kur antsa'ay," yaw puma kitotat
pu' yaw puma pangqw ninma. Pay
pi yaw pam hak nuutsel'ewayniqw
puma pay yaw tsaatsawnaqe yaw
oovi pangqw a'ni watqa. Niiqe yanhaqam yaw puma kikmongwiy piw
aw tuu'awvayaqw yaw pam kikmongwi'am haalayti. "Kur antsa'ay,"
yaw kita, "pay nu' yan hin navot-
niqe oovi umuy aw hoona. Pay
puye'em son hak it tutskwat qa
himuy'ta," yaw kita. "Noq kya pi
antsa nuy tutaplawqw oovi pay nu'
antsa awniy," yaw pam kita. Niiqe
pay yaw pam suyan unangwti
puma hakiy mongwiy'vanyaniqw.

Pu' yaw pam tuwat awniiqe yaw
antsa aw pituqw pay yaw pam piw
panta, qööhiy yaw aqwwat tayta.
Pu' yaw pam aw pitutoqe suupan
pay yaw pam as qa navotnat aw
pituqw pay yaw kur maasaw
navotqe pu' aw pangqawu, "Yeese'ey," yaw kita.

"Owiy," yaw kita, "antsa um yaw
nuy tutaplawqw oovi nu' angqöy,"
yaw aw kita.

"Owiy," yaw pam kitat pu' yaw
qatu'a'awna.

Pu' yaw pam kikmongwi oovi pep
qatuptuqe pu' yaw tsoongoy ang
tangata. Pu' yaw puma pep tsoo-
tsonglawu. Pu' yaw puma yukuqw
pu' yaw pam kikmongwi put aw
pangqawu, "Ta'ay," yaw kita,
"antsa yaw um yep it tutskwat

person, I will enlighten him in
certain ways and share some things
with him," Maasaw explained.

"Very well," the men assented,
whereupon they headed back. But
since the man they had encountered was so terrifying, they became
frightened once more and ran off
as fast as their feet would carry
them. They relayed Maasaw's
message to their leader, who was
elated. "Great, that's what I
wanted to know; that's why I sent
you there. I knew all along that
someone had to have ownership of
this world. And since he's asking
for my presence, I suppose I'll go
to see him. The chief was greatly
relieved that they would have
someone to guide them in this
upper world.

So the leader, in turn, made for
the fire and when he got there,
Maasaw was sitting just as before,
staring into the flames. The leader
was under the impression that his
arrival had gone unnoticed, yet
Maasaw was very much aware of
it and welcomed the man. "Come
sit down," he said.

"Sure," the leader replied. "Indeed, I was told that you requested
my presence and so I've come."

"Yes," Maasaw answered and once
more bade his guest to sit down.

The latter complied, then filled his
pipe, and the two smoked for a
while. After they had finished, the
chief spoke first. "Now," he said,
"I understand you own this entire

soosok himuy'taqat yanhaqam
puma ihongvi'a'yam tuu'awvayay,"
yaw pam aw kita.

"Owiy," yaw kita, "nu' it yep
himuy'ta, tuuwaqatsit. Pu' nu' piw
pay yang aqwhaqami it tuuwaqatsit
ang pootiy'numngwuy," yaw kita.
"Noq antsa uma tsangaw nöngakqe oovi uma inumum yephaqam
yesniy. Niikyangw uma hapi nuy
mongwiy'kyaakyangw yep yesniy,"
yaw kita. "Antsa nu' it tuuwaqatsit
himuy'kyangw pu' nu' piw it qatsit
aw tunatyawtay. Pu' mokqa atkyami ikiy aw sinotimantaniqat put
nu' pep piw aw tunatyawtay,"
yaw pam put aw kita. "Nu' hapi qa
himu nukpana. Niikyangw nu' it
mokiwuy piw himuy'taqw oovi
himuwa qa hiita akw hinkyangw
mookye' inumimantaniy. Inuminiqw pu' nu' put paas tavikyangw
pu' nu' yangqw put kivaytsiwat
aw wiikye' pu' nu' pangso atkyami
piw sukwat qatsit aw put tavimantaniy. Yan hapi nu' yaapiy umuy
yep tumalay'taniy," yaw pam kita.
"Noq oovi uma yaapiy yephaqam
inumi enang tuuvingtiwiskyaa-
kyangw yep inumum yesniy," yaw
pam put aw kita.

"Kur antsa'ay," yaw pam kita.
Paasat pu' yaw pam pangqw
ahoyniiqe pu' yaw pam yanhaqam
mongsungwmuy aa'awnaqw pay
yaw puma tuwat haalaytotiqe yaw
pangqaqwa, "Kur antsa'ay, kwakwhay," yaw kitota. "kur antsa
itam yaapiy put tutskwayat ep
yeskyaakyangw antsa yaapiy put

land. My strong men conveyed this
information to me."

"Yes," Maasaw replied, "I'm the
owner of this earth. I roam and
look after the land into its farthest
reaches. I'm really glad you've
made your way into this world to
live here with me, but you should
do so with me as your leader. I
truly own this place and also take
care of life. Furthermore, I make
sure that whoever dies comes to
reside in my home down below,"
Maasaw revealed. "I'm no evil
being, however. I'm simply the
keeper of death. This means that
anyone who dies with a pure heart
will come to me. As soon as he
does, I'll welcome him and take
him to the opening of a kiva from
where I send him down to the
underworld to another life. Hence-
forth I'll tend to you in this manner," he explained. "For that
reason I want you to pray to me,
too, from now on while you inhabit
this land with me."

"Very well," the chief replied,
whereupon he returned and passed
on Maasaw's revelations to his
fellow leaders. Gladdened in their
hearts they cried, "We must be
grateful, indeed. From this day on
we'll definitely live on Maasaw's
land and look up to him as our

mongwiy'yungwni. Itam aw naa-
wakinkyaakyangw yaapiy yesniy,"
yaw puma kitota.

leader. We'll always pray to him as
we live out our lives," they agreed.

Next, Maasaw created the sun to provide light and warmth for the
newcomers.

TEXT 31

Niikyangw pam yaw tuwat qa
taalat ep qatu. Pas yaw qa haqam
taala, qa haqam yaw himu taawa.
Qa haqam yaw i' himu muuyaw.
Noq pay yaw puma kur hin qa
piw taalat ep yesni. Son yaw pas
puma ngas'ew qa hiita taalay'-
yungwniqe pu' yaw puma put aw
hiihin poptaya. Hiita hapi puma
akw pep talniy'yungwniqey put yaw
puma as yukuyani. Noq pu' yaw
pam maasaw pumuy amumi yan
tutapta, "It hapi pösövit angqw
uma put yukuyakyangw pu' uma
put piw aw pavasiwyaqw pu' pam
riyayaykuni. Pu' uma put riyakna-
yaqw pu' pam yang oovi yanmakyangw pu' pay pam as son suupan
qa talniy'tamantaniy."

Pu' yaw puma oovi put tutavotyaqe
pu' yaw puma oovi as pantotiqw
pay yaw pam antsa as oomi wupkyangw pay yaw qa pas suyan
talniy'ta. Pu' yaw puma piw put
aw wuuwantota. Noq pu' yaw pam
it tutskwat himuy'taqa piw amumi
pangqawu, "Ta'ay, pu' uma itwat-
yaniy," yaw kita. "I' hongvi. I' son
hisat haqami hintiniy," yan yaw
pumuy amumi tutapta.

Maasaw himself lived in total darkness. There was no trace of light
anywhere. The sun and moon did
not exist. For the people who had
just emerged, however, there was a
need to live in a world of light.
They would have to have some sort
of light and so they experimented
with a variety of things. They
would attempt to create something
which could serve as a source of
light for them. So Maasaw instructed: "You can produce this
light from cotton. Then gather
over it in prayer and it will begin
to rotate. Once you get it rotating
and it travels across the sky, it
should give off the light you desire."

The people did as told, but when
their creation finally ascended the
heavens, it only emitted a dim light.
So they mused over the matter once
more. Again Maasaw turned to
them and suggested, "Try a sifter
basket this time. It is strong and
will last forever."

Noq paasat pu' yaw puma piwya-
kyangw pu' yaw puma pay piw put
tutavoyat su'an yukuyaqe yaw
puma paasat pu' it pösövit akw it
tutsayat nömya. Pantotit pu' yaw
puma it mosayurpatsvut atsva pu'
piw akw enang nömyat paasat pu'
yaw puma put piw tunösmokyaa-
toynaya. Pantotit pu' yaw puma
piw put pitsangwtoynaya. Noq put
yaw puma piw pantaqat paasat
pu' yaw piw aw tawlalwakyangw
pu' yaw piw put riyaknaya. Pu' yaw
pam riyakkyangw pu' yaw piw
hihin oovetikyangw paasat pu' yaw
pam pavan riyayayku. Oomi'iwma-
kyangw pu' yaw piw pavan a'ni
halayvit r iyayaykuqe pu' yaw
paasat suyan talniy'ma. Pas pi yaw
suyan taalawva.

Yantoti yaw pumaniqw pu' yaw
pam pangqawu, i' tutskway'taqa,
"Pantani," yaw kita. "Ta'ay, ima
hapi son as hin qa maatsiwni," yaw
kita.

Yaw pam kitaqw pu' yaw pam hak
wuuti pumuy asna. Niikyangw yaw

The people tried a second time,
heeding Maasaw's advice. They
covered the sifter with a layer of
cotton,[4] which in turn was wrapped
with a bison hide. Then they
fastened to it a small pouch filled
with food. Having also painted
some facial features on their creation, they again chanted over it,
eventually causing it to spin. No
sooner did it begin spinning than it
gained altitude and began whirling
with even greater momentum. As
it climbed higher and higher, its
speed steadily increased and it
brightly illuminated the sky. Broad
daylight had appeared.

When this much was accomplished,
Maasaw cried, "That's the way
it's going to be. But now these two
lights must have a name."

Immediately a woman set to bap-
tizing them by ritually washing
their hair. She washed the hair of

---

[4]Powell's passage relating to the creation of the sun is noteworthy in that it twice
operates with the number seven which, as a rule, is totally un-Hopi in concept. Again,
Ma-chi-ta, correctly Matsito, is erroneously assigned the place of Maasaw. "Still it was
cold and dark, and the people murmured and cursed Ma-chi-ta, and he said: 'Why do
you complain? Bring me seven baskets of cotton;' and they brought him seven baskets of
cotton. And he said: 'Bring me seven virgins;' and they brought him seven virgins. And
he taught the virgins to weave a wonderful fabric, which he held aloft, and the breeze
carried it away to the sky; and behold! it was transformed into a full-orbed moon. The
same breeze also carried the flocculent fragments of cotton to the sky, and lo! these took
the shape of bright stars. And still it was cold; and again the people murmured, and Ma-
chi-ta chided them once more, and said, 'Bring me seven buffalo robes;' and they
brought him seven buffalo robes. 'Send me seven strong, pure young men;' and they sent
him seven young men, whom he taught to weave a wonderful fabric of the buffalo fur.
And when it was done, he held it aloft, and a whirlwind carried it away to the sky, where
it was transformed into the sun" (1972: 26).

pam it mootiwatniiqat asnaqe pu'
yaw pam oovi put muuyaw yan
tungwa. Noq pam hapi yaw i' pay
qa pas suyan talniy'taqawa pan
tungwniy'va. Noq pu' yaw pam it
muuyawuy angk yukiltiqat asnaqe
pu' putwat yaw pam taawa yan
tungwaqw pu' yaw puma piw put
riyaknaya. Noq pam yaw pas suyan
talniy'ta.

the first creation and named it
"moon." That was the object which
radiated the dim light. Then she
washed the hair of the second
creation. On that she bestowed the
name "sun." Following this ceremony, they once again got the sun
to rotate. It really gave off a brilliant light.

When the newly emerged people requested Maasaw to become their
leader, he refused and appointed the younger of two brothers[5] as their
chief. "The Hopi people asked him, that since he is the first person here,
and that they came to him, he should be their leader in this new land,
but Maasaw said no. He said, 'You have many intentions or plans that
you want to do in this life. I will not be your leader now until you have
completed all the things that you want to do in this life; then I will be
your leader.' The Hopis said, 'Since you know us, our hearts and our
intentions, I think it would be proper for you to appoint someone to be
our leader. Someone from among us.' This Maasaw agreed to do, so he
gathered the people and he went to two brothers and he chose the
younger brother to be the leader of the people and he told him that
from that day on he would be the father of those people here and to take
care of this land" (*Hopi Hearings* 1955:80).

After acquainting the people with the element of fire (see Chapter
5), distributing to them maize as a staple food and teaching them how
to sow and grow crops (see Chapter 6), Maasaw issued his famous
pötskwani to them, "rules for living and maintaining the proper way of
life."[6] In the existing English literature the concept of *pötskwani* is

[5]For further information on the two brothers see Katchhongva (1975: 8) and *Hopi
Hearings* (1955: 124).

[6]According to other traditions, Maasaw conveyed his life plan to the Hopi only
after completion of their migratory wanderings. The occasion was provided during their
encounter with the god at Orayvi, as is evident from the subsequent quotations in the
Hopi Hearings: "It was at Orayvi here the Great Spirit who gave this life plan to us"
(1955: 44). "We of Orayvi knew that Orayvi is the mother of all our life pattern, because
it is here that these things were laid down for us" (1955: 257).

generally rendered as "life plan," "life pattern," or "road plan." Younger Hopi who are no longer familiar with the term often substitute the word *tutavo* "instructions/teachings." "Prophetic statements" given to the Hopi in conjunction with the laws of the *pötskwani* are commonly known as *navoti*, literally "knowledge gained from hearing, i.e., not from seeing or experience."

For mnemonic reasons Maasaw's life-teachings were incised in *owatutuveni* or "stone tablets," a gesture akin to the way in which Moses received the Ten Commandments. The tablets themselves were fashioned from hardened cornmeal.[7] Two excerpts from the *Hopi Hearings* are cited in regard to the tablets. "Then Maasaw realized that he did not make any provisions for himself because he had given land and life to these people, so he asked the women to grind some corn so that he could make a stone tablet, and when that was made out of cornmeal, our life plan and the things that they were told were put in on the stone tablet. Two were made of the same thing and each brother received one of them to carry in this life, and they were instructed to never let go of it because it will be upon these stone tablets that this Hopi life will be based. In this way they were instructed to live this life and to work and help the people in taking care of this land. Maasaw said they must never forsake, never doubt his teachings and instructions, for if they ever doubted it and forsaked this stone tablet and all its teachings, they will cause a destruction of all life in this land, so they were warned to always remember and carry on these instructions for all his people..." (1955: 81).

"Here's another thing. When Maasaw asked the women to grind the cornmeal he wanted to make sure the White man would [not] forget these instructions and in order for him to have something he told the Spider Woman to get some cornmeal so when she did he made a batter which was flattened out and with his magic power he turned the corn-meal into a stone tablet and gave one to each of the nephews, one which was to be the White man and the other was the Hopi" (1955:81-82).

The growing importance of these tablets is borne out by the manifold references to them during the *Hopi Hearings*.

"We also know that the Hopi people obtained this sacred stone tablet which was placed in the hands of those great leaders of the Hopi people when they first came here. It has written all these teachings, the life plan of the Hopi, and it is upon this stone tablet we base our life and all of our religious ceremonies are connected to it" (1955:6).

---

[7]For a Hopi reference to the *owatutuveni* or stone tablet see Chapter 4, Text 42.

"When the people settled and began to organize how they would live, a stone tablet was made and placed in the hands of the proper leaders. All Hopi life is based on this stone tablet" (1955:50).

In conjunction with the *pötskwani*, inscribed in the stone tablets, Maasaw also bestowed the name Hopi on the younger of the two brothers.[8] "So he set a date, up to sixteen days, at which time they would gather again, so after the fourth day they would be able to move on. When that time came, Maasaw set up an altar and things he used in upholding this life and land, and here we were to offer our prayers and receive this life plan, and we were to stay up at night in order to keep watch over this great gathering where the life plan was to be given to us. After this was done he took this altar or *tüponi* and placed it in the hands of the younger brother and told him, 'I give you this symbol which represents land and life and I appoint you as the leader to take care of this land. Your name shall be Hopi and you must lead your people in this life along the good life which I have given you. Take care of your children. Take care of this land and life so that all people will be well and shall live long lives, that there shall be plenty of food for all people. When the life is long you will reach the time when you will have to use a cane and that is when you have reached your old age, and there will be no sickness even to the end of your lives.' This is what he told the Hopi people. 'You must never harm anyone. You must never make wars against any people.' These were the teachings that were given to the people at that time" (1955:80). A Hopi reference to this naming event is given in Text 32.

TEXT 32

Noq yep pu' yaw itam antsa put maasawuy amum hiisavohaqam yanyungqw pep pu' yaw kur itamuy kwilalaykuyaniqat aw pituqw ep pu' yaw pam itamuy piw tsovala. Niikyangw pep pu' yaw pam itamumi it hiita maatakna. Paasat pu' yaw pam pep soosokmuy sinmuy amumi wuuwakyangw pay yaw antsa haqawatuy amumi hin

After we had lived alongside Maasaw for a while, it became time to start our migration. Maasaw, therefore, had us assemble once more and revealed to us a curious object. Then he thought about the ways and characters of different people who were gathered there. Then he gave one person the strange object to hold, which

---

[8]The older brother is consequently identified as the Hopi's "white brother" (Katchongva 1975: 9).

navotiy'ta. Niiqe pu' yaw pam put
kur it owatutuvenit hakiywat
mavoktoyna. Pantit pu' yaw pam
put hakiy mavoktoynaqey put yaw
pam asnakyangw pu' yaw pam put
paas tungwa. Noq pam yaw kur
hak hopini. Yan yaw pam put
tungwa.

turned out to be a stone tablet.
Next, he washed the hair of the
person holding the tablet and, to
complete the ritual, gave him a
name. Henceforth this person was
to be known as Hopi. That was the
name Maasaw bestowed upon him.

Finally, Maasaw decided that it was time for the people to leave the
Sipaapuni, the place of their emergence, and set out on their migrations
across the continent.

TEXT 33

Noq pu' yaw pam maasaw wuuwanta pay yaw kur puma son pep
put amum yesniniqw pu' yaw pam
oovi pumuy amumi pangqawu,
"Ta'ay," yaw kita, "pu' hapi uma
pas suyan taalat ep yeese. Noq pay
uma kur son inumum yep yesniy,"
yaw kita. "Pay pi uma naat haqami
tunatyawwisa. Oovi uma pangsoq
hapi hoyoyoykuniy," yaw kita. "Pu'
son pi uma qa hiitakw hapiyaniy.
I' tutskwa hapi aqwhaqami naat it
paatuwaqatsit aatsatsava pan-
yungway. Noq pam hapi i' pa̱a-
tuwaqatsi pangniikyangw pam it
tutskwat epniiqe pas wuuyaq'ay,"
yaw kita. "Put uma hapi son ang
qa nööngantiwiskyaakyangw pu'
uma haqami wuuyaq tutskwat aw
ökikyangw paasat pu' uma haqami-
yaqey piw pangsowat ökiniy," yaw
amumi pam kita.

Maasaw came to the conclusion
that the people could not reside
with him. So he told them. "Now
that you live in a world full of
light, you cannot stay here with
me. You're still bent on reaching
another destination. I, therefore,
want you to set out for that goal.
But you'll need some means of
transportation. This land in its
entire reach lies in the middle of
the oceans. These seas are much
larger than the land. You must
cross them before you reach a large
body of land and then your destination," he explained.

Waters summarizes the significance of the four directional migrations. "Before Maasaw turned his face from them and became invisible, he explained that every clan must make four directional migrations before they all arrive at their common, permanent home. They must go to the ends of the land—west, south, east, and north—to the farthest *paaso* (where the land meets the sea) in each direction. Only when the clans had completed these four movements, rounds, or steps of their migration, could they come together again, forming the pattern of the Creator's universal plan" (1963:35).

In connection with his decision, to dismiss the people across the land, Maasaw also distributed different languages among them.[9]

TEXT 34

Noq pay hiisavohaqam pi pas puma pepeq yesqw pu' pam maa-saw pumuy amumi pangqawu, "Ta'ay, pay aqw hayingwtiy. Uma son nawus qa naanahoyyani. Pay son uma pas yepsayani. Uma angqe' haahaqe' kuktotani," kita amumi yawi'. "Noq oovi uma pew-yaniy," yaw amumi kita.

Noq pu' yaw oovi pam haqamniqw pu' paasat yaw haqawa awniqw pu' yaw pam put aw, "Ta'ay," kitat pu' yaw pam paysoq put aw tongok-ngwu. Aw tongokq pay yaw pam ayo' nakwsukyangw pay yaw hinwat tuuqayta. Pu' yaw piw suukya awniqw pay yaw pamwa pay piw anti. Pay yaw piw hinwat tuuqay-tangwu. Paasat pu' pay yaw pam

Exactly how long the people had been residing there is not known, but one day Maasaw said to them, "All right, the time has come. You'll have to migrate into dif-ferent directions. You cannot remain in only this one place. I want you to leave your foorprints in various places. Come here to me," he beckoned.

Obediently someone stepped up to Maasaw who only muttered, "Now," whereupon he slightly touched the person. And no sooner had Maasaw placed his hand upon the person than he walked away and spoke a different language. Somebody else then approached Maasaw and the same thing hap-pened to him. He, too, ended up talking in another tongue and was

---

[9]While some emergence myths attribute this "Babylonian feat" to *yaapa,* the "mock-ingbird," our version, which holds Maasaw responsible, is confirmed in the *Hopi Hearings:* "He has given different people their languages and way of life, and their way of worshipping, so that all plans of life would work out in the way he wants this life to be placed on this earth." (1955: 98).

mitwat lavayiyat qa maatsiy'-
tangwu. Qa sun yaw puma yu'a'ata.

Pu' yaw pam pepehaq pumuy
soosokmuy pantsana. Niiqe puma
yaw oovi soosoyam qa suukw lavayit
tuuqayyungwa. Pay yaw peetusa
kur sun lavaymakiwyaqe puma yaw
oovi pay hingqaqwaqey pay peetuy
lavayiyamuy maatsiy'yungwa. Pay
pi pam maasaw son piw pumuy
qa hiisa'niiqamuy sun yu'a'atotaqa-
muy naahoy oya. Paapiy pu' yaw
puma qa sun yu'a'atota. Qa sun
tuuqayyungqe puma yaw qa naa-
matsiy'numya. Kur yaw puma
paapu hin naanami yu'a'atotani.
Paasat pu' yaw puma pepeq naanahoyya. Hak hapi yaw hakiy an
tuuqayte' yaw put amumningwu.
Paasat pu' yaw puma hiihiitu
himusinom, si'oot, yotsi'em,
kumantsim, tasavum, kooninam
naanahoyya. Pas yaw pam pep
pumuy lavayit soosokmuy huytaqw
pep pu' puma naanahoyya.

no longer capable of understanding
the first person. They both spoke
differently.

Maasaw did this to all of the people
there. As a result they no longer
shared a single language. Only a
handful in each case had received
the same language, so that these
people understood the language of
a few others when they carried on
a conversation. Maasaw divided
those few into different groups on
the basis of the language they
shared. From that day on people
spoke in different tongues and
hence were no longer able to
understand one another. They
simply could not converse with
each other any more. And so the
people departed and trekked off
into different directions. Whoever
spoke the same language as the
next person went with him. Now all
the various Indian races went
apart, among them the Zunis, the
Apaches, the Comanches, the
Navajos, and the Pai people. They
all went their separate ways after
Maasaw had distributed the different languages among them.

Prior to embarking on their migrations, each clan is also said to
have been equipped by Maasaw with a *paa'uypi* or "water planting
implement."[10] While this connection between Maasaw and the phenome-

---

[10]Instructions on how to repair a broken *paa'uypi*, or on how to replace it when
necessary, are also conveyed to the Hopi by Maasaw. For details see Waters (1963: 34).

non of water is fairly unusual, it is by no means unexpected. In prayers to Maasaw, the god is sometimes implored for moisture.[11] The reference to the magic water jar is cited by Waters. "To each clan Maasaw then gave a small water jar. In the years to come, he said, they would be slowly migrating over the earth, and many times there would be no water where they settled. They were then to plant this jar in the ground and, thereafter, for as long as they remained there, water would keep flowing out of this *paa'uypi.*"

Maasaw went on, that one certain person "must be ordained to carry this water jar for the whole clan. He must be a holy person whose life is perfect in every way. Four days before you are ready to move on, this water carrier must go without salt and he must pray. Then he will carry the jar until you arrive at the next stop on your migration. For four days more he will pray and fast and go without sleep before planting the jar again. Then again the water will start flowing, and he may take up his normal life" (1963:34).

The land chosen by Maasaw for the Hopi as a destination of their wanderings would be marked by a large star.

TEXT 35

"Niikyangw uma hapi naat haqami-wat hoytaqe oovi uma son yepsa yanyungwni. Pu' yaapiy uma hapi oovi nankwusanikyangw haqaqw pam taawa yaymakqw pangsoq hapi uma nankwusani. Put hapi uma nay'kyaakyangw yaapiy yesni. Pam umuy mukintani. Pu' pam piw it tutskwat mukintaqw putakw pu' i' hiihiimu umuunatwani wungwiwmamantani. Putsa akw himu wungwiwmamantani. Pu' uma panwiskyaakyangw naat uma

And then he added, "But I know that there is still a place you're striving to reach. For that reason you can't stay here forever. When you leave, go into the direction where the sun rises. From this day on you'll live with the sun as your father. He'll give you warmth. He'll also heat the earth so all your crops can grow. Only by means of his heat will things grow. Eventually, as you travel along, you'll see

[11]Compare, for example, Talayesva (1942: 287). Beaglehole reports in conjunction with a harvest Sopkyaw, that the impersonator of the real Maasaw is approached prior to his departure by men and women who "give him prayer feathers and meal with prayers for a long life, rain, good crops and many children" (1937: 47).

haqe'yakyangw pu' uma it wuko-
sohut tutwani. Put uma tutwe' pep
pu' hapi uma suus yesvani. Pu'
uma hapi pep kitsoktote' pu' uma
hapi pep suus yesvani. Pam hapi
pep pas umuututskwani. Put pay
son hak umuy naanaqasnaniy,"
yaw aw kitat pu' yaw piw pangqawu, "Niikyangw oovi pay hapi i'
umuuso, kookyangwso'wuuti, atkya
hin put umungem pasiwnaqa pam
hapi pay umumumniy," yaw kita.
"Noq ason hapi put uma aw tuu-
vingtotani, hin uma yangqw nankwusakyangw pu' uma hintoti-
niqw'öy, haqami umawatya-
niqw'öy," yaw kita.

a huge star.[12] Where you sight this
star, you'll settle permanently at
that spot. There you'll found a
village and dwell forever. The land
where that happens will be yours.
No one will compete with you for
it. On account of this your grandmother, Old Spider Woman, who
made plans for you down in the
underworld, will accompany you.
Inquire of her what you're supposed to do when you leave here
and which direction you are to
take," Maasaw instructed.

In his farewell words, Maasaw finally revealed to the Hopi their
ultimate goal, Orayvi.

TEXT 36

Paasat pu' yaw pam maasaw put
pötskwanit amungem yuku."Ta'ay,
pay hapi uma yangqw nankwusani.
Uma yep umuuqatsiy piw aw tunat-
yaltotini. Naavaasyani uma'ay. Qa
naanap hin uma yesni. Pay uma
angqe' aatsavalni. Pu' uma pay
nanaalaktinumyaqw pay tatam
umuukiki angqe' hongyani. Pu' it
hiihiita qötsvit, mötsikvut uma

It was then that Maasaw gave
instructions for the people on how
they and future generations were to
conduct their lives. "All right, you
will now journey forth from here.
Mark well how you conduct your
life. Be kind to one another and
don't live dissolutely. Spread out
across the land and be sure to
establish settlements. As you trek

---

[12]According to Hermequaftewa, the star was a sign actually given to the Hopi by
Maasaw. "There was a sign given to them by Maasaw. Whenever the Great Star appeared
in the sky there the Hopi would settle for all time. Wherever they were then, there they
were to take food from their waists and settle down to live" (1954: 3).

kiihaykye' pangalantotani. Pu' pam
umuukiki as pay sonqa kiiqötotini-
kyangw pay pam naat son ang
aqwhaqami qa susmataqmantani.
Pam hapi pay son tuuvoyni. Itakw
hapi i' piw susmataqtini hiisaq nu'
umuy tutskwat aa'awnaqw'ö. Ason
uma yep hapi put mongvastoti-
kyangw paasat pu' uma oraymiye'
pep pu' uma ason suus yesvani.
Oovi uma orayvit hepwisniy," yaw
amumi kita.

Niiqe pu' oovi pam hin orayvi
soniwniqat, haqamniiqat paas yaw
pam put pumuy aa'awna. "Pay
uma tutwaqw pay nu' son piw qa
navotni. Pay nu' son piw umuy qa
pan unangwtapnani. Uma hapi
orayve yesve' uma hapi pas sus-
kyahaksinomniwtini. Uma hapi pas
tutskwangaqwniiqat hiita nunukngwat himuy'vayani. Pam hapi pas
it tuuwaqatsit hot'öqa'at'a. Pang
orayviy ang pas qa himu qee'e.
Paniqw hapi uma oovi orayvit
hepwisni. Uma hapi tutwani," yan
yaw amumi tutapta.

along, heap such things as ashes
and trash near your villages because your communities are bound
to fall into ruin one day. But
ashes and trash will be easily
recognizable and never disappear.
They will serve as markers of how
much land I granted you. Later,
upon completing your migration,
proceed to Orayvi and settle there
for good. So be on your way and
search for Orayvi," he instructed
them.

Thereupon Maasaw described in
detail the features and the location
of Orayvi. "Once you find Orayvi,
I'll learn about it. I'll instill that
feeling in you that you've found
your destination. After colonizing
Orayvi, you'll become wealthy
people. You'll gather treasures
from the land, for it constitutes
the backbone of this earth. There
isn't anything that doesn't exist in
the vicinity of Orayvi. For this
reason I want you to go there.
You're destined to find it," he
directed them.

4

The Land Connection

In the Hopi view of things Maasaw is the autochthonous proprietor of *tuuwaqatsi* "land and life" in its solid form, and *paatuwaqatsi* "water and life" in its liquid form. Beaglehole's informants, for this matter, refer to Maasaw as "Earth Father" (1936:6).

TEXT 37

Pay pi antsa itam hopiit naat pu'
sipaapunit epeq nöngakkyangw
yaw put hakiy maasawuy aw pas
susmooti öki. Niiqe oovi itamuy-

We Hopi had barely made our
emergence at the place called
Sipaapuni when we encountered
Maasaw as the very first being.

niqw pam hapi soosok yep it tuuwaqatsit, paatuwaqatsit himuy'ta,
pay pas kyaahisat, naat pas yay-
ngwangaqw.

Thus, according to our traditions,
he has been the owner of all the
land and seas since time immemorial.

As god of the surface of the earth, Maasaw is in particular the *genius loci* of the land claimed by the Hopi as their own. The geographical boundaries of this land, which is occasionally termed *mastutskwa*, or "Maasaw's country,"[1] are delineated in a legend collected by Stephen. In the tale, which begins with a quarrel among the gods motivated by the partition of the lands, Maasaw strides off a large tract for himself and his later protégés, the Hopi. "Maasaw first travelled south, then cir- cuitously toward the east until he reached his starting point. He called this area his land. The exact limits are unknown but it is surmised he started from a point about where Fort Mojave is situated, thence south as far as the Isthmus of Panama, skirted eastward along the Gulf of Mexico and northward by the line of the Rio Grande up into Colorado, thence westerly along the thirty-six parallel, or thereabouts, to the Rio Colorado, meandering along its tributaries, and so on, southward to his starting point at Fort Mojave. This was Maasaw's land originally, the land of the Hopiitu" (1929:55-6).

Generally, Maasaw is thought of as the sole and aboriginal inhabitant of the upper world at the time when Hopikind reached the surface of the earth. In some traditions, however, ownership of the earth is shared between Maasaw, Spider Woman, and her two grandsons.

TEXT 38

Inavotiniqw antsa hisat qatsiyay-
niwqat epeq ura ima hakim yep it
tuuwaqatsit himuy'yungqam piw
tuwat maamatsiwya. Noq i' maasaw pumuy mongwi'am. Noq pu'
i' qöö'aya'amniqa kookyangwso'wuuti. Pu' put so'wuutit mömat-
niqam pöqangwhoya, palöngawhoya. Panis hapi puma paasa' yep

According to my knowledge, at the
beginning of life those beings
present here who owned the earth
had names just as we do. Maasaw
was the headman and the house-
keeper was Old Spider Woman. In
addition, there were her grand-
children Pöqangwhoya and Palöngawhoya. These four were the

---

[1] A reference to the concept of *mastutskwa* is found in Swanton (1953: 352) under the spellings of "Mastutc'kwe" and "Maastoetsjkwe."

it tuuwaqatsit himuy'yungqw
angqe' qa hak haqam naato qatu.

Pu' itam pew sinoti, yan hopi-
matsiwtaqamu. Niiqe oovi itam
mooti it tuuwaqatsit aw tuukunya.
Yantaqat akw i' qataymataq
qatuuqa itamumi tutskwat no'a.
Qa yepsa tutskwat, ayo'wat paatuwaqatsit yupqöymi piw enang
itamuy put maqa.

sole proprietors of this world at a
time when no one else existed.

Then we who are called Hopi
came to inhabit this place. We
were the first to set foot on this
earth. For this reason Maasaw, the
god who lives invisibly, transferred
this land to us. He gave us not
only the land here, but also that
which lies beyond the oceans.

As to the god's bestowal of the land on the Hopi, sources of oral
tradition, for obvious reasons, vary considerably in regard to the motivation and even the time of this act. In a mythic account from Second
Mesa transmitted by Wallis, Maasaw already assured Shrike, the messenger from the underworld, that he would be willing to divest himself
of the land. "I shall give you my land," is a promise actually volunteered
by the god (1936:4).

In my version of this episode Maasaw informed the bird that he
would not completely entrust the land to the petitioning Hopi. To be
sure, he would permit the people to settle and live on his land, but he
would retain title to the earth.

TEXT 39

Noq pay pi yaw pam a'ni himuniiqe pay hakiy angqaqwniqw pay
yaw pam hakiy suuhova'ikwngwu.
Niiqe pam yaw oovi kur put hakiy
pay hova'ikwqe yaw put pay
nuutaytaqw yaw antsa motsni aw
pitu. Noq pam yaw pepeq uuyiy
qalaveq taqatskiy'ta. Noq pangso
yaw pam motsni put tuwaaqe pu'
yaw pam pangsoqhaqami tsokiiti.

Noq antsa yaw pam ep qatu-
kyangw yaw naqlap kwaatsiy
taviy'ta. Pu' yaw pam as kwaatsiy
naat pu' aw maavuyaltiqw pay
yaw put motsnit kiisiwni'at put

Maasaw, of course, is a being
invested with greater than mortal
powers and capabilities. For
instance, he can smell an approaching person right away. And
since he had picked up the scent
of someone, he was waiting for
whoever it was to show. Sure
enough, it was a shrike who arrived, alighting on top of Maasaw's
hut at the edge of the field.

As Maasaw squatted by the fire,
he had a mask placed next to him.
He was just at the point of reaching out for it when the shrike's

maasawuy atpip maatsiltiqw pay
yaw pam oovi nawus put qa ep
kwusu. Pu' yaw pam motsni panis
epeq tsokiitikyangw pu' yaw, "Too,
too, too, too," yan yaw töqti.
Pu' yaw pam maasaw put aw yan
yorikkyangw pu' yaw aw pangqawu, "Ya um pitu?"

"Owi."

"Kur antsa'ay. Pay um pew
hawni."

Paasat pu' yaw pam oovi pangqw
aw hawt pu' yaw aqlap qatuptu.
Noq pam yaw put paas tavi. Niiqe
pu' yaw aw pangqawu, "Qatu'uy,"
yaw aw kita.

Paasat pu' yaw pam maasaw put
aw namtökqw pu' yaw pam motsni
yan yori. Pay yaw pam pep uuyiy'-
taqa pay yaw itamun tokoy'ta.
Noq pay pi yaw pam kur hin qa
navotiy'ta pam motsni hiita oovi
waynumqw. Pay pi a'ni himuniiqe
oovi pay yaw aapiy navotiy'ta.
Niiqe pu' yaw aw pangqawu,
"Ta'ay, son pi um qa hintiqw
waynumqe oovi yaasatniqwhaqam
pew inumi pitu. Pi qa hak hisat
yephaqam waynuma."

"Owiy," yaw pam motsni kitat pu'
pam put aw tu'awiy'ta hintiqw
puma pangqw atkyangaqw pangso
put hongvi'aytotaqat. Pu' yaw pam
pangso pumuy amungem qatsi-
heptoqey. "Noq yaw antsa um yep
qatuy. Pu' antsa itam tuwat pep
atkya yeesey. Noq pep itaaqatsi
sakwiti. Pas itam kur hin hiniwto-
tini. Itam soosok hiita ang a'ni
neeneepew tumalay'yungway. Pas

shadow became visible beneath
him, so it was too late to pick it
up. And no sooner had the shrike
perched on the field shed, than he
chirped out, "Too, too, too, too."
Maasaw looked up at him and
greeted him. "So you've come?"

"Yes."

"Very well. Come on down here
to me."

The bird flew down as bidden and
landed next to Maasaw. The latter
cordially welcomed him. "Sit
down," he said.

When Maasaw turned toward the
shrike, the bird was able to look
at him. He noticed that the owner
of those crops there had a body
just like us humans. Being endowed with magical powers, the
god already knew beforehand the
reason for the bird's mission.
Nevertheless he said to him, "All
right, you must have come with a
purpose. No one has ever traveled
here before."

"Yes," the shrike replied, whereupon he explained to Maasaw why
the inhabitants of the underworld
had appointed him to be their
messenger and to seek life for
them. "So what they told me is
true, you really live here. We, in
turn, dwell down below, yet our
existence has become a shambles.
We are troubled and confused.
There is no cooperation among
people and no harmony. People

itam qa lomaqatsiy'yungwa. Itam
paapu qa namisuutaq'ewyay. Itam
koyaanisqatsit yeesey. Noq paniqw
oovi nuy angqw pew ayatotay.
Niikyangw pu' piw pangqaqwa sen
yaw itam son angqwye' yep umum
yesniy. It yaw nu' uumi maqaptsi-
taniy," kita yaw awi'.

Yan yaw pam put aw lavaytiqw
pu' yaw maasaw put unangwmi
taatayi. Pay a'ni hin tunatya yaw
ep apqölpe. Noq oovi pay yaw
pam qa pas suyan haalayvewat
hu'wana, "Pi uma'ay. Pay pi uma
angqwyaniqey naanawakne' pay pi
uma angqwyaniy," yaw aw kita.
"Noq nu' yan'ewakw yep okiw-
hintay. Qa himu inuupe nukngwa.
Qa taalat nu' ep qatu. Noq pay
pu' oovi uma piyani. Put aw uma
suutaq'ewye' uma antsa angqwyaniy," yaw kita. "Niikyangw nu'
hapi son umuy pas it tutskwat
maqani. Nu' hapi umuy it pas
maqe' nu' hapi son it ahoy naap-
tini. Pay uma hin qatsiyesqey pay
uma naato hisat piw put aqw
ahoy ökini. Pu' nu' umuy it maqe'
nu' kur umuy hintsanniy. Nu' son
hapi paasat umumi tuyqawiy'-
taniy," yaw aw kita. "Noq pay pi
uma angqwyaninik angqwyani.
Nen pu' uma hapi yep pay haak
inumum yesniy," yaw aw kita.
Pu' aw kitaaqe pay yaw nakwha.
Angqw awyaniqat pay yaw nakwha.

Pu' yaw motsni haalayti. "Kwakwhay," kitat paasat pu' yaw pam
puuyaltikyangw pu' ahoy nakwsuqe
pu' ahoy atkyayaqamuy amumi
hin navotqey put tuu'awma.

cannot stand each other any
longer. Our way of life is *koyaanisqatsi,* utter chaos. That state of
affairs has induced them to send
me here. I was told to inquire if
we could possibly come here to live
with you. So I am to ask your
permission."

The god looked into the bird's
heart. He saw that there were
great aspirations within. Thus,
quite saddened, he reluctantly
replied, "That's up to you. If you
desire to come, then do so by all
means. I'm barely eking out an
existence here. I own nothing of
value and I live in total darkness.
So it's your choice. If you're willing
to put up with these hardships,
then come. But I will not entrust
this land to you. If I do that, I'll
never get it back. One day you will
return to the same way of life that
you are living now. If I turn this
land over to you, I wouldn't know
what to do with you, nor would I
have any control over you. Still,
if you really care to come, you are
welcome to do so. You can stay
here with me for the time being."
With these words Maasaw gave
them permission to come to him.

The shrike was elated. "Thank
you," he cried and flew off to
return and deliver Maasaw's
response to the people below.

To survive on his land, Maasaw urged the Hopi to adopt his way of life, which is distinguished by poverty and hardship. Obviously, their chances of success would be enhanced if they were also to follow his religious practices.

TEXT 40

"Ta'ay, noq oovi kur uma nuy yep hin qatuqw uma put aw suu-taq'ewye' pay uma inumum yep yesni. Nen uma it yep tuuwaqatsit akw mongvasyani. Pu' kur uma piw yep it iwimiy nu' put yep hintsakmaqw put uma aw suu-taq'ewye' put uma enang akw mongvasyani." Yan pam pumuy amumi lavaytikyangw pu' pam pumuy amungem piw tuwat son pi qa hiita hintaqe put pam pumuy amumi oya, tiiponit.
"Niikyangw uma naat a'ni hiita tunatyawvaya. Pu' uma hapi it hiita qa lomahintaqat aqw ökye' naat uma hapi nuy paklawnayani." Yanhaqam yaw pam piw pumuy amumi lavayti.

"Very well, if you are inclined to live my kind of life, you may reside here with me. In that case you will benefit from the use of this land. If, in addition, you are willing to adopt the religion which I practice, you will derive further benefits for your life." With these words Maasaw relinquished to the people various items in his posses-sion, among them also a *tiiponi*, the emblem of his religion. "But," he continued, "you have arrived with great ambitions and expec-tations. When you [in the process of realizing them] fall into your evil ways again, you will make me weep." In this fashion Maasaw talked to them.

The Hopi can thus consider themselves only as temporary tenants on Maasaw's land, as is expressly stated in Text 41. The concept of tem-porary tenantship is expressed by the plural verb *haakyese* "to live/to stay for the time being."

TEXT 41

Itam yaw naat pay yep haakyese. Naat pam itamumi it tutskwat qa pas no'a. Pay itam pi panis ang haak mongvasyaniqat oovi pam itamuy nakwhana itam yep yesni-qatniqw pay ii'it pi puma wuu-wuyom oovi navotiy'yungwa.

They say that we merely live as tenants on this earth. Maasaw has not bestowed ownership of this land on us yet. He granted us permission to settle here for the sole purpose that we could benefit from the land. The elders are familiar with all these stipulations.

TEXT 41

As a symbolic token of the land covenant between Maasaw and the Hopi, the god had Spider Woman fashion two *owatutuveni*, literally "stones with multiple markings." The tablets are said to indicate, among other things, the dimensions of the land allocated to the Hopi.

TEXT 42

Paasat pu' yaw pumuy oovi nan-kwusaniqw paasat pu' yaw pay i' piw yep kiy'taqa, maasaw, put kookyangwso'wuutit paas piw pan put owatutuvenit pepeq mas-kyatoyna. Noq pu' yaw oovi i' kookyangwso'wuuti put sukw kwusuuqe pu' pam yaw hiita ang penta. Pu' pam yukuuqe pu' pam piw sukwat anga'. Yantit pu' yaw pam put pumuy mömuy amutpipo hoyokna. Paasat pu' yaw puma maasawuy amum aw hikwsuqw pu' yaw pam ang paki. Pay pi hiita pi ang peena. Niikyangw pam hapi yaw yep it tuuwaqatsit pas soosok tungwaniy'ta.
Hiisaq i' yep tuuwaqatsi payutumpoq qalawtaqat put yaw pam tu'awiy'ta.

As the people were about to start forth on their migration, Maasaw entrusted Old Spider Woman with two stone tablets. Old Spider Woman took the first and drew something on it. With the second she did the same thing. Then she nudged the two tablets in front of her grand-children, who together with Maasaw breathed upon them. As a result, her inscriptions were etched into the stone. What exactly was drawn on the stones is not known. But their markings are said to describe the land in its entirety. They delineate the dimensions all the way to the edge of the sea.

The number of tablets reportedly given to the Hopi by Maasaw varies from one informant to another. Waters speaks of four tablets, of which one was given to the Kookop clan and three to the Bear clan. One of the Bear clan tablets is adorned along its edge with two snakes reputed to symbolize "the two rivers that would mark the boundaries of the people's land"[2] (1963:32). Text 43 once more confirms the significance of the tablets which are held extremely sacred.

TEXT 43

Noq pu' yaw antsa itam pep put owatutuvenit makiwyaqw pu' yaw pam put aw lavayti, "Ta'ay, yep hapi nu' umuy it tuuwaqatsit maqa. Haqami qalawtaqat nu' put umuy maqa. Put hapi nu' yep umuy mavoktoyna. Aqwhaqami ima yep uutim kurukmaqw pumuy hapi um yep timuy'kyangw paas aqwhaqami tsaamiy'mani. Lolmat ang um tsaamiy'mani. Antsa yokvaqw himu aniwtiqw put uma noonoptiwiskyaakyangw aqw-haqami wuyomiq umuutimuy amumum umuuqatsiy ö'qalyani. Sinom wuutaqtokvantiwni, so'wuu-tiharkutokvantiwni."

Yan yaw pam put hopit öqalaqw pu' yaw pam put owatutuvenit mavokoy'taqa maasawuy aw pang-qawu, "Kur antsa'ay. Is kwakwhay. Niikyangw yaapiy hapi itam ung nay'kyaakyangw antsa panhaqam yesni."

Having relinquished possession of the stone tablet to the Hopi, Maasaw said to its keeper, "All right, I've granted you ownership of this earth. It's yours as far as it extends. That's what I've placed in your arms by giving you this tablet.[3] Once your children have multiplied throughout this land lead them with care. Guide them in goodness. When it rains and crops grow, strive in life for old age as you sustain yourselves with food. People are to die in their sleep as old men and as old women."

Thus Maasaw encouraged and reassured the Hopi, whereupon the keeper of the tablet replied, "Thank you very much, indeed. From this time on we'll think of you as our father as we live."

---

[2] For pictorial representations of both sides of these four tablets see Waters (1963: 32-33). The two snakes supposedly signify the Colorado and Rio Grande Rivers (Waters 1963: 32). In the *Hopi Hearings* only one snake is mentioned and said to symbolize "the guarding of this land and life. As long as we remain fast and adhere to the teachings of the tablet the Snake will hold back the punishment" (1955: 55).

[3] An early land reference in conjunction with the tablet is found in Wallis: "Maasaw gave this story inscribed on a stone, to the Hopi. He said: 'The whole earth is mine. As long as you keep this, it all belongs to you' " (1936: 16).

Prior to the Hopi embarking on their migrations Maasaw, in a farewell speech, emphasized that the land belongs to all people, not just to the Hopi. Furthermore, they were told never to part with it.

TEXT 44

Pu' yaw pam maasaw imuy hopii-tuy mongwiyamuy aw pangqawu, "Ta'ay," yaw aw kita, "yuk hapi uma pu' itutskway aw nöngakqe yep hapi uma oovi yaapiy yesni. Noq uma pew it itutskway aw yayvaniqat nu' nakwhay. Pu' i' hapi yep soosokmuy sinmuy himu'amu. Qa hopitsa i' tuts-kwa'ata. Uma hapi qa naanap hinkyaakyangw aqwhaqami umuu-hopiqatsiy ang hintsakwise' putakw uma nayesniy'yungwniy. Nen uma wuuyavo yesni," yaw pam maasaw put aw kita. Pu' yaw pam piw pangqawu, "Niikyangw uma hapi it tutskwat qa hisat yep yuu-yuynani. Uma hapi yep it umuu-tutskway pas qa hakiy aw no'a-yaniy. Uma pas qa hakiy maqa-yani. Qa hakiy uma aw huyayani. Uma hapi it angqw nitkyalalwani. Put uma yuy'kyaakyangw yesni. Kur uma hisat hakiy it aw huya-yanik pay uma paasat kur hiita

With that Maasaw turned to the leader of the Hopi. "Well then," he said, "now that you've emerged into my world, you'll live here from now on. I gave you per-mission to come up to my land. But this land belongs to all people. It's not the sole possession of the Hopi. For the time to come make sure you lead a constructive life. Practice the gentle ways of your culture. By these means you will thrive and enjoy a long future. And," added Maasaw, "never ever disturb this land. Do not cede your land to anyone; don't ever give it away. Above all, don't sell it to anybody. After all, it is to provide your nourishment. Hold this land dear like a mother as long as you live. If you sell it you will no longer reap crops. Be prepared: one after another people will approach you and put you to the test in this matter."[4] After these

---

[4] As intimated in the *Hopi Hearings*, Maasaw especially warned the Hopi against the land-hungry White man. "The Hopi people were further warned that the white man, as he would come moving in this direction, he would claim every piece of land over which he went including the trees, rocks and everything under it. We were to watch. We were not to become confused. He also said they will come and ask for land and if you give them a small piece of land and it is given to them they will ask for more, for this particular people is a very clever and scheming people. Do not become bewildered or confused. Hold on to your land holdings which have been given to you. They have been given to you and therefore are yours. Don't give up the land. Above all, hold on to your tradition which is grounded in this land. If once you give your land, your tradition will begin to dry up and lose its value" (1955: 87).

ang natwanlalwani. Naat hapi
umumi naanangk ökiwkyaakyangw
son naat umumi qa unaheptotani."
Paas yaw it yantaqat pam maasaw
put aw piw enang tutaptat pu' yaw
pumuy maatavi.

detailed instructions to the leader,
Maasaw removed himself from the
Hopi.

Following their migratory treks across the continent, the various Hopi
clans slowly but surely convened on Maasaw's land as commanded by the
god. Once again the Hopi met Maasaw face to face. The encounter with
the god varied considerably, depending on clan tradition. Invariably,
however, he gave the Hopi permission to settle on his land.

The First Mesa Snake clan, in an etiological legend explaining how
it obtained this permission, tells of the god appearing "in a horrible
shape" with "blood all over his body" to test their courage. "When he
got close they were scared to death and fell on the ground. But the
leader did not fall, because he had looked at this thing before and he
was the only one who didn't get scared and didn't fall. So, after this
happened he went over to where this leader was sitting, and in order
to scare him he went to the leader and put his arms around him, and in
order to really scare him he has his way of making a sound, but the
leader did not get scared, so this thing that approached him felt of his
pulse from the back and the front. When people are scared, the heart
beats faster, but this man was calm and this thing looked him in the eye.
He saw that there was a black mark away from both of his eyes. He said,
'No wonder. You are a snake. That is why you didn't get scared.' By that
remark he meant that he had a strong heart. 'Because you didn't get
scared, you have got the best of me. I will have to forfeit the land that
I call my own" (*Hopi Hearings* 1955:340-41).[5]

The legendary encounter between Maasaw and the Hopi at Orayvi
lacked all the dramatic aspects of the one that occurred at Walpi. Again,
there are conflicting traditions as to how the meeting came about. One
rendition of the story focuses on Matsito, the Bear clan leader from

[5]Compare also Stephen (1939: 204), where the same episode is narrated. "You and
your people are strong of heart. Look in the valleys, the rocks, and the woods, and you
will find my footsteps there. All this is mine, but by your courage you have won it. All
this I give you, all this is yours forever, because you met me and were not afraid."

Songoopavi,[6] as the hero of this event. Matsito, after leaving his home village, had gone into exile at a place in the vicinity of Kaktsintuyqa.[7] There, a nightly fire in the direction of Orayvi began to arouse his curiosity.

TEXT 45

Pu' matsito yaw hiisavohaqam pi pep oovi yankyangw pu' yaw pam oomiq wuuvi. Yaw oomiq wupkyangw pu' yaw kaktsintuyqat tatkyaqöymiq tumpoq qatuptuqe pu' yaw angqe' taynuma. Niikyangw pay yaw as pu'niqw pam yaw qa hiita haqami tuway'tangwu. Noq pay yaw aapiy hiisakishaqam talongvaqw piw yaw pam hisat mihikqw ayoq oraymiq qööhit tuwa. Pepehaq yaw qööhiwtangwuniqw pam yaw pangqw put tuway'taqe pam yaw oovi pangsoq put aqw tunatyawtangwu. "Ya sen hak piw pepehaq qööhiy'tangwu? Suupan as nu' pay naala yepeq," yaw pam yan wuuwankyangw hisat mihikqw pangsoq tayta.

Pu' yaw as pam hisat taalö' aqwniqw pay yaw qa haqam himu

Having spent some time there Matsito ascended to the top of the mesa. He established himself at the south rim of Kaktsintuyqa and looked about. In the beginning he did not see any signs of life whatsoever. A few days later, however, he discovered from this vantage point a light over by Orayvi. A fire was burning there, and now that he had spotted it, he kept a watchful eye on it. "Who on earth has that fire going there? I thought I was the only one here," he kept wondering as he sat there, one night, looking in that direction.

One day Matsito decided to seek out the place with the fire, but

---

[6]Matsito was the younger of two brothers affiliated with the ruling family in Songoopavi. From the perspective of this Second Mesa village, Matsito is portrayed as "lazy and dishonorable, taking advantage of his birthright" and is finally driven out by his older brother. "Later malcontents from Songoopavi joined him, thus forming the nucleus from which sprang the pueblo of Orayvi" (Hargrave 1930: 3).

As recounted by the Orayvians, Matsito was the headman of Songoopavi. "Matsito's younger brother became enamored of his, the chief's, wife which resulted in a quarrel between the two men. Matsito decided to leave the village, so his worthless brother became chief." Later, when Matsito's hiding place was discovered, many Songoopavians, "who also had no confidence in the executive ability of the ruling chief, abandoned their homes and joined their old chief on the Third Mesa. This group, the better people of Songoopavi, then founded Orayvi" (Hargrave 1930: 3). See also Waters (1963: 109-10).

[7]Compare the Glossary under "Kaktsintuyqa."

tövumsi. Qa haqam yaw himu
taq'iwtaqa'eway. Qa himu yaw
qötsvi haqam. Pu' yaw pam aapiy
pay qa suus pangsoq as put aqw
pootaqw pay yaw pas qa haqam
töövu, tövumsi, qötsviningwu.

Noq pu' yaw hisat mihikqw piw
pepeq qööhiwtaqw pu' yaw pam
aqwa'. Niiqe yaw aqw pituqw
antsa yaw hak qööhiy aw qatu.
Pu' yaw pam put hakiy aw pituqw
pu' yaw pam aw pangqawu,
"Qatu'uy," yaw pam hak aw kita.
"Um hak piw waynuma?"

"Owiy," yaw pam matsito aw kita.
Pay yaw hak piw anhaqam soniwa.
Hak yaw qalkyaqe pööpöngiw-
kyangw, sohotkiwkyangw höm-
somta. Pay yaw piw hak an taaqa.
"Ya pay um yep yaasat qööhiy'-
tangwu?" yaw aw kita.

"Owiy, pay nu' yep yan qööhiy'tangwu," yaw aw kita.

"Noq um haqam kiy'tay?" yaw aw
kita.

"Pay nu' yangqw taavangqöyngaqw
kiy'ta. Pay nu' pangqw pew wup-

there was no charred wood to be
found. Not a shred was in sight
that seemed to have been burned,
not even ashes. From that time on
he checked out the site on repeated occasions, yet there were no
traces of embers, charcoal, or
ashes present.

One night when the fire was
burning there again, he headed
over to it. This time, however,
someone was sitting by it when he
arrived. As Matsito approached
the stranger, the latter addressed
him, "Sit down, are you also
traveling about?"

"Yes," Matsito replied. There was
nothing peculiar about the
stranger's looks. Across his forehead his hair was cut in bangs,
his sideburns reached down to the
bottom of his ears, and in the
back his hair was tied in a knot.
He turned out to be a man just as
he.[8] "Is it you who always has this
fire going at this time of the
night?" Matsito inquired.

"Yes, that's me," the man en-
lightened him.

"Then where do you live?" Matsito
continued to query the stranger.

"My living quarters are on the
west side of this mesa. I usually

---

[8]Talayesva recalls the Hopi elders saying that on three occasions, when Matsito
approached the fire, the light went out. "But on the fourth time he saw a human form
holding his great bloody head in his hands. The deity admitted that he was the god of
Fire and Death who guards the mesa and assured our ancestor that he could stay" (1942:
287-88).

ngwuy," yaw aw kita. "Noq son pi um qa pas hiita oovi waynumay?" yaw aw kita.

"Owiy. Noq um yep it himuy'tay?" yaw aw kita.

"Owiy, noq himu'uy?" yaw aw kita.

"Pay hapi sen as um hin nuy nakwhanaqw pay nu' yephaqam uqlap qatuptuniy," yaw aw kita.

"Ta'ay, pay pi um pantiniy. Pay pi yep qeniy. Pay pi um antsa angqw pewnen pay yep hoop pi pay haqamwat neengem kiitaniy," yan yaw aw lavayti.

Noq pu' pam oovi kya pi paasat yan aw nukwangwlavaytiqw pu' yaw pam oovi pangqw pangso yama, orayviy hopqöymi. Niiqe pep pu' yaw pam oovi haqam tuwat namortaqe pep pu' yaw pam tuwat qatuptu.

come up here from there," he informed him. "But I suppose you are here for a good reason."

"Yes. Do you own this place here?" he enquired.

"That's right. Why do you ask?" he probed.

"I just wondered if you'd give me permission, I could live here somewhere next to you."

"All right, go ahead and do that. There is space here. By all means come here and make your home east of here somewhere," the stranger said.

After this favorable response Matsito moved over to the east side of Orayvi. There he selected a site and settled down.

According to the version recorded by Voth, the Hopi, while residing at Songoopavi, "heard that Skeleton [i.e., Maasaw] was living where Orayvi now is, and so they all traveled on towards Orayvi" (1905a:23). In the ensuing scene of meeting the god, the Hopi consented to live the simple life of Maasaw. His only possession, a planting stick, appropriately could be likened to a scepter symbolizing ownership of the land. Maasaw, in turn, granted the Hopi permission to establish residence on this land.

TEXT 46

Noq pu' yaw itam oovi antsa pangqaqw nankwusakyangw pu' yaw antsa itam yep orayve pu' it qataymataqqat qatuuqat, maa-sawuy, aw öki. Noq pam maasaw

Thus we set out on our migration, and indeed, at Orayvi we en-countered Maasaw, the god who lives unseen. From his abode in Orayvi he had made it a habit of

yaw pep haqam orayve kiy'taqey
pangqw yaw pam atkyangaqw
wungwupkyangw pu' itamuy nuu-
taytatongwu. "Sen pu' haqam
peqw ökini," yan wuuwankyangw.
Noq put maasawuyniqw i' tuuwaqatsi pay qa himu. Pam pi pay
naala a'ni himuniiqe oovi pay naat
qa talöngvaqw pay soosovik yep
tuuwaqatsit ang nakwsungwuniiqe
oovi wuuwantaqw itam hopiit hapi
pay pangso oraymi put an suy'kini.

Niiqe pam yaw oovi orayviy kwiningya kuywanvave yaw itamuy
nuutaytani. Oovi yaw antsa pumuy
aw ökiqw yaw pam pumuy haalay-
tiqe yaw amumi pangqawu, "Uma
öki?"

"Owi."

"Ta'ay, yeese'ey." Pu' yaw piw
amumi pangqawu, "Ta'ay, uma
yorikyani. Yep hapi sulaktutskway.
Qa haqe' paayuy. Qa haqam himu
hoqlö. Uma hapi sulaktutskwave
yesvaniy. Noq uma hapi iqatsiy aw
suutaq'ewyaqe oovi angqw pew
inumi öki. Noq oovi nu' umumi
pangqawni, kur uma pas antsa
nuy hin qatuqw put aw uma
suutaq'ewye', inun yesniqey naanawakne', pay uma yep yesvaniy."

Noq pay yaw puma suutaq'ewya.
Noq paasat pu' yaw pam piw

ascending to the mesa top every so
often to come and await our
arrival. "Maybe they'll come
today," he would think as he
waited. The vast expanses of this
land are, of course, quite insignificant to Maasaw. Because he
is endowed with greater than
human powers, he can traverse
the entire earth before morning
arrives. Hence he had assumed
that we Hopi, too, would arrive
at Orayvi as quickly as he had.

He had promised to wait for us at
a location north of Orayvi known
as Kuywanva.[9] When we finally
showed up, he was elated. "You've
arrived?" he exclaimed by way of
greeting.

"Yes," the Hopi replied.

"All right, welcome." Then he
continued, "Now, look about. The
land here is arid. There's no river
here nor is there a forest. You're
going to inhabit a desert. But
since you did not hesitate to live
my way of life, you came here to
me. Therefore, let me tell you
this: if you are willing to lead my
kind of life, if you really desire to
do so, go ahead and settle at this
site."

The Hopi expressed their willingness, whereupon Maasaw added,

[9]Voth specifies Natuwanpikya, "a place a very short distance west of Kuywanva,"
as the meeting place between Maasaw and the Hopi (1905a: 23). According to one
tradition the god used to amuse himself at that location "by playing a game to test his
skill" (Katchongva 1975: 10). The act of *natwanta* or "testing oneself," consisted of
holding a stone in one's stretched-out hand and then trying to insert it in the hole of a
boulder by walking towards it with closed eyes.

pangqawu, "Ta'ay, nu' hapi pay
panis sooyay'ta. Panis nu' poshumiy'ta, kuywikiy'ta, usimansa-
kwiy'ta. Panis nu' yanta. Kur nu'
hiitakw umuy yep pas pa'angwani.
Noq oovi nuy hintaqw put uma
aw suutaq'ewye', qa kyaanana-
wakne', yanhaqam inun okiw-
yesninik pay uma yep inumumyani." Pu' yaw puma paas put
hu'wanaya. Hin pam yaw qatuqw
pay yaw puma pas put su'an yesniqey kitotaqe yaw paas naa-
nakwha.

Paasat pu' yaw puma pep put
qatuuqat yaw aw pangqaqwa,
"Ta'ay," yaw kitota, "antsa itam
naanami öki. Noq pay oovi sonqa
um itaamongwiniy," yan yaw
puma put maasawuy aw maqaptsi-
tota. "Pay paapu itam ung mongwiy'yungwe' paapu qa itaaqatsiy
piw sakwitotani. Pay oovi sonqa
um itamumi mongw'iwtani," yaw
puma put aw kitota.

Noq pay yaw i' qataymataq qatuuqa pay yaw qa nakwha. Niiqe
yaw amumi pangqawu, "Qa'ey,"
yaw kita, "pas kya pay son naat
pantani. Pi pay um pew imuy
tsamvaqe pay son um qa naap
amumi mong'iwtani, naap um
moopeq'iwtani. Naat uma a'ni
hiita tunatyawvayay. Ason umuy
put ang kuukuyvaqw, uma put aw
antsatsnaqw ason pepeq pu'
nu'niy," yaw amumi kita. "Ason
pay uma yep it hin umuutunatyay,
hin uma yesniqey put ang umuy
kuukuyvaqw, pep pu' nu' ason pay
ahoy piw umumi pite' pu' umumi
hin wuuwani. Pu' kur pay umuy

"All I own is a planting stick,
some seeds, a canteen of water,
and a tattered piece of wrap. No
more, no less. There is nothing I
can help you with. But if you're
willing to face the life I stand for,
if you're not too particular and
can live in poverty as I do, you
may stay here with me." To this
the Hopi wholeheartedly agreed.
They promised to live under the
same conditions.

Then they said to him, "All right,
we have truly encountered one
another. For that reason you have
to be our leader now." They
petitioned Maasaw, "With you as
our headman we won't destroy our
life again. Hence you must rule
over us."

But he who lives unseen declined.
And he stated his reason. "No,"
he said, "I don't think this is
possible yet. You led these people
here, hence you must assume the
leadership yourself. You must
personally fill this high position.
All of you came with great ambitions. The day you've seen those
ambitions through and fulfilled
them, I'll assume that leadership
position. Once you've realized your
plans and lived the life you want
to live, I'll return and give some
thought to your request. If you're
still leading a good life then, I'll
consider your suggestion. For the

naat lomahinyungwniniqw pep pu' nu' ason umungem piw aw hin wuuwani. Pay haak oovi uma naapyani," yaw kita. "Pay pi as nu' mootiy'makyangw pay nu' piw naat nuutungktato. Niikyangw oovi nu' yaapiy nakwsuni. Talvew nu' nakwsuni. Niikyangw pay nu' naat piw sonqa ahoy pituni." Yan yaw pam amumi lavaytit pu' yaw pam naatupkya.

time being, however, you'll be on your own," Maasaw declared. "I'm the first but I'm also going to be the last. Now I'll go forth from here and head towards the rising sun. But I assure you I'll return." With this message to the Hopi, Maasaw hid himself from them.

The scene in Text 46 above, in which Maasaw declined to assume the offered leadership role, is also transmitted by Voth. In his version, the god specifically addressed the land question. When asked, "Will you give us some land?" the god complied with their wish indicating, however, that one day he would reappropriate his land. "When the White Man, your elder brother, will come back here and cut off the heads of the bad ones, then I shall own all this land of mine myself. But until then you shall be chief. I shall give you a piece of land and then you live here." Thereafter the god "stepped off a large tract of land" which he allotted to the Bear clan (1905a:23).

Maasaw, characterized by Hermequaftewa as "the Creator of our land" (1954:1), asserted his original ownership of the land when the *pahaana* or "white man" first set foot on this continent: "Then this person came to us from across the great water and from another land. We call him and his kind Pahaana, the white man. Maasaw, being a spirit, met the Pahaana as they came upon our shore. The white man did not ask anyone for permission to come upon the land. Maasaw spoke to him and said, "You should ask for permission to enter on this land. If you wish to come and live according to the way of the Hopi in this land, and never abandon that way, you may. I will give you this new way of life and some of the land." Maasaw, being a Great Spirit, looked into the hearts of the Pahaana and knew that they had many things that they wanted to do in this land not according to the way of Maasaw. The white man asked Maasaw if there were some people already occupying the land. Maasaw said "Yes, their houses are already standing. There are villages already established. They have their fields, everything—their way of life." Maasaw, alone, can give this life and land according to the Hopi Way. He did so to the Hopis and all the peoples that came with them first, because they prayed for permission and followed the plan of life of Maasaw. No other people should claim any part of this land, rightfully, therefore" (Hermequaftewa 1954:5).

In his role as owner and guardian spirit of the earth Maasaw also assumes protectorship of those who travel on his land. To be granted a good journey the Hopi traveler formerly would leave a votive offering at one of the god's shrines. According to a First Mesa tradition Maasaw himself instructed the Snake clan, when it first came to Hopi country, to deposit on the cairn that had been constructed for the god such simple things as "a bit of wood, a tuft of grass, or a portion of their burden on it." This was supposed to let him know that the traveler was thinking of him. "For him Maasaw would have kindly regard and would protect him on his future journeys, but those who neglected to make an offering would incur his anger and be in danger of death. Nearly every trail, now, has a cairn upon it at some point, and when a tired Hopi passes it he takes a bunch of grass and rubs his head, arms, legs, etc., and places the tuft and a small portion of his burden on the heap, placing a stone on the tuft, or a bit of wood, to hold it secure. At the same time he asks Maasaw to protect him; if returning from a journey he thanks Maasaw for his protection" (Stephen 1936:151).

That Maasaw was also considered as tutelary god of travelers, at Third Mesa, can be gathered from Talayesva's autobiographical account. Prior to setting out on a salt expedition, his father, in order "to insure a good journey and to prevent weariness...stopped near the Maasaw shrine, made a corn meal path leading westward, and placed on it a prayer feather with its breath line pointing in that direction" (1942:233).

A recent testimonial basically confirms this tutelary aspect of Maasaw, limiting it, however, to one who travels across the god's land at night.

TEXT 47

Noq himuwa haqami mihikqw hoyte' pay qa hinwat haqam hintit aqw pitumantaniqat, it hakim yan tunatyawkyaakyangw maasawuy aw okiwlalwangwu. Pay itam sopkyawat sinom okiwatsa akw put aw itaaqatsiy ö'qalya.

When a traveler is on the road at night, we hope that he may reach his destination unharmed. For this we also beseech Maasaw. And all of us by means of prayer beg him for a long life.

On the basis of a couple of passages in the literature, Tyler suggests that Maasaw also has functioned as a god of boundaries. Parsons states that Stephen "notes the use of certain field marks and of a boundary stone between Songoopavi and Orayvi, a figure of Maasaw" (1936:390).

The stone, which is illustrated in *Hopi Journal*, has round shallow holes with a black rim painted around them to mark the eyes and nose. According to Stephen "the head was carved and the face holes painted to keep the young people from removing it. To keep Navajos also from destroying it. The name of Maasaw [is] attached to it for [the] same reason also" (1936:390). Titiev knows of a *qalalni'owa* or "boundary stone," "marked with the head of Maasaw" which "commemorated that deity's original claim to the entire domain" (1944:62). Tyler concedes that these instances do not sufficiently prove widespread use of Maasaw as a figure on boundary stones; nevertheless, he believes that they illustrate the fact that the concept was established among the Hopi.

My own research does not bear out his hypothesis. While it corroborates the existence of stone boundary markers, it also establishes the

Figure 6.—Shrine of Wukomaasaw or "Great Maasaw." Compare also Text 130. According to Fewkes, it was one of the best known of all the shrines at First Mesa. "This shrine... has a rock on one side but is made up largely of twigs and branches that have been thrown upon it by those passing with firewood. In the same shrine may likewise be found small clay vessels, prayer sticks, and various other offerings. These are not confined to the shrine but are found also in front of the opening, as in the case of the small bowl shown in the figure." See Fewkes, Jesse Walter. "Hopi Shrines Near the East Mesa." *American Anthropologist* 8 (1906), p. 353.

custom of marking a particular clan holding with a stone, depicting on it the totemic emblem of that clan. Thus, the Maasaw image was probably not used as a general symbol for marking any field boundary, but was reserved in this function to members of the Maasaw or Kookop clans.

TEXT 48

I' yang paavasva mamkiwqw oovi pang himungyamuy paasayamuy qalalniyat ep pam haqam naa-toyla'am, wu'ya'am, pey'tangwu. Meh, itamuy patkingyamuy ep oomaw pey'taqw pu' honngyamuy ep honmaqtö. Pu' tsorngyamuy ep pam tsiro, pu' kookyangwngyamuy ep kookyangw, pu' qalangyamuy ep taawat qala'at. Pu' imuy tap-ngyamuy ep i' taavoningwu. Pu' qa pamniniqw pay it sowit kuk'at ep pey'tangwu. Pu' piw imuy masngyamuy ep i' maasawuy qötö'at pey'tangwu.

Since the fields are all allocated to people here, the borderline of a given clan field is marked by the emblem of its respective clan or clan ancestor. For example, a field of the Patki clan is identified by a cloud, a Bear clan field by a bear paw, and a Bluebird field by a bluebird. At a Spider clan field a spider is depicted and at a field belonging to the Forehead clan, the sun's forehead is drawn. At the plot of the Rabbit clan a rabbit is pictured. Instead of the entire rabbit, just the footprint of the rodent may also be represented. By the same token there is a depiction of Maasaw's head at the planting ground of the Maasaw clan.

5

Fire, Light, and Darkness

Maasaw's relationship to the element of fire and, in a broader sense, to the phenomena of light and darkness, is an elaborate one and not always free of contradictions. Although predominantly associated with the darkness of night, the god invariably comes to be characterized as the "owner" (Courlander 1972:23), "giver" (Courlander 1972:43), "bringer" (Carr 1979:19) or "controller" (Nequatewa 1936:126) of fire. Maasaw, in this respect, has all the makings of a culture hero and bears a certain resemblance to the Greek Prometheus. Unlike the Titan, however, Maasaw did not have to steal the fire to pass it on to humankind.

According to one tradition, the god provided man already in the Third World with the knowhow of fire-making. To this purpose he sent the hummingbird from his abode in the upper world to teach the people "how to create fire with a fire drill" (Courlander 1972:23). Generally, it is not until after the emergence of the Hopi from the underworld, though, that the god bestows his gift on them.

TEXT 49

I' maasaw qööhit himuy'ta. Noq oovi sinom pay sonqa maasawuy angqw piw put tuwiy'vaya yuk tutskwayat aw nöngakqe.

Maasaw is the owner of the fire. Hence one may assume that people gained their knowledge of fire from the god after they emerged into this, the upper world.

When first found in the upper world of utter darkness, Maasaw is seen sitting by a fire. While some of my own recordings have the god "facing the fire" and "staring into the flames," Nequatewa's emergence version stresses the fact "that he would not turn his face toward the fire" (1936:25). This latter version better befits a god of death who is proscribed from day and roams in the realm of blank night. As Text 50 points out, he is only abroad during the hours of darkness and must shun any source of light in order not to impair his vision.

TEXT 50

Pam maasaw pi pay yaw mokpuni-ngwuniiqe oovi qa taalat ep tuwat waynumngwu. Niiqe pam oovi haqam qööhit, taalat aw pite' pam put qa aw yorikngwu. Pam tuwat ayoqwat, qa taalat aqwwat, nam-tökngwu. Put kya pi poosi'at pas suyan taalat akw hiita qa tuway'ta-ngwuniqw oovi pam tuwat panti-ngwu.

Maasaw is a dead being, hence he goes about in the darkness of the night. Thus, whenever he comes upon a fire or light, he avoids looking at it. Instead, he turns towards the dark. He does this because his vision may be impaired by extreme brightness.[1]

---

[1] In a story recorded by Voth, the god is surprised in deep sleep by a group of Hano men who are on a rabbit drive. Essentially blinded by the daylight, he madly rushes about, only to dash repeatedly into some rock wall and puncture his head in the process (1905a: 123).

In an obvious reversal of what is customary for the living, the god of death is said to sleep during the day. This belief has also filtered into a Hopi folk saying, which jokingly refers to one sleeping during daylight hours. As a matter-of-fact, anybody who sleeps late in the morning can be chided by this saying.[2]

TEXT 51

Himuwa wuuyoqa taalö' puwngwu-niqw put aw pangqaqwangwu, "Um himu maasaw'ewayniiqe tuwat taalö' puuwi. Qatuptu'u. Um qa pantani. Nawus maasaw taalö' puwkyangw pu' mihikqw waynumngwu."

When an older person sleeps during the daylight hours, people say to him, "You're just like Maasaw because you sleep during the day. Get up! You can't do that now. It's Maasaw only who rests during the day and goes around at night."

The admonition not to wash one's hair in the evening, the onset of nighttime, is tied to Maasaw's strong association with darkness. Noteworthy in this connection is the Hopi belief, that the time period from noon onward is already considered to belong to the dead.

TEXT 52

Hakimuy aw pangqaqwangwu, hak yaw qa tapkiqw aa'asngwu. Paasat-niqw hakiy aa'asqw i' maasaw yaw hakiy aw astongwuqat pang-qaqwangwu. Noq oovi hopi pan navotiy'ta: Hak put moovit akw asninik hak talavay taawanasami

People are instructed not to wash their hair in the evening. If a person washes his hair at that time, Maasaw is said to come and wash his head together with that person. Therefore, the following is common knowledge among the Hopi: Whenever a person intends to shampoo his

[2]That sleeping during the day is considered quite improper in the eyes of the Hopi is evidenced by a number of additional proverb-like sayings which address this habit: *Hak taalö' qa puwngwu.* "One doesn't sleep during the day." *Hak taalö' qa kwangwavuwngwu.* "One does not sleep well during the day." *Hak taalö' puuwe' qa haalaykyangw taatayngwu.* "One who sleeps during the day does not wake up happily."

paasavo pantingwu. Pu' aapiy
taawanasapviipiy pam yaw imuy
maamastuy qeni'amningwuqat
kitotangwu.

hair with yucca root, he should do
so during the span from morning
until noon. The time from noon
on is said to belong to the dead.

Since Maasaw roams the land during the hours of darkness, the Hopi
are usually quite apprehensive, if not afraid, of being out at night. Some
people are reputed to become so obsessed with this fear that they develop
tsawintuya or "anxiety sickness," a disease akin to nyctophobia, the fear
of darkness.[3]

The risk of straying into the path of the god is particularly high in
the month of Kyaamuya (approximately December). For this reason
certain nighttime activities are taboo during this part of the year.

TEXT 53

Hak kyaamuyva mihikqw qa
ösösötinumngwu. Hak yaw pan-
tsaknume' maasawuy wangwaylawngwu.

One does not go about whistling at
night during the month of Kyaamuya. Whoever does so, summons
Maasaw.

TEXT 54

Hak yaw mihikqw qa ösösötoy-
nangwu. Hak yaw pantsakye' hak
yaw maasawuy wangwaylawngwu.

One should not make whistling
sounds at night. Whoever does so
is said to be calling for Maasaw.

TEXT 55

Hak kyaamuyva mihikqw qa
ngumantangwu, ispi hak yaw
paasatniqw maasawuy amum
ngumantangwu.

A woman should not grind corn at
night during the month of Kyaamuya, because they say that she
would be grinding together with
Maasaw at this time.

---

[3]For additional information on *tsawintuya* compare Chapter 8. The concern about
not whistling at night is, in Text 54, extended beyond that winter month.

TEXT 56

Hak yaw kyaamuyve qa tutumayto-
ngwu. Noq oovi maana nguman-
taqw tumaya aqw kuyvaqw pam
yaw pay maasaw put aw tutu-
maytongwu.

One does not go to court a girl in
the month of Kyaamuya. For when
a girl grinds corn and the wooer
peeps in [to her through the wall
opening], Maasaw is said to come
to court her.

TEXT 57

Hak yaw kyaamuyve mihikqw qa
iipaq qöqööngwu. Hak yaw paasat-
niqw qöqööqw i' maasaw yaw
hakiy aw kookostongwu.

One does not build a fire outdoors
at night in the month of Kyaamuya. People claim that if one
does so, Maasaw will come and
borrow burning embers from that
person's fire.

TEXT 58

Hak yaw kyaamuyve qa moptaa-
pamtangwu. Hakiy yaw put pan-
tsakqw hakiy yaw i' maasaw aw
moptaapamtatongwu.

One is not supposed to pound on
yucca roots in the month of Kyaamuya. Whenever one does that,
Maasaw is said to come and join
one in that activity.

TEXT 59

Hak yaw kyaamuyve qa kiilaw-
ngwu. Hak yaw kyaamuyve kiilawe'
hak yaw neengem maskimiq
na'saslawngwu. Hak yaw pante'
pay songqa mokngwu, kiihut
yukuta'.

One is not supposed to build a
house in the month of Kyaamuya.
Whoever does so prepares himself
to go to Maski. When one does
that, one surely dies upon completion of the house.

The taboo in Text 60 is only indirectly linked with Maasaw in that
it refers to the dead. However, since the dead are part of the god's
domain, and since the taboo expressly addresses an activity at night, it is
also cited here.

TEXT 60

Hak yaw kyaamuyve mihikqw qa pööqantangwu. Hak yaw kyaamuyva mihikqw hiita tuulewnit hintsakqw pu' yaw ima yep atkya maskive yesqam puma yaw angqw pew tunatyawyungqe puma yaw hakiy poosiyat nawkiyangwu. Pu' yaw hak yan qa tala'vostingwu.

During the month of Kyaaamuya a man should not work at his loom at night. People say that when weaving is done within that time period, the residents at Maski, the "House of the Dead" in the underworld, heed this and will arrive to take the weaver's eyes. Then he will turn blind.

It comes somewhat as a surprise, therefore, and also seems contradictory to Maasaw's avoidance of light, when the god plays a major role in the creation of the sun and the moon. On the other hand, the god's providing daylight and nightlight for emerging humans can be seen as a logical extension of his willingness to give mankind command of fire. The following excerpt from a Second Mesa emergence myth is highly noteworthy in that Maasaw suggested a human sacrifice to keep the sun rotating at its proper speed.[4] Ultimately, man would have to die to guarantee the perpetual movement of the sun.

TEXT 61

"Owiy," yaw kita, "pay nu' yep it tutskwat himuy'kyangw antsa nu' qa taalat ep tuwat yannumngwu-niiqe oovi pay nu' qa hin put hiita talniy'taniqat yukuniqey wuuwantay," yaw kita.

"Haw owi?" yaw kita. "Noq pay nu' ung tuuvingtani. Sen itam son yep umum yesniy?" yaw kita.

"Pay pi uma yep inumum yesniy,"

"Yes," Maasaw replied, "I own this land and travel about in darkness. It never occurred to me to create anything which would provide light."

"Is that right?" the leader said. "Let me ask you then if we could possibly live here with you."

"Sure, you can live here with me,"

---

[4]In Wallis' Second Mesa emergence version, human children are sacrificed to make both the moon and the sun move (1936: 8-9). For another account of the creation of these stellar light sources see Chapter 3, Text 31.

yaw kita. "Niikyangw son uma yep
qa taalat ep yanyungwnik suutaq'ewyaniy. Uma hapi atkya
taaway'yungngwa. Noq oovi uma
hapi yep piw taawat yukuyaniy,"
yaw pam kita. "Noq nu' oovi uumi
tutaptani hak hin put yukungwu-
niqw'öy," yaw pam kitaaqe paasat
pu' yaw pam oovi put mongwit aw
pangqawu, "Ta'ay, it um tsöpvukyat haqamnen put um yan
pongokput tukuniy," yaw aw kita.
"Paasat pu' um put angqw yaw-
maqw pu' nu' yep put aw taw-
lawni. Pay pi itam su'an yukuqw
pay pam son umungem qa talniy'taqw uma taalat ep yesniy,"
yaw kita.

Paasat pu' yaw pam ahoy kiy
awniiqe pangqw pu' yaw pam
hiihiita himuy kimakyangw pu'
yaw put tsöpvukyat enang ep
kwusiva. Pam yaw put pas sus-
lomahintaqat pangso yawmaqe pu'
yaw put pongotku. Pu' yaw pam
maasaw put aw tawlawt pu' yaw
pam put yukiq hoopoq tuuva.
Panti yaw pamniqw pu' yaw pay
hiisavoniqw pay yaw pang haqe'
tsotsmoniqw pangqaqw yaw pam
kuyva. Niikyangw yaw pongokpu.
Pangqw pu' yaw pam yamak-
kyangw pu' yaw pam yang oova
yanmakyangw pay yaw qa pas
talniy'ma. Pay yaw pas hin taala.
"Pay as pam talniy'kyangw pay
kur pam qa su'an yukilti," yaw
pam maasaw kita. "Noq pay pi
hintiqw pi. Noq pay nuy aw
wuuwaqw pay kya as pam wi-
huy've' pu' talniy'taniy. Paasat pu'
sen pam a'ni riyakye' pu' mukip-

Maasaw replied. "But I doubt
you'll be willing to put up with
this darkness. Down below you had
a sun. Therefore you'll need to
create a sun up here, too. I'll
give you instructions on how to do
that." With that he commanded
the chief, "All right, find an
antelope skin and cut it into a
circular shape. After that bring it
over and I'll sing over it. If we do
this right, our creation is bound to
illuminate this world and you can
live in the light," he said.

The leader did as told. He returned home and came back with
all sorts of things, including an
antelope hide. He had brought the
finest skin there was, out of which
he cut a circular piece. Next,
Maasaw sang over it and then
flung it towards the sky in the
east. It was not long before the
hide rose behind a hill which
happened to be there. It was
round as it emerged but when it
traveled across the sky, it was not
very bright. It was an odd sort of
luminescence. "It does radiate
light but evidently it wasn't done
properly," Maasaw admitted. "I
really don't know why. But thinking about it I believe the hide
disk might give more light if it
were covered with grease. That
should speed its spinning. In turn
the disk should grow so hot that it

kye' pu' sen pavan uwikye' paasat
pu' sen pavan talniy'taniy," yaw
kita. "Noq itwat pu' um aw
yorikqw pam hapi mihikqw
umungem talniy'tamantaniy," yaw
kita. Pam kur yaw i' muuyawni.

Put yaw kur pam maasaw mooti
yuku. Paasat pu' yaw pam piw
pangqawu, "Ta'ay, pu' um piw
ahoynen pu' um it sowi'ingwvukyat
haqamni. Niikyangw put um pas
susyaasaqat a'ni pööngalat um
angqw yawmaniy," yaw kita.

Pu' yaw pam oovi pangqw piw
ahoyniikyangw pu' piw put ep
kwusivaqw pu' yaw puma piw put
pan pongokput tuku. Noq pu' yaw
pam maasaw pangqawu, "Ta'ay,"
yaw kita, "it hapi ura nu' piw
pangqawu. Itam it wihut akw hapi
lelwiqw pu' nu' tuuvaqw paasat
pu' pam sen a'ni öqalat riyayay-
kye', pavan mukiite' pu' sen pavan
uwikniy. Paasat pu' sen pavan
talniy'taniy. Niikyangw i' hapi
sonqa sinot hiikyay'taniy," yaw
pam put aw kita. "Noq oovi um
hiitawat uutiw'ayay, maanat, pas
aw unangway'taqey put um nawus
tavini. Niikyangw itam son nawus
put qa niinani. Pay pam put
wihuyat akw enang riyayataqw
pay pam maana son hisat qa
sulawtini. Sulawtikyangw pu' pam
songyawnen yep umungem talniy'tani. Pu' kur nu' pay piw qa
an yukye' pep pu' nu' piw uumi
hinwat tutaptaniy," yaw aw kita.

Pu' yaw pam kikmongwi pangqawu, "Ta'ay," yaw kita, "pay
antsa nu' sukw maanat tiw'ayay'-

would flare up and so shine more
brilliantly," Maasaw suggested.
"The creation you just saw will
give you light at night." Evidently,
that was going to be the moon.

After this first creation Maasaw
once more commanded the
chief, "Now, go back again and
search for a buckskin. Bring the
largest and thickest you can find."

So the chief returned a second
time and when he arrived with the
buckskin, they cut this, too, in a
circular pattern. Then Maasaw
said, "As you recall, I suggested
we daub this hide with grease.
Once I throw it, it will probably
start to rotate rapidly, acquire
intense heat, and consequently
flame up. At that point it should
give off more light. But this
undertaking will cost a person's
life," he informed the leader.
"You'll have to sacrifice the niece
who is most dear to you. I'm
afraid we'll have to kill her. The
girl must die so that the disk can
spin with her grease. In a way, her
death will provide the light for
you. If I again fail to do this
right, I'll have more instructions
for you later," Maasaw said.

The chief replied, "Yes, as a
matter of fact I do have a niece.

tay. Pam naat pas puhuwungwiw-
taqw pay nu' son nawus qa put
taviniy," yaw pam kita.

"Kur antsa'ay, kwakwhay," yaw
pam maasaw kita.

Pu' yaw puma put maanat wihuyat
put sowi'ingwvukyat ang lelwiqe
paas put wipkinaqw pu' yaw
maasaw pangqawu, "Ta'ay, kur
itam piw tuwantaniy," yaw kita.
Pu' yaw pam put a'ni tuuvaqw
pavan yaw pam hin töqti. Hiisavoniqw pu' yaw hihin angqaqw
taalawva. Pu' yaw paasat pay pam
pas suyan talniy'kyangw yaw
angqw yamakto. Pu' yaw angqw
kuyvakyangw pas yaw pavan
paalangpu angqw kuyva. Pantikyangw pu' yaw pam oomiti-
kyangw paasat pu' yaw pam
teevengewat hoyta. Paasat pu' yaw
pam panmakyangw pu' yaw paasat
taawanasapviipiy atkyami siroktoq
paasat pu' yaw kur tapkiwmaqw
pu' yaw pam teevenge paki. Aqwhaqami yaw pakimaqw pu' yaw
pam maasaw pangqawu, "Ta'ay,
kwakwhay. Yantani. Itam hapi
su'an yukuy," yaw kita.

Noq yaw pam kikmongwi yaw
angqe' yorikqw pay yaw maasaw
paasat qa haqam. Pay yaw kur
pam haqami. Pam yaw tuwat qa
taalat epningwuniiqe yaw oovi
taalawvaqw yaw kur haqami.
Niiqe pas yaw oovi ep mihikqw pu'
yaw pam kikmongwi piw awi'.
Awniqw pay antsa yaw pam ep

She's just passed the stage of
childhood. I suppose I have no
choice but to sacrifice her."

"All right, thanks," Maasaw
replied.

And so they applied the girl's fat
to the buckskin. When the hide
was really greasy, Maasaw said,
"Well then, let's try again." With
that he hurled the disk out with
such vehemence that it emitted an
odd sound. Before long a faint
light began to appear and then it
manifested itself in brilliant brightness. As the disk became visible
over the horizon it was completely red. Slowly it rose and
embarked on a westward course.
As it traveled upward, it reached
midday, from which time on it
steadily slid downward in the sky.
By evening it dipped under the
horizon in the west. After it had
disappeared completely, Maasaw
exclaimed, "Now, thanks indeed!
This is the way it should be. We
did it properly this time."

When the leader looked about,
Maasaw was nowhere in sight.
Apparently he had vanished. Since
he had always lived in darkness, he
simply disappeared when it turned
daylight. So the chief had to wait
till nightfall before he was able to
approach Maasaw. As on the
previous occasion, the god had a

piw qööhiy'kyangw pay yaw piw
huur moto'kyangw pangso qatu.
"Ya um pitu?" yaw kita.

"Owiy," yaw kita.

"Antsa'ay," yaw kita. "Itam hapi
su'an yukuy," yaw kita. "Oovi nu'
uumi pangqawni: I' hapi ura
sinot hiikyay'tani. I' sinot hapi
wihuyat akw uwiwitaqe oovi pam
a'ni mukiitikyangw pu' pam piw
a'ni talniy'tay. Yaniqw oovi yaapiy
son himuwa hapi qa mokmantani.
Pu' pam sinot wihuyat akw piw
naat taytamantani, uwiwitaman-
tani. Noq humuwa pantiqw pay
uma engem paahototamantani.
Pu' pam humuwa pante' pam hapi
pay inumi sinotimantani. Pu' pam
tuwat yep inumum qa talpuva
hinnummantanikyangw pam pi
pay umungem put taawat warikniy'tamantani. Oovi pay himuwa
pantiqw pay uma qa pas hin aw
wuuwantotamantaniy." Yanhaqam
yaw pam put kikmongwit aw
lavayti.

camp-fire blazing and sat by it
facing the flames with his head
pressed to his chest. "You've
come?" he greeted the chief.

"Yes," the latter answered.

"Well," Maasaw continued, "we
were successful in our undertakings. So let me explain the
following to you now: keeping the
sun going will be possible only at
the expense of human life. Only
by flaming with human grease can
the sun burn with such heat that it
will produce enough light. For this
reason people will have to die
from now on.[5] With the grease of
the dead the sun will stay alive
and keep on burning. And whenever someone dies, I want you to
make a prayer feather. At the time
of his death the deceased person
becomes one of my people and
joins me roaming about in darkness while he keeps the sun going.
So don't be troubled when someone passes away." This is what
Maasaw revealed to the people's
leader.

---

[5] In an emergence version, recorded by Parsons, it is Coyote who suggests that death
is the answer to keeping the sun going: "Then the sun came out, but it could not move.
Then the people were talking, 'Something is wrong. Why can it not move?' Then they
asked each other, 'What can make it go?' At last Coyote said, 'Nothing wrong with it.
All is fixed as it should be. Nothing wrong, but if somebody should die right now, then it
would move.' Then, just there, a girl died and the sun began to move. When it got to the
middle of the sky, it stopped again. 'Well, what is the matter?' they asked again. Coyote
said, 'Nothing is the matter, nothing is wrong. If somebody dies right now, it will move.'
Then the son of one of the head men died, and that made the sun go again. 'It is only by
somebody dying every day—morning, noon and evening—that will make the sun move
every day,' said Coyote." (1926: 171).

As is evident from the emergence episode above, Maasaw vanishes from sight as soon as the sun, his own creation, manifests itself above the horizon. Assuming the cloak of invisibility, he becomes the *qataymataq qatuuqa*, "the one who lives unseen." From now on only a fire at night attests to his existence.

TEXT 62

To be sure, Maasaw dwells here on earth, but he prefers to live his life unseen. He usually will not reveal himself to people for he does not want to disturb them by that experience. Since he travels about at night, he does so using fire. If one truly desires to see him, Maasaw will surely oblige.

Pu' maasaw pi pay as yep qatu-kyangw pam pay piw qataymataq qatu. Pam son haqam hakiy aw naamataqlawni, pam son hakiy pan yuuyuynani. Pu' pam pi mihikqw waynumngwuniiqe pam oovi qööhit akwningwu. Pu' hak pas antsa put aw yorikniqey naa-waknaqw pay pam piw son hakiy qa nakwhanani.

Figure 7

While walking the earth at night, Maasaw carries a *kopitsoki* or "fiery cedar bark torch" to light his way.

TEXT 63

Yaw antsa maasaw mihikqw yang waynume' pam yaw it kopitsokit yawnumngwuniiqat piw kito-tangwu. Pam put yawnumqw pam uwiwitimangwu. Put pam paa-lay'numngwu. Noq put qööhi'at haqe' hoyoyotimakyangw haqami

Whenever Maasaw goes about at night, he is said to carry a torch. It is the fire from this torch which moves along, burning, and which he uses to light his way. Each time the god pauses, the light from his torch burns steadily, but occasion-

Figure 8

Figure 9

Maasaw petroglyphs at Tutuventiwngwu (Willow Springs, AZ). Figure 7 clearly depicts the god with his torch. The "abbreviated" versions in Figures 8 and 9, on the other hand, seem to portray him holding his dreaded club. Photographs by E. Malotki.

huruutiqw pam pep uwiwitangwu, pu' ephaqam wupa'leletangwu. Pu' ephaqam pay piw pam soosoy tokngwu. Pu' pam haqamiwat piw naalakqw pu' pam piw uwikngwu.

Noq pam kopitsoki pay laaput angqw yukiwkyangw pu' pay ang mootsitsikvut akw toonaniwtangwu.

ally the flames will leap high into the air. At other times, the fire will completely cease to burn. The instant Maasaw moves on to another place, the fire usually starts flickering again.

Maasaw's torch is fashioned from juniper bark, and is entwined with strands of split yucca leaves.

A fire moving at night, especially one whose intensity fluctuates, thus becomes the very hallmark for the presence of the god (Text 64). Places where he rests are marked by the embers from his campfire (Text 65).

TEXT 64

Maasaw pi mihikqw suutokihaq waynumngwuniiqe oovi pam yaw pay susmataqningwuniiqat itana pangqawngwu. Pam haqamniqw put qööhi'at pay hiisay ep uwiwitakyangw pu' wuuyoqtingwu. Pu' paasat pam haqami nakwsuqw pam uuwingw put amum ang hoytimangwu. Pu' pam haqam piw pan hakiy aw naamataqtanik pam pep piw hin'ur uwiwitangwu. Pam pi pay maasawen pay pan susmataq hoyoyotimangwu, pu' piw tootoktimangwu. Pay pan pam hakiy aw naamataqtangwu.

My father insists that Maasaw is easily discernable, due to the fact that he travels about in the middle of the night. Wherever he is, a small fire will flicker and then increase in size. Upon proceeding to another location, the fire moves along with him. Whenever he wants to reveal himself to a person, the fire will burn intensely. If the fire really represents Maasaw, it will move along alternating between bursts of bright illumination and periods of dimness. This is the way in which the god makes his presence known.

TEXT 65

Pay pangqaqwangwuniqw haqam maasaw qatuqw put pay töövuyatsa tuway'yungngwu. Pam pay pan hakimuy amumi naamataqtangwu. Pay töövusa haqam mamatsilngwu.

Hopis maintain that at the location where Maasaw dwells, one can only see the embers from his fire. In this way he shows his presence. Only the embers are visible.

Although Maasaw prefers to live his life invisible, he does reveal himself to mortals once in a while. People who doubt his existence or brag about what they would do if he were truly to appear, may actually provoke such a showing of the god. While normally a sudden light will suffice to cow any braggarts,[6] to those sincerely desiring proof of his existence he may expose himself as an awful creature swinging his firebrand. Text 66 is a vivid account of such an incident.

TEXT 66

Hisat yaw ima wuuwuyoqam paaqavit ep imuy hakimuy lööqmuy taaqatuy L.-t kiiyat epeq yu'a'atota. Noq puma yaw hakim put peevewnangwu, maasawuy. Pu' yaw puma oovi pan naawakna: "Pas as pam hisat itamumi naamataqtani. Pas nu' as hisat put haqam aw pas naap yorikni." Noq puma hapi yaw pay it naap a'ni unangway akw yan naawakna. Sen pi yaw pam himu pas antsa haqam qatu. Hin pi yaw pam himu soniwa. Yan yaw puma put pevewinvewat yu'a'ata. Pu' yaw puma hakim piw naasungwam.

Noq orayve yaw puma panti. Noq pu' yaw puma hisat mihikqw aqw hopqöymiqwat kwayngyaptato. Niiqe puma yaw aqw tumpoq pituqw piw yaw pepeq amutpip kootalawvat pu' piwningwu. "Ya

Many years ago some elders were at the house of L. in Paaqavi, where they were talking about an experience two men had had. These two men were skeptical about the existence of Maasaw and had expressed the following desire: "If only he would reveal himself to us once. I would very much like to see him personally somewhere." It was their aggressive character which made them wish these things. They wondered if the god really existed and were curious as to his appearance. In this doubting way the two men spoke, who also happened to be buddies.

The following experience they had took place in Orayvi. One night they headed to the east side of the village to relieve themselves. Upon getting to the mesa edge they noticed, much to their surprise, that there below them the glow from a fire was flickering. "Who

---

[6]Titiev cites an instance of such hubris, as a group of young braggarts disregard an old man's warning to discontinue this kind of boasting. "That night Maasaw appeared as a mysterious light, whereupon the young men fell all over each other, beat up the older man, and scattered" (1972: 130). Compare also the episode in the Kwan kiva in Chapter 12, Text 135, where the god leaves evidence of his existence in the form of cornhusks.

sen hak himu piw pangqaqw
qööhiy'tay?" yaw puma naatuving-
taqe pu' yaw puma pas aw tumpo.
Niiqe puma yaw laho'makyangw
aw tumpo nangk hoyoyota. Noq
pu' yaw pam mootiy'maqa oovi
aqw pas tumpoq pitukyangw pu'
yaw pam pas pavan hin yorikniqe
pu' yaw pam aqw tsooraltit pu'
aqw taatayi. Su'aw yaw pam oovi
aqw pantiqw yaw ep tuuwive himu
wunuptu, wupataqa yaw haki'.
Niikyangw yaw hak oomiq taykyangw yaw hak hiita yawta. Noq
yaw pam himu töövu'iwta. Pu' yaw
pam oovi paasat piw pavan aqw
hoyo. Noq paasat pi yaw piw
suyan muytala.

Noq pu' yaw pam aqw yorikqw
pepeq yaw hak sun wunuwkyangw
yaw hak tuupelmo matyawkyangw
wunuwta. Noq pay yaw as hak
taaqa. Pu' yaw pam paasat pas
aqw pavan hoyokq paasat pu' yaw
pam hak kur kopitsokiy'taqe put
yaw wiiwilaqw pu' yaw put angqw
wupa'leleykuqw pavan yaw paasat
suyan taalawva. Noq pas pi yaw
pam himu hak qa soniwa. Pavan
yaw pam himu ungwvukuwta.

Yan yaw pam put hiita yorikqw
pu' yaw pam angkniiqa aw pangqawu, "Ya um qa tuwa? Ya
himu'u?" yaw pam put aw kitaqw
paysoq yaw pam aqw kuytaqa put
aw, "Uh, uh, uh," kitalawu.

Pu' yaw piw as tuuvingta, "Ya um
hintiy?"

on earth would have a fire going
there?" they inquired of one
another, whereupon they edged
closer towards the rim. They were
crawling on their hands and knees,
one behind the other. When the
man in front reached the rim, he
was anxious to see what the glow
was all about, so he lay down on
his stomach and peered over the
side. The instant he glanced down
something stood up on the ledge
below, some man of gigantic
stature. He had his eyes cast
upwards and held something in
his hand, which appeared to be
glowing embers. The man in front
now moved a bit closer. At the
time this took place there was
bright moonlight.

As he peered over the edge, he
saw someone standing there quite
still with one palm of his hand
resting against the cliff. It was
clearly a man. As he inched even
closer up to the rim, he was
able to discern that the giant
below him apparently bore a
torch. Each time he twirled it
around, large flames leaped from
it and the visibility became very
clear. What a grotesque looking
creature this man was! His whole
face was covered with blood.

This was the sight he beheld as
the man behind him asked, "Don't
you see anything? What is it?"
But the one peering over the side
could only utter, "Uh, uh, uh."

Once more the man behind him
inquired, "What's the matter with
you?"

Noq pay yaw pam pas put aw qa hingqawngwu. Paysoq yaw pam put aw, "Taq, taq," kitalawu.

Paasat pu' yaw put sungwa'at pangqw put ahoy langakna. "Ya um hintiy?" yaw aw kita. Noq pay yaw pas nawutstiqw pu' yaw pam kur yan unangwtiqe pu' yaw aw pangqawu, "Tuma nimay," yaw kita. "Is utiy!"

Pay yaw pam qa sööwu pep put hiita aw yorikqey yu'a'atat pay yaw pam pangqw waaya. Pas yaw puma pituqw paasat pu' yaw pam put aw yan lalvaya. Pam maasaw hapi yaw put pas aw pan naamaa-taknaniqe oovi pam yaw pas aqw kuyvaqw pu' yaw pam kopitsokiy pavan wiiwilaqw pu' yaw paasat antsa suyan taalawvaqw pu' yaw pam put maasawuy paas piptsa hin pam soniwqw. Pay yaw pam panis put aw pan yorikt pay yaw pam mashuruuti.

Yan yaw puma put pas naap yori. Pas yaw puma paasat pu' tuptsiwa, pay yaw kur pam himu pas antsa qatuqw.

But the man in front would not answer his questions. All he was able to stammer in return was, "Taq, taq."

At this point his friend wrenched him away from the rim. "What happened to you?" he demanded. It took a good amount of time until the other had regained his senses. "Let's go home," he blurted out. "How awful!"

He didn't pause to share the experience with his friend. Instead, he bolted away from the scene. It was not before the two arrived back home that he did give an account of what he witnessed. It had, of course, been Maasaw's intention to show himself to the man. Thus, when he vigorously whipped his torch about, its light became so bright that he was able to observe in detail the features of the god. Immediately upon viewing him, however, he became petrified from fright.

This the two men personally experienced. It was only then that they were convinced that Maasaw truly existed.

A mythological explanation for the god's connection with fire at night is provided by Yava. According to him, Maasaw's initial encounter with fire occurred in Maski, the Hopi "realm of the dead." At that time he had not yet reached his god-like status. Tradition has it that Maasaw was thrown into the *koysö*, the open fire pit into which all evil Hopi can expect to be cast for punishment. However, Maasaw "escaped from it and returned to the land of living things. It was the fire in the pit, they say, that burned off his hair and made horrible scars all over his body, and that put flames in his mouth. If you see a flame or a kind of flare moving in the dark, that's Maasaw's breath, and you'd better get away from there as fast as you can" (Yava 1978:107).

A moving fire at night is generally perceived with dread by the Hopi. Courlander cites an experience along these lines from one of his informants: "We young men were going up there for a rehearsal of the butterfly dance, during the night....Before we got halfway to Orayvi we saw a fire coming, moving. And we knew that it was Maasaw. He moved. Before we got to the top of the cliff, we beat it back, threw everything away. So we knew that this evil spirit is around" (1982:99).

Titiev relates an instance of a pregnant woman who developed labor pains during a cornbake, generally held at night. While being taken home for delivery, "a light which soon faded out" was seen near the village. "This proved to be Maasaw, and the woman died in childbirth just outside her pueblo" (1972:167-8).

Furthermore, a fire at night is generally regarded as a bad omen.[7] This belief is explained in the subsequent statement:

TEXT 67

Meh, hak ephaqam haqam qööhit tuwangwuniqw pam hapi pay qa lolma. Hak put tuwe' hak yaw tuu'awtangwu. Pam yaw hakiy hiita qa lolmat aawintangwu. Sen hak hintini, sen haqawa hakimuy amungaqw hintini, sen hak haqam mokni. Pam hapi yaw pay pas qa nukngwa hak put uuwingwuy tuwaniniqw. Noq pam himu qa lomahintaqa hintiqw pam put qööhit tuwaaqa pay kur qa tuu'aw-tangwu. Noq pan himu hintiqw pu' paasat hakim suyan nanap-tangwu pay pam kur qa tuu'aw-taqat.	Look, at times a person may suddenly sight a fire. That is not good. The one perceiving this fire is said to be having a vision which signifies a bad omen. This person may come to harm, or some mis-fortune may strike a member of his family. It is also possible that somewhere someone will die. It is not good at all to sight a fire. When something unfortunate occurs after sighting a fire, it becomes clear to the person said to have had a vision, that the sight-ing of the fire was not a hal-lucination.

Closely associated with fire are, of course, both wood, the material which fuels its flames, and the phenomenon of warmth. As to the wood

---

[7]Additional examples, illustrating both the fear that a moving fire at night instills, and the belief that such a flare constitutes a bad omen in the form of an accident, disease, or death, can be gleaned from Courlander (1982: 99) and Yava (1978: 107).

association, one of Titiev's informants identifies "a peculiar crackling sound" of the wood burning in the stove as "the voice of Maasaw" (1972: 186). Stephen has recorded a myth in which the gods bestow their gifts on a youth who is told that he will become the first chief and father of the Hopi. This youth is the only survivor of the original group of Hopi that managed to escape to the upper world. It turns out that Maasaw's presents to him are the "secret of fire and the uses of wood" (1929:55). This connection, not elsewhere attested to in the literature, is corroborated in Story 2 (ATR 10) where the god initiates the young protagonist into the proper ways of gathering fire wood. He even teaches the boy a magic ditty that enables him to make short shrift of the laborious task.

Warmth as a byproduct of fire is an obvious link to Maasaw in his capacity as fertility spirit. This link, between the germinating and growth-inducing power of heat and Maasaw, is already established in the pre-emergence phase at the occasion when the messenger from the underworld first discovers the god. "He found a field in which corn, watermelons, beans, etc., were planted. All around this field a fire was burning, which was kept up by wood, and by which the ground was kept warm so that the plants could grow" (Voth 1905a:12). Fewkes actually suggests that Maasaw is "a personification of fire as a symbol of life" (1903:40). Tyler, who picks up on the symbolic essence of fire as a life-generating force, mentions two widespread connections in this regard. "Fire is associated with the masculine sun whose generative powers are obvious to all. Less obvious to us, perhaps, ...is the association of the fire drill, and hence fire, with the male element" (1964:21). In citing Robert Graves, who suggests an interpretation of phallic magic for the whirlings of the male drill in the female stock, Tyler identifies the fire-bringer Maasaw as a potent fertility figure with strong sexual overtones (1964:21).

The role of Maasaw as a masculine fire-god is also manifest in the attested literature. Fewkes reported the unmasked impersonation of the god at one point during the Wuwtsim ceremony when the "new fire" is kindled[8] (1920:600). Hidden by a blanket the Kwan head, as the god's

[8]For a detailed account of the ceremonial act of producing the "new fire," during Wuwtsim, see Fewkes (1900: 92-93). Interesting in this connection is the fact that corn pollen was dropped in the slots of the fire-board and fire-stone before the spindles were inserted. Compare also Fewkes (1892: 195), where the same custom is reported. For additional information on the production of fire consult Fewkes (1892: 218), where illustrations of the fire-making apparatus are given. See also the Glossary under "Fire making."

impersonator, accepts the sacrifices of the Wuwtsim, Al, Kwan and Taw
society initiates which, in the form of pine needles, are thrown into the
new fire (1900:94 and 1895:438). This fire, which is considered sacred,
is then carried to all the other kivas as well as the four directional shrines
by means of a cedar bark torch (Fewkes 1920:600). Parsons warns
against considering the fire-making as a key to the whole Wuwtsim, as
was done by Fewkes. "This fire-making ritual is one both of sacrifice or
offering to Maasaw, and of omen; the time taken to ignite, as measured
by the number of songs sung during the process, is prognosticative of a
good year or a bad" (Stephen 1936:959). For Third Mesa, Parsons also
reports the custom of a fire sacrifice, referred to as *qööhit paaho'at* "fire
paaho," to Maasaw within the context of the Maraw ceremony (Stephen
1936:927). Stephen calls the god *qöömongwi* "fire chief" at one point in
his lengthy notes on the Snake-Antelope ceremony (1936:927).

   While Waters views the new-fire ritual as a dramatization of the
"first cold dawn of Creation," he draws a connection between Maasaw as
god of fire and the sun. Interesting in this regard is the emphasis on
coal as fuel rather than wood. "A new fire is kindled by flint and native
cotton. It is kept going with coal from the countless outcrops nearby,
accompanied by prayers to Maasaw, deity of the Nadir, of death and the
underworld, where coal comes from. Maasaw gets his power from the sun
to keep burning the fires in the underworld and deep in this earth,
which are manifested during the eruption of volcanoes — the new fire thus
representing the cosmic power directed from the sun to Maasaw, who
then projects its germinating warmth to the earth and mankind. The
ritual kindling of the fire takes place at dawn before the sun is up. It
symbolically begins to warm only the upper crust of the earth. Then,
as the sun rises, later rituals represent the germination of seed, the
appearance of vegetation, and the maturity of crops at harvest. Brands
from the new fire are then carried to light fires in the other three kivas"
(1963:140-1).

   As transpires in Waters' passage, Maasaw as owner of the fire is also
linked to volcanism. This is confirmed in a Hopi legend concerning the
over 900-year-old eruption of Sunset Crater, which recently could be
salvaged.[9] When a fire, set by the revengeful Ka'naskatsina, burns out of
control, a kachina elder cries out:

---

[9]To be published in a monograph by Northland Press (Flagstaff) in 1987 — Malotki
and Lomatuway'ma, "Earth Fire: a Hopi Legend of the Sunset Crater Eruption."

TEXT 68

"Is ohiy, pay hapi pas amumiq pituy," yaw pam kita, "pep qöö-hiy'yungqamuy aqwaa'. Puma hapi pepeq atkyaqwat qööhiy'yungqam it maasawuy sinomatniiqe puma hapi pepeq put engem it qööhit aw tunatyawyungwa. Puma hapi pas qa nun'okwatuy. Noq pay hapi pam qööhi sumataq pas naami pitu."

"Dear me, I believe the blaze has reached the people who tend the fire underground. They are relatives of Maasaw. They keep the fire there for him and know no pity. I believe the two fires have joined together."

As a caretaker and benefacter to people who believe in him, Maasaw uses the firebrand traditionally associated with him to guide his protégés to safety in the darkness of the night. This is borne out in the Hopi Texts 69 and 70. Although the length of these texts stands in no relation to this relatively minor tutelary aspect of the god—detailed descriptions of his ceremonial dealings with fire would be a great deal more desirable—the texts, nevertheless, exemplify very nicely to what degree Maasaw is still affecting the minds of modern-day Hopi.

TEXT 69

Imuy itimuy taaha'am, ura hak K.-niipu, yaw hisat homol'ongaqw nimakyangw masiipamiqhaqami tasapmuy amum paasavo tsokiwma. Pangqw pu' yaw pam naap. Panmakyangw pu' yaw pam haqami paanaqmoki. Pay pi hak hiihikwlawe', yan unangway'me', nu'an paanaqmokngwu. Noq pam yaw panti, paanaqmoki.

Noq naat angqe' i' wukovö qa pangningwuniqw pam yaw oovi hisatvönawit. Niiqe pam yaw pangniikyangw yaw ahoy yorikqw

Once K., the deceased uncle of my children, was returning home from the town of Winslow. He had hitched a ride with some Navajos as far as Masiipa. From there he proceeded on foot. At some point he became thirsty. This feeling of thirst typically occurs when a person becomes sober after having been on a drinking binge. And this is what happened to K. He badly needed a drink of water.

At that time the big highway did not exist yet, so he walked along the old trail. At one point, as he looked behind him he noticed,

piw yaw put angk yaasavawya
qööhi kwangwahoyoyotima. Pay
yaw pam suupan wuuwa, "Is uti,
kur pi piw inumum." Noq pam
hapi yaw maasaw. Pu' yaw pam
pangqw put angk panmakyangw
pas yaw put qa maatavi. Niiqe
pam yaw put pas peqw kiimiq
pitsinat pu' yaw put maatavi. It
pam oovi pas yan yorikiy'ta. Noq
pay pi yaw pam suyan maasaw.
Pam hapi put pas peqw wiiki. Pu'
yaw pam as piw qatuptuniqey
unangwtiqw paasat pu' yaw pam
uuwingw suupan pas pavan piw
hihin wuuyoqtingwu. Pu' pay pi
pam sonqa aw pan wuuwa, "Kur
nu' qa huruutiniqw oovi pam kya
pi pantingwu." Paapiy pu' pam
nawus piw aapiytangwu.

Yan piw yaw pam put pangqaqw
wikqw pam piw pas it naap
lalvaya. Niikyangw pam pay
panwat put aw naamaatakna. Pay
pamsa qööhi angk kwangwaho-
yoyota. Pay pam oovi hakiy tuptsiwniy'taqat pas qa peevewnaqat
pan hakiy ayo' tavingwu. Put hapi
pam aw awiwa. Pam pi qa nukpana. Pam pi sinot tumalay'ta.
Noq oovi himuwa a'ni unangway'-
kyangw put peevewnaqw pam pay
paasat son put hiita ep ayo' tavini.
Son hakiy put peevewnaqat pam
ookwatuwa, naamahin pi pam
nu'okwa. Pu' piw naamahin pam
hak put aw qa tuptsiwniy'taqa
hiita akw pas okiwhintaniqw son
pam put ookwatuwni.

much to his surprise, that there
was a small fire following him.
He quickly realized, "My gosh,
how amazing, a fire going along
with me!" This was, of course,
Maasaw. The fire trailed behind
him and would not let go of him.
It was not until it had guided
him here to the village that it quit
following him. K. personally
experienced this with his own eyes.
There is no doubt that it was
Maasaw who had accompanied
him all the way here. Also it seems
that every time K. felt the urge to
sit down, the fire increased in size.
He must have thought at that
point, "I guess I'm not supposed to
stop; that's why the fire behaves
like that." This compelled him to
continue on his way.

In this manner Maasaw escorted
K. home. He has personally narrated this event. Maasaw had
revealed himself in this fashion to
him. It was only a fire which
followed him with such ease, yet
thereby the god brings one who
believes in him, and who does not
doubt his existence, to safety. That
is Maasaw's role. He is not evil,
rather he takes care of people.
Hence a person who is incon-
siderate and defiant by nature,
and doubts his presence, will not
be safeguarded by him. Such a
skeptic finds no pity with Maasaw
even though the god is usually
benevolent. Even if this disbeliever
is in grave danger or in another
bad situation, Maasaw will not
sympathize with him.

While in Text 69 Maasaw leads a drunk Hopi to the safety of his home, in Text 70, below, a movie-goer who is returning from a late performance is ushered by the god through the night.

TEXT 70

Noq pu' pam P. yan maatsiwqa pay naat tiyoniikyangw pam kiqötsmomiq it matamintaqat tiimayto. Noq pu' yaw ep mihikqw pam yukiltiqw pu' yaw pam pangqw naap nima. Niiqe pam oovi pay suwiptaniqe pu' pam ayoq oraymiq wupt pangqw pu' pam pay aqw kwiniwiq kuywanvamiq kuyvat pu' pam aqw kwiniwiq. Nit pay yaw pam pangsoq nalmaqasti. Pay pi qa talqw pam oovi aqw kuyvat pu' yaw pay pepeq wunuptu. Noq yaw ayaq qöma'waveq angqw naat pu' aqw hawqw pepeq poniwtaqat epeq yaw sikisve wunu. Noq sen pi yaw pam pepeq hintiqat yan yaw pam wuuwa. "Pay pi nu' put aqwnen put amum kiimiq pituni," yan yaw pam wuuwaqe pu' pay pam pangsoq put sikisvet aqwa'.

Noq suyan pi yaw pepeq sikisve qööhiy'taqw pu' yaw pam oovi pangsoqa'. Pu' yaw pam hihin qa aqw yorikqw pay yaw pam qööhi kur tooki. Pu' yaw pam piw aqw yorikqw pay yaw paasat epeq yaasava uwiwita. Pu' pay yaw pam pan wuuwa, "Pay pi kya sen pam maasaw'u." Noq pam maasaw pi ayaq hotvelay taavang pumuy hisat yesngwuniqw pepeq pumuy kiiya-

When P. was still a young, unmarried man, he went to the village of Kiqötsmovi to attend a motion picture show. By the time the movie was over it was black night. Heading home on foot, P. decided to take a short cut. He took the trail up to the village of Orayvi from where he continued on northward to Kuywanva and then again bore on in a northerly direction. It was at this moment that he suddenly became afraid of being alone. It was very dark, so having passed over the ridge of Kuywanva he halted. Directly beneath the curve of the road which descends from Qöma'wa he saw a vehicle parked. It occured to him that it might have broken down, so he thought, "I guess I'll head over to that car. That way I might get to the village by catching a ride with the driver." With that he set out towards this car.

There was clearly a car there with its headlights on, so he headed in its direction. Then, having only momentarily taken his eyes off it, he realized that the light had disappeared. Upon taking a second look, he saw a fire with long flames. Immediately the idea struck him, "Perhaps it's Maasaw." At a place west of Hotvela, just below where P. and his family had

muy atpipaq pi pam qatu. Pu'
pam pi pumuy wu'ya'am. "Pay
kya pam'i. Kya pam nuy wikto,"
yan yaw pam wuuwaqe pu' pay
yaw pam oovi aqw waymakyangw
yaw aqw paas tunatyawma.

Niiqe pu' yaw pam aw haykyalniy'-
maqw pay yaw pam uuwingw
hoyoyoyku. Noq pam yaw put
aqwwat naat hoytaqw pay yaw put
mutsqöhi'at tooki. Noq pay yaw
pam put aw qa pas hin wuuwanta.
Pay pi yaw pam mutsqöhi unangway'tangwuniiqe pay yaw naap
hisatniqw mokngwuniqw oovi. Pu'
yaw pam pangqw put angkniqw
pu' yaw put mutsqöhi'at hintiqw
pay piw ahoy uwi. Paapiy pu' yaw
pam hihin wuuyaq puutsit qööhiy'ma. Pu' yaw pam put angk-
niiqe pam haqe' qööhi hoytaqw
pay yaw pam suupangqe' put
angk. Pay yaw pam oovi qa wuuyavo put angk. Pu' yaw pam qööhi
aqw qöma'wat oomiq wupto-
kyangw aqwhaqami tuuwaya.

Pu' yaw pam aqw oomiq angk
wupqe pu' yaw pam angqe' tay-
numqw pay yaw qa haqam qööhiwta. Pangqw pu' yaw pam ayo'
hihin teevenge ang hisatkaree-
tavöningwuniqw pangso yaw
pamniiqe pang pu' yaw pam
hiisavonit pu' yaw pam haqam
ayo' lasqe paapiy pu' pay yaw pam
yuumosa naapvönawit. Niiqe pam
yaw oovi aqw ayoq pisatsmomiq
wupqe pu' yaw aqw kwiniwiq
taytaqw ang pu' yaw pam piw
qööhi hoyta.

Pu' yaw pam pangqw hawt pu'·

formerly lived, Maasaw is said to
make his home. He is their clan
ancestor. "Perhaps it's him. He
may have come to fetch me."
Thoughts like these crossed his
mind as he walked towards the
light keeping a close watch on it.

When he neared the fire, it began
to move along. Suddenly, his
flashlight gave out. But that didn't
bother him much. After all, a
flashlight had batteries and they
could go dead at any time. As he
continued in pursuit of the peculiar phenomenon, for some un-
explainable reason his flashlight
came back on again. From that
point on its beam of light was also
broader. He now pursued the fire
exactly along the course it was
taking. P. was not far behind it
when it ascended Qöma'wa and
disappeared over the rim of the
mesa top.

He continued tracking it up to the
top, but by the time he arrived
and looked around, there was no
fire visible anymore. So he went
slightly west to where the ancient
wagon route was located and
followed it for a while until he
veered off onto a foot trail and
walked straight along its path.
After climbing the top of Pisatsmo,
he looked northward, and once
again there was the fire moving
along before him.

Having descended from Pisatsmo

yaw pam aapiy aqw pönawit. Noq
pepeq pi nan'ivo paasa. Yukwat
sipal'uyiy'taqaniqw pu' yukwat
morivasa. Niiqe pam yaw oovi
pumuy amuutsava yamaktokyangw
pu' pam angk pitutoq pay yaw
piw put mutsqöhi'at tokto. Pu' yaw
pam angk pisoqtiqe pu' yaw pam
put aqw pööpamiq wiiki. Niiqe
pu' pam pay oovi put eepeqta.
Songyawnen momiqwat yamakt
pu' yaw pam aapiyta. Pu' yaw
pam ahoy yan yorikqw pay yaw
qa himu angk. Paasat pu' yaw
pam piw aapiyniikyangw yaw
yorikqw pay yaw apyevehaqam
qööhilti. Paapiy pu' yaw pam put
angk aw kiimi. Pu' yaw pam piw
yorikqw pay yaw paasat qa himu
haqam qööhiniqw pu' yaw pam
paapiy piiw. Pu' yaw pam angqw
hotvelay taavangqw aw atvelmo
hawqw pay yaw piw ayam tsii-
saskit aqlap qööhilti. "Kur pay i'
kya pi pam'i," yan yaw pam
wuuwa.

Pangqw pu' yaw pam put angknii-
kyangw su'aw yaw pam oovi put
angk pitutoq pay yaw pumuy
kiiyamuy iipwat qööhilti. Pephaqam yaw uwiwita. Pu' yaw pam
angqw awniiqe pu' yaw aw pituqw
pay yaw pam paasat kur haqami.
Pangso yaw pam put maatavi.
Kiiyat yaw pam put aw wiiki. Pu'
yaw pam aapami pakiiqe pu'
aapay ang wa'ökt pas yaw paasat
pu' pam tsawnaqe yaw soosoy
tililiyku.

he proceeded along the foot trail.
Here fields lay on each side of the
path; one had peach trees, the
other was a bean patch. He traversed
these fields and began drawing
closer to the moving fire when his
flashlight began to dim again.
This time he quickened his stride
and caught up with the fire as he
reached the highway. As it turned
out, he had actually overtaken it.
He had come out in front of it and
then continued on. When he
peered over his shoulder, there was
nothing behind him. Therefore he
pushed on but, when he looked
ahead, the fire once more had
materialized before him. From
that point on P. followed it to the
village. Upon taking another look
he found that the fire had vanished,
so he kept on going. As he
arrived at the bottom of the slope
which lies to the west of Hotvela,
the fire appeared next to the
church. "That must be him," he
thought to himself.

P. proceeded after the fire and
just as he was approaching it, it
lit up in front of his house. There
it kept burning. He made for it,
but when he came upon it, it was
no longer there. Having led him to
his home, the fire had finally
abandoned him. Upon entering,
P. reclined on his bedroll, and it
was not until that moment that he
became frightened and began to
shiver all over.

6

Agriculture and Life Force

Maasaw, the great Hopi representative of death, who owns both land and fire, is also a major fertility power. "The connecting idea," Curtis reasons out, "seems to be the conception that the growth of plants is dependent on warmth, and warmth is the product of fire" (1922:102). This link is already established during the emergence phase of Hopi mythology, when the Hopi found the god "nursing his small paradise of vegetation inside his ring of fire" (Tyler 1964:20).[1] While there are

---

[1] Compare Voth (1905a: 12). The messenger who is dispatched to explore the dark upper world finds "a field in which corn, watermelons, beans, etc., were planted. All around this field a fire was burning, which was kept up by wood, and by which the ground was kept warm so that the plants could grow."

Courlander has Maasaw himself give the *raison d'etre* for fire: "You see... there is no light, only grayness here. There is no warmth, and I must build fires to make my crops grow" (1972: 28).

versions of the emergence myth in which either Muy'ingwa[2] or Sootukwnangw[3] bestow the first crops on the Hopi, the majority of traditions
credit Maasaw with giving this gift. Portrayed as an industrious farmer
whose implement *extraordinaire* is his planting dibble, the god can to
some extent be regarded as a role-model for the agriculturist Hopi.[4] This
image of Maasaw as the "mythical proto-farmer" takes shape in an
episode of a Hopi emergence legend. In this passage the clues that
identify Maasaw's abode are nearly all of an agricultural nature.

TEXT 71

"Ta'ay, kur um aw yamakye' oray-
mini. Epeq taavang owatukwit
tatkyaqöyngaqw tuusöve i' himu
qataymataq qatuuqa, maasaw,
hapi kiy'tay. Pangso umni," yaw i'
kookyangwso'wuuti aw kita. Pay
pi pam a'ni himuniiqe pay yaw
oovi piw navotiy'ta. "Um pangso
hepni. Pu' kur um pep qa tuwe'
pu' um angqw taavangqöymi
wupatsmomini. Pep hapi pam
paasay'ta, pep pam uuyiy'ta. Pam
hapi pay sonqa pepni qa kiy
epnen'e," yaw aw kita. "Noq
pu'haqam uuyi'at nuvawiwtaniqw
pam pay son oovi qa pepni," yan
yaw aw paas tutapta.

"All right then, once you find
your way into the world above,
fly to Orayvi. West of there lies a
butte by the name of Owatukwi.
There, on its south side, is an
overhang where this invisible being
known as Maasaw resides. Go
there," Old Spider Woman directed the shrike. Spider Woman,
of course, is endowed with greater
than human powers and, therefore, had knowledge of all these
things. "Look for Maasaw under
that overhang. If you can't find
him, head on west to Wupatsmo
where he owns a field and grows
his crops. He's bound to be at the
field if he's not at home. This
time of the season his crops should
be ripe, so I'm sure he'll be there,"
Old Spider Woman pointed out to
the bird.

---

[2] Compare Bradfield (1973: 257) who contrasts Muy'ingwa, an important vegetation
deity, with Maasaw. While the fertility role of the latter is linked to *tuuwaqatsi*, "the earth
surface" of the Above, the former is seen to be operative as a germ god in the Below. See
also Stephen (1929: 10).

[3] Concerning Sootukwnangw's role as a donor of seeds see Stephen (1929: 55).

[4] "Skeleton always planted and the food was never gone... Skeleton gave them
roasting ears, and watermelons, melons, squashes, etc., and they ate and refreshed
themselves" (Voth 1905a: 13).

Paasat pu' yaw pam oovi pangqw nakwsu. Puuyaltikyangw pu' antsa angqw pam pew yama. Pu' antsa yaw pam pangso orayminiiqe pu' yaw ep pitu. Ep pituuqe pu' yaw pangsoq haqami kiiyat aa'awnaqw pangso yaw pami'. Pu' yaw aw pituqw pay yaw qa qatu. Pu' pam pi paas tutavot hinmaqe pu' yaw pam oovi put hakiy hepnumqey qa tuwaaqe pu' yaw pam paasat angqw taavangqöymi wupatsmomi'. Pangso yaw pamniiqe yaw antsa hakiy uuyiyat aw pituto. Noq pep wupatsmove hapi yaw pam kur antsa paasay'ta, i' himu maasaw.

Pangso hapi yaw yokve' pang munvangwu. Pang yaw munve' pang yaw tsivookyatingwu. Pep hapi orayviy aatavang yaw pam uylawu, maasawu. Niiqe pay yaw pam oovi antsa uuyi'at nuvawniy'taqw yaw pam ep pitu. Pu' yaw pam pep kohot piw paas maskyay'ta. Pay pi hak uuyiy ep pite' pay tuutu'tsangwuniqw oovi. Noq yaw paasat taawanasaptiqw yaw pam pep put aw pitu. Noq yaw pam paasat qööhiy'ta. Pam hapi yaw kur tuutu'tsani.

The shrike departed. He winged skyward and, indeed, by penetrating the heavens, he succeeded in entering this upper world. Continuing onward he arrived at Orayvi and sought out Maasaw's residence as he had been directed; but when he came to the overhang, Maasaw was not home. Since the bird had been given explicit instructions about what to do in such a case, he proceeded westward to Wupatsmo. Sure enough, on his way there he neared someone's plants. So it was true: the god Maasaw had a field at Wupatsmo.

After a rainfall the water generally flooded the area there and deposited loamy soil. Maasaw had chosen this spot west of Orayvi to sow his crops. The crops were fully ripe when the shrike happened to arrive. The bird also noticed that Maasaw had a neat stack of firewood set aside, for when a farmer comes to his field, he usually roasts corn over an open fire. By the time the shrike arrived it was noon and Maasaw had a fire blazing. No doubt, he was planning to roast corn.

To assure plentiful crops, the Hopi farmer plants portions of his field especially for Maasaw and, after the harvest, deposits the products as offerings at Maasaw's rock (Stephen 1940:103). In addition, he solicits crops from the god in prayer.

TEXT 72

Pay pi hak hiita wuuwankyangw maasawuy engem put yukungwu, nakwakwusit. Pam pi pay soosok hiita himuy'taqat pangqaqwangwuniqw pay hak oovi naap hiita pi akw so'on'iwte' put aw naawaknangwu. Sen pasva himu wuuhaq aniwtiniqat pay puuvut hiita hak aw naawaknangwu.

A person has something special in mind when he prepares a prayer feather for Maasaw. The god is said to possess all things; therefore, when one is very much in need of something, one begs him for it. For instance, one may pray to him for an abundance of crops in the fields.

In his role as fertility god, Maasaw is primarily responsible for the distribution of corn. He thus forms the very basis of Hopi culture. Two Hopi testimonials underline this important gesture of the god:

TEXT 73

Noq pu' yaw puma oovi antsa tutskwat makiwyakyangw pu' put amum yep yesniqey kitotakyangw pu' yaw puma antsa pangqw nankwusani, peqwhaqami hopiikimiq. Noq pu' yaw puma pangqw nankwusaniqw pu' pam maasaw pumuy amumi it natwaniy, qaa'öt, akw puma nayesniy'yungwniqat amutpip pongyaata. Niiqe pu' yaw pam paasat put naanan'i'vaqw oyaata. Kwiningyaqw yaw pam it sikyaqa'öt aqw sunasamiq hooviy'taqat tavi. Pu' taavangqw yaw sakwawsat, pu' tatkyaqw pu' yaw paalangput. Hoopaqw pu' yaw qöötsatniikyangw pu' yaw pam it qöötsatnit pu' it takurit amuutsava it kokomat taviqw pam yaw pu' it oongaqwniiqat tu'awiy'ta. Noq pu' yaw atkyami piw sukw taviy'taqw pam yaw i' tawaktsiniikyangw pam yaw it sakwaputnit

After the people had been granted possession of the land and had acknowledged that they would inhabit this world with Maasaw, they were ready to proceed to the area now known as Hopiland. Prior to their leaving, however, Maasaw set out before them his main crop, corn, to provide for their sustenance. He arranged ears of corn in a circle for each of the six directions. To the north he assigned a yellow ear with its butt pointing inward. The west was represented by a blue corn, the south by a red colored one, and in the east he placed a white ear. Between the white and the yellow ears he put the purple corn, which symbolized the zenith. The sweet corn, in turn, was laid between the blue and the red

pu' it palaqa'öt amuutsavanii-
kyangw pam yaw it atkyangaqw-
niiqatwat tu'awiy'ta. Yanhaqam
yaw pam put sunasamiq hooviy'yungqat pongyaata.

Noq pu' yaw pam pumuy amumi
pangqawu, "Hak hiitawat naa-
yongwe', hiitawat aw kwangway'tus-
we' hak put namortamantani.
Hak hiita namorte', put ep kwuse',
put nitkyay'mamantaniy," yaw
amumi kita.

Pu' yaw puma oovi put qaa'öt
ang naanangk ömalalwakyangw
yaw puma nanaptaqe yaw puma
kur qa sun tuuqayyungwa. Noq
pay i' tasavu pas tutuyqawiniiqe
pam yaw pas susnukngwat, pas
suswupaqa'öt, pas susmooti namorta. Pu' pay yaw himuwa angqw
aw nakwse' pu' yaw ang paasat
tuwat sukw kwusungwu. Noq pay
yaw kur qa qaa'ötsa pongyaata.
Pay yaw puma aw yoyrikyaqw pay
yaw ep antsa nuutuptsiwtaniqa
nöösiwqa pongya'iwta, pu' soosoy
himu poshumi enang. Noq pu'
pay yaw puma ang put ömalalwakyangw ayo' naakwusta.

Noq pu' yaw i' hopi susnuutungk
namortaqw paasat pay yaw pas i'
sowiwasa, hiisavawya ep peeti.
Pay yaw i' hopi kur put navotiy'ta,
yaw pam qaa'ö hiisavawya sonqa
yaavo pituni. Pu' yaw pam maasaw aw pangqawu, "Um sakina.
Pay um suuput namorta. I' hapi
pay as naamahin yaasayhoyanii-
kyangw i' hapi pay pas son haqami
hisat ökiwtiniy," yaw kita. "Um
naakyantsana." Panhaqam yaw

ears. It represented the nadir. In
this manner Maasaw arranged the
corn ears whose ends all pointed
to the middle.

Following this, Maasaw said to the
people, "Select whichever ear you
find attractive; choose whichever
you desire. The one you pick you
can take along as food for your
journey."

One after the other the people
selected an ear of their liking, and
in doing so became aware that
they did not speak the same
language any more. The Navajo,
who was a greedy person, was the
first to make his selection. He took
the longest and the best ear. Then
somebody else approached the
array of corn and made his choice.
But apparently Maasaw had not
only displayed corn ears before
them, for when the people looked
at the place where the corn had
been, they discovered that there
was enough food present for everyone. There was also an entire
assortment of seeds. And so the
people helped themselves to the
food and then moved on.

The Hopi was the last to choose.
The only ear remaining by that
time was a stunted one. However,
the Hopi knew that this short ear
would last forever. Maasaw con-
gratulated him. "Lucky you," he
said, "you really picked the right
ear. Even though it's small in
size, it will never give out. You can
be proud of yourself." Maasaw's

pam aw lavaytiqw yaw pam
pii'oyti.

Pu' yaw aapiy mima peetu himusinom pay put hiihiita tuusaqat
qa qaa'öt namortotaqe put oovi
pan uylalwakyangw noonova. Noq
puma himusinom yaw oovi nanap
hiita tunösmakiway'yungwa. Noq
i' hopi naala yaw kur suuput it
sowiwat namortaqe pu' pam yaw
put yankyangw pu' pangqw nakwsu. Pu' puma yepehaq hopiiki-
veq huruutotiqw aapiy naat itam
put poshumit aasakis yaasangwuy
ang uylalwa. Akw itam peqwhaqami naat nayesniy'yungwa.

words filled the Hopi with pleasure.

People of other races selected
various grasses instead of corn and
cultivate these to sustain themselves. Consequently, every group
received its own staple food. The
Hopi apparently were the only
ones to make the correct choice.[5]
They selected the short stubby ear
of corn and they took it with
them. From that day they settled
here in Hopiland and have been
planting this seed year after year.
To this day they still utilize it to
endure.

TEXT 74

Paasat pu' yaw pam pep pumuy
sinmuy tsovalniy'kyangw pu' yaw
pam pumuy amutpipo hiita oya.
Hiihinyungqat qaa'öt, poshumit,
tuusaqat yaw pam pep pongyaata.
"Ta'ay, yep hapi nu' umungem it
maskyata. Hak hapi hiita akw
qatuniqey put namortamantani.
Niikyangw hak somatsinen suuput
hapi namortani."

Naat yaw pam pu' oovi kitaqw
pay yaw hak sinsonngaqw a'ni
hingqawkyangw yamakto. "Pay nu'
itniy," yaw pam kitakyangw pu'
yaw pam pangso nakwsukyangw
pu' yaw pam pang put pas suswu-
pat qaa'öt kwusut pu' yaw put

While Maasaw had the people
gathered there, he placed some
things before them. He spread out
on the ground many types of corn,
all sorts of seeds and grasses. "Well
then, I've prepared all this for
you. Choose now what you care
to sustain yourselves with. Anyone
who's good at guessing will pick
what is right for them."

No sooner had Maasaw ended his
instructions than someone from
the middle of the crowd came
forth talking loudly. "I'll have this
one!" he kept shouting as he
approached the site. Upon select-
ing the longest ear of corn he held

---

[5]Compare also Katchongva (1975: 6), where the selection of the corn is characterized as "a test of wisdom. The shortest ear was picked by the humblest leader."

oomiq iita. "Ta'ay, inumi yoyrikya'ay. It hapi nu' akw naataviy'-
tani." Noq kur pam yaw hak
tasavu. Panhaqam yaw kur pam
qatsiy'tani. Hiita nunukngwat yaw
pam tutuyqawmantani.

Paasat pu' yaw mimawat sinom
tuwat namorlalwa. Pu' yaw puma
oovi pantsatskyaqw pu' yaw suukya
peeti. Pam yaw pay okiw hin'eway
qaa'ö pep akwsingwa. Paasat pu'
yaw hak taaqa pangso nakwsuqe
pu' yaw pam put ep kwusu. "It
hapi nu'niy. I' hapi huru. I' pay
inumi a'ni aptsiwtay. Naamahin
pi' i' as yaasayhoya." Noq pam
yaw kur it sowiwat namortakyangw
pam yaw hak kur hopi.

it high over his head. "Hey, look
at me. With this I'll nourish
myself!" It so happened that this
man was a Navajo. This would be
his way of life. He would use
greed to obtain all the good
things.

Now the rest of the people were
making their choice. As they did
so, only one thing was left over,
one ear of corn, about which there
was nothing attractive. At this
point a man came up and helped
himself to it. "This is the ear I'll
have. It's a hardy specimen. This
is sufficient for me, even though
it's rather small." This man, who
had chosen the shortest ear of
corn, was the Hopi.

Of the six corn ears which Maasaw aligned along their main directional associations, the *kokoma*, a deep purple corn, is specifically related
to him.[6] In the literature *kokoma* is usually assigned the color label
"black".[7] The reason for this erroneous color identification may stem
from the fact that the ceremonial color linked with the zenith, for which
this corn symbolically stands, is black. According to Hopi lore, Maasaw
wears a belt fashioned of purple corn around his waist symbolizing his
power of maize fecundity. One should note the assurance of a bountiful
harvest in Text 75, and capability to extract moisture which is believed to
reside in the god's seed corn, in Text 76.

TEXT 75

Pam maasaw pi pay it kanelsakwitsa yuwsiy'tangwuniikyangw
pam yaw piw it kokomqa'öt

In addition to a dilapidated
woman's dress Maasaw wears
purple colored corn about his

[6]Compare Stephen (1929: 10). "The Hopi obtained from Muy'ingwa all their typical
plants except the squash and *kokomqa'ö*, and these Maasaw gave to them."

[7]Compare Titiev (1944: 61).

kwewtangwu. Pu' hisat hakiy aw pangqaqwangwu, "Hak haqam maasawuy aw pite', hak put qa mamqast awnen pu' put qa'ökwewyat nawkingwu. Hak pante' pu' put ayoqwat uyismiq uuye' hak a'ni put aniwnangwu," hakiy aw kitotangwu.

Pay pi hopiit it sukw qaa'öt pan tuwiy'yungwa, kokomqa'ö. Pam yaw tuwat it maasawuy himu'at. Put yaw i' maasaw tuwat qaa'öy'taqat pay kitotangwu.

I' maasaw pi pay put kokomqa'öt itamuy sinmuy amungem pan kwewnumngwu. Noq oovi pam hakiy aw pituqw hak qa tsawne' put nawkye' pu' hak put poshumtat pu' yasmiq uyngwu. Hak put yasmiq poshumiy aw huumingwu. Pu' hak put pan neengalat pu' put uyqw, kur ep taala' qa yokvaqw, pu' hakiy uuyi'at paanaqso'iwtaqw, pu' yaw pam maasawuy qaa'öyat angqw hak poshumtaqw, pam yaw oomi oo'omawtuy amumi pumuy amungem kuytongwu.

waist in the form of a belt. Long ago, people used to say to a person, "Whenever you encounter Maasaw, walk up to him without fear and help yourself to the corn in his belt. After doing that and sowing the seeds of this corn the following planting season, you will reap a profuse amount."

The Hopi term for this species of corn which belongs to Maasaw is *kokoma*, "purple corn." People speak of Maasaw owning this type of corn.

TEXT 76

Maasaw roams the land wearing a belt of *kokoma* corn for us. Thus, when the god chances upon a mortal and the mortal does not panic, but removes a cob from Maasaw's belt, he can produce seeds from it and then plant them the following year. The kernels shelled from this corn are added to the regular seeds that year and then the mixture is planted. If during the ensuing summer a shortage of rain results in the plants becoming parched, the seeds which are taken from Maasaw's corn are said to ascend to the sky to fetch water from the clouds for the thirsting plants.

Within the context of the Sopkyaw ceremonial (see Texts 90 and 92, below) the impersonator of Maasaw once actually ground corn. Since the chore of corn-grinding is reserved exclusively for Hopi females, the performance of this activity constitutes a trait of antithetic behavior so typical for the deity of death.

TEXT 77

Pay pi sinom pangqaqwangwuniqw
yaw hisat maasaw sopkyawmaqat
ep pitungwu. Nen pu' pam yaw
pumuy höhöqyaqamuy amumum-
ningwu. Nen pu' pam orayviy
tatkyaqöyngaqw wuuve' pu' pam
yaw pepeq owat ang ngumamay-
kungwu. A'ni halayvit ngumamay-
kut pu' angqw kiiminingwu. Put
mataaki'at pi pay yaw as hisat
pepeq qatsngwuniikyangw pu' pi
pay pam sonqa haqami.

People relate that in the past
Maasaw came at the occasion of a
Sopkyaw and that he intermingled
with the workers who were taking
the ears off the corn stalks. Later,
after making his ascent to the top
of the mesa from the southwest,
the god would grind corn on a
stone. He always ground with
extremely rapid strokes and then
headed on to the village. The
mano or handstone with which he
carried out the grinding was still
present there a while back, but
now it has probably disappeared.

While the use of Maasaw's belt is limited to growth magic in regard
to maize, his *maawiki* or "club" is thought to hold all the seeds of interest
to the Hopi agriculturist.[8]

TEXT 78

Noq pay pi pangqaqwangwuniqw
yaw put maasawuy maawikiyat
aasonve i' poshumi mookiwtangwu.
Pam pi yaw a'ni pasvaniiqe oovi
soosok hiita natwanit poshumiyat
pangqw mookiy'tangwu.

People claim that the inside of
Maasaw's club is filled with planting seeds. He is also reputed to
be an excellent farmer. For this
reason he has within his club
every variety of planting seeds.

As a major vegetation deity Maasaw also seems to enjoy a special
connection to string beans.[9] An indication of the god's closeness to this

[8]Curtis (1922: 178) describes the club as "about ten inches long and two inches in
thickness, which is hollow and filled with seeds of all kinds known to the Hopi farmer."

[9]Indirect evidence for Maasaw's close connection with string beans can be derived
from the necklace worn by the Masaw kachina. According to Titiev's sources the sheep-
horn necklace is said to represent "string beans" (1972: 140).

agricultural product can be found in the Hopi folk belief that he uses the strings of the vegetable to sew his shoes.[10]

TEXT 79

Pu' hakim it maawiwngwut noonove' hakim put taapawiyat paas oo'oyayangwu. Nen pu' hakim öö'öye' pu' ang qenitote' pu' hakim pay put maspayangwu. Hakim yaw qa put kiy aasonve haqami o'yangwu. Hakim yaw put aapave o'yaqw, put yaw maasaw angqw hakimuy amumi taapawtatongwu. Nen pu' pam put tootsiy akw angqe tuu'iingwu.

When people dine on string beans, they carefully place the strings aside. Upon finishing their meal and cleaning up, they throw the strings out. They are never left inside the home, because in that case Maasaw comes to pick them up. He uses them to sew his shoes.

How a disbeliever in Maasaw's fondness for the strings of these beans fares is vividly recounted in the following passage:

TEXT 80

Itam hisat maawiwngwut noonovaqe öö'öyaqw, pu' pam iwuutiniqa as ura put taapawiyat qöönaniniqw pu' pam taaha'at aw pangqawu, "Um pay put qa qöönaniy. Um yuyiq iipoq put oyaqw, pu' i' qataymataq qatuuqa yangnen put ömaate' sonqa haalaytini. Pam put tootsiy akw tuu'iingwuniiqe pam put tuwat akw pan mongvasiy. Um oovi qa qöönat um iipoq oyaqw, pay pam put sonqa tuwani."

Once when we had been eating string beans and were satiated, I recall that my wife was inclined to burn the strings. Her uncle, however, told her, "Don't burn the strings. Take them outside so that when Maasaw, the one who lives unseen, comes by here he can help himself to them. He will be grateful for he sews his shoes with them and makes use of them in that way. So don't burn them but leave them in front of the house. He's bound to find them."

[10]Compare Chapter 10, Text 133, where "shoes" are claimed to distinguish the good from the evil Maasaw. Only the latter is thought to wear shoes.

Pu' iwuuti aw pangqawu, "Son pi pam yangqe'ni."

"As'awuy, pay pitungwuy."

"Pay nu' qöönani."

"Pay um tis qa qöönat pay um iipoq oyaniy," ura kitalawqw pu' pam put pay qa pantit pay iipoq oya.

Niikyangw pam put peevewna. Sen pam pas antsa put yukutongwuqat nuy tuuvingta. Pu' nu' aw pangqawu, "Pay sonqa yukutoni. Niikyangw pay son soosok kimani. Pay pam hiisa' lomahinyungqatsa ang poopongt pu' pay antsa son put qa kimani," nu' aw kita.

Noq pu' ep mihikqw pam taaha'amniqa nimaqw pu' itam wa'ömti. Noq nu' pi pay suupuwvangwuniiqe antsa panti. Noq hisatniqw pu' kur kya pi pam pituuqe pu' put iwuutiyniqat aw naamataqta. Pu' pam kur mashuruutiqe as a'ni hingqawlawu. Pu' yaw pam put suyan piptsa. Hin hak soniwqa taaqa aw pituqw put nuy pam aa'awna.

My wife replied, "He'll never come by here."

"Of course he will; he does come around."

"Well, I'll go ahead and burn them."

"I beg you, instead of burning them, place them outside," I remember her uncle urging her. So she didn't burn the strings and deposited them outdoors.

But my wife remained skeptical. She inquired of me if Maasaw truly came around to get the strings. I answered, "I'm sure he'll come and fetch them. But he won't take them all. He'll probably pick out only a few good ones. Those he'll take along."

After her uncle had left for home that night, we lay down to sleep. As I usually fall asleep right away, I did just that. At some time into the night Maasaw apparently stopped by and revealed himself to my wife. She had a nightmare and screamed out loud. Not that the screaming helped. Later she said she had gotten a good glimpse of Maasaw and she related to me what the man who approached her had looked like.

Maasaw's strong fecundity function is further substantiated by Texts 81 and 82. The proverbial saying, in the first of these, is based on the accomplishment of a feat requiring extraordinary physical strength.

TEXT 81

Yepeq songoopaviy taavangqöyveq maasawuy qötö'at qaatsi. Niikyangw pam pay qa pas antsa put qötö'at. Pam pay yaasay a'ni putu, wuko'owa. Noq hakiy aw pangqaqwangwu, "Um kawayvatngat wuukoq aniwnaniqey naawakne', um masqötöt aqwnen pu' um put tsopaatani. Pam pep tuukwit epeq tsöki. Pam a'ni putu. Kur um put tsöpaate' pu' um put tsöpkyangw put tuukwit angqe naalös qöniltit pu' ahoy aw piw tsokyani. Um pante' pay um son paasat qa wuukoq kawayvatngat aniwnani," hakiy aw kitotangwu.

On the west side of Songoopavi lies the head of Maasaw. Actually, it is not his real head; it is only a very heavy, large stone which figures in the following saying: "If you want to produce huge watermelons, go to Masqötö or "Maasaw's Head" and lift the rock there. It rests on a pillar and is extremely heavy. If you manage to pick it up, carry it around the pillar four times before you set it down. After accomplishing that feat you can be sure to grow large watermelons."

Passage 82 explains a custom[11] that was once practiced in conjunction with entering Maasaw's cave shrine, an important station along the ancient Hopi salt trail to the Grand Canyon. The condition of certain food remains, in the cave, constituted an omen for growth and expectations related to food in general.[12] Maasaw is believed to own a grinding bin in his subterranean domicile.

[11]Talayesva recalls a prayer to Maasaw uttered by the salt expedition members prior to the war chief's setting foot in the cave. "Great Maasaw, accept our gifts [i.e., the prayer feathers and cornmeal] and grant us a smooth path and an easy journey. Send rain so that our people may live in plenty, without sickness, and sleep in old age" (1942: 240).

[12]Titiev, in his account of a Hopi salt expedition, confirms this belief and cites additional details concerning the portentous significance of things discovered in Maasaw's cavern. "Here there is a milling stone, exactly like those to be found in all Hopi houses, and the intruder looks it over very carefully for omens. If fresh food from recently gathered crops is seen, it is a bad omen, but if Maasaw seems to have been grinding old corn, then it is a favorable sign and means good crops for the next season. At the same time the observer must note whether or not the occupant of the cave has stored up a large amount of fuel and whether or not there is a good supply of corn at hand, for if Maasaw seems well fortified in both respects it means that the Hopi will have a hard winter and a poor yield from their farms" (1937: 250).

Compare also Talayesva (1942: 240). When, upon exiting from Maasaw's cave, the war chief was asked what news he had for the Hopi, he replied: "I saw four old corncobs and some dried beans. The grinding stone had some very old meal on it."

Pay antsa yuyiq öngtupqamiq
ima hopitaataqt hisat öngmokwis-
ngwu. Noq pay pi lavaytangwuniqw puma yangqw aqwye', pu'
aqw pas tumpoq ökye', pu' puma
pepeq pay naat tokngwu. Pas ason
qavongvaqw paasat pu' puma aqw
hantangwu. Noq pu' puma aqw
hanwiskyaakyangw puma haqam
tuusöt nukpana yan matsiwqat aw
ökingwu. Pangso puma haqami
ökye' pu' puma imuy naat pu'-
yaqamuy amumi tutaptotangwu,
yaw pumuy aqw yungqw haqam
himu nöösiwqa aasaqawtani.

Noq antsa yaw puma haqam
mataningwuniqw pangso yaw
puma ökiqw antsa yaw ang ngum-
niningwu. Noq pu' yaw puma aw
yoyrikyaqw, kur yaw pam pu-
hungumninen pam hapi yaw qa
lolmaningwu. Noq pu' pay yaw
hisatngumninen pam yaw pay hiita
lomahintaqat tu'awiy'tangwuqat
yan puma lavaytangwu. Pam yaw
ayo' qavomi hin i' itaanatwani,
itaanösiwqa, itamungem pew
na'sastiniqat put hapi yaw pam
tu'awiy'tangwu. Noq pu' antsa i'
puhuhimu pam yaw qa lomahintaqat yan puma pangsoq sasqa-
yaqam it lavaytangwu. Noq
paniqw oovi hak yaw pepeq pan
hiita nukngwat aw yorikye', hak
yaw put qa kwangway'ngwuqat
kitotangwu. Pu' paasat it piw
sööngöt hisatwavut öngmokwisqam
tutwe' yaw haalaytotingwu. Pam

In the days past, the Hopi men
used to go on salt journeys to
Öngtupqa, that is, the Grand
Canyon. In their narratives they
relate, that after they started out
from Orayvi and reached the
canyon rim, they usually spent the
night at the top and did not
start their descent until the next
morning. On their way down they
came to a cavern known by the
name of Nukpana ("The Evil
One"). Upon reaching this site,
those men who were making this
expedition for the first time, were
informed that on entering the
cave they would find food strewn
about.

And, indeed, this was true. At
one place in the cave they came
across a metate with some cornmeal on it. If upon inspection the
flour turned out to be freshly
ground, this was an unfavorable
sign. But if by chance the cornmeal was old, then this was supposed to be a good omen. It fore-
told how our crops and our food
would be provided for us in the
near future. Those who have
undertaken this journey agree that
new things found in the cavern
portend adverse food and crop
conditions. Consequently they used
to say that the man who discovered
something good there should not
be desirous of it. On the other
hand, the salt expedition members
were elated whenever they came
across some old corn cobs. These,
according to tradition, indicated

yaw soosoy himu natwani naa-
ko'naniqat tu'awiy'tangwu.

that all the various crops would
be produced in abundance.

Figure 10.—Nukpana, the home of Maasaw, at the bottom of Salt Trail
Canyon. The cave, found by the author on May 19, 1986, is approximately
twenty feet wide at its entrance and, allegedly, has not been visited by any
Hopi for over two generations. Photograph by E. Malotki.

Maasaw's relation to fertility is not a narrow one. To be sure, his
germinative powers are predominantly linked to the vegetable kingdom,
in particular, to products cultivated by man. This aspect of Maasaw, as
a germ god, is clearly based on his ownership of fire and the land. However, the earth also supports life, animal as well as human. Indeed,

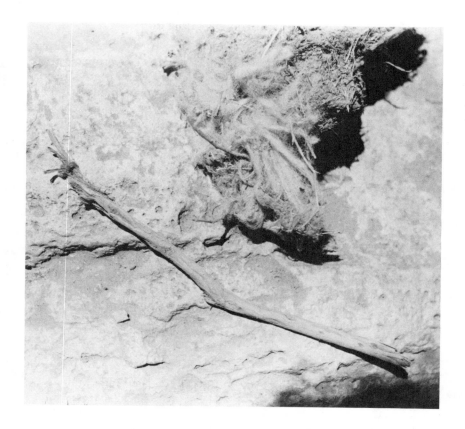

Figure 11.—A stick with a single cotton loop, and a bunch of woolen strings embedded in packed dirt and clay, provide evidence for a positive identification of Maasaw's home. These items, to which prayer feathers were once attached, were found by archaeologist Peter Pilles who accompanied the author into the cave. Photograph by E. Malotki.

while the god of death is responsible for man's return to the earth, that is, to the home of the dead in the underworld, it is this very underworld from which Maasaw allowed mankind to emerge to new life in the first place. In the light of this natural blending of life and death, which are both intimately affected by him, Maasaw must also be seen as a god of life.

Tyler goes one step further and suggests that "human fertility is also within his realm of activity, in the sense that human methods of fertilization are thought to be archetypes of vegetal reproduction" (1964:20).

Stephen, in a curious sidenote to a comment on the symbolic significance of the circular band, generally painted next to the neck or brim of a pottery vessel, depicts Maasaw as a messenger concerning human fertility. As a rule, "if the woman who decorates the vessel is old and past the child bearing period, she paints a complete surrounding band; if she has had a child recently or expects to ever have a child, the band is not quite complete; she leaves a small space of a quarter or half inch unpainted. Young unmarried girls are not permitted to use this surrounding band in their pottery decoration." According to Stephen, "this decorative style continued for a long while, until the women ceased to bear children. Then Muy'ingwa sent Maasaw to tell the women that if they hoped to bear children again, they must leave the 'gate of breath' open so that he might perceive the token of their desire" (Wade 1980: 23).

In a sense, then, one can postulate that the parturitive powers attributed to the god include the vegetal, animal[13] and human realm. That this conclusion is not an overinterpretation of Maasaw's fertility role is corroborated by the statement in Texts 83 and 84. Dreaming about the god not only extends a person's life span, it is also a good omen for bountiful crops and livestock.

TEXT 83

Pay pi itam put maasawuy aw naanawaknangwuniqw oovi yaw hak put tuumoklawe' hak qatsiy aw hoyoknangwu. Pu' hak piw hin hiita ang mongvas'iwmaniqey paniqw hak yaw piw put tuumoklawngwu. Niikyangw hak yaw qa tsawnangwu, hak yaw tuwat na'qalangwu. "Kur antsa'ay, kwakwhay, nu' put tuumoklawu. Iqatsi hapi aw hoyo. Pu' nu' hiita uuye' pu' nu' hiita a'ni aniwnamantani. Pu' ima ivokom, kaneelom, kawayom, waawakast aw wuuhaqtini." Yanhaqam hak yaw tuwat oovi öqaltingwu put tuumoklawe'.

Because we constantly pray to Maasaw, it is held that dreaming about him prolongs a person's life. To accomplish things is another reason for dreaming about the god. But one must not become frightened; rather one must encourage oneself. "All right, thanks, I've dreamt about Maasaw. Now my life span has been extended. And whenever I plant, I'll produce plenty of crops. Also my livestock, my sheep, horses, cattle will increase." For these things to come about one strives after dreaming about the god.

---

[13]Compare Stephen (1929: 55) where, in an origin myth, the youth destined to become the first chief and father of the Hopi received from Maasaw "deer, antelope, bear, turkeys, eagles, in fact all animals which live upon the earth or water or in the skies."

Text 84 constitutes a prayer for both longevity and a bountiful harvest.

TEXT 84

Pay hopiit pi pangqaqwangwuniqw pam yaw hak maasaw pay hisat qatu. Noq oovi himuwa wuuyavo qatunik pu' piw put an hongvininik, pam pay put maasawuy aw put oovi naawaknangwu. Noq pay antsa hak sakine' pay hak wuuyavo piw qatungwu, qa hisat hintangwu, qa tuutuyngwu. Pay pi hak panis aw naawaknangwu. Pay pi itam hopiit putsa hiita okiwnawakinpit tuwiy'yungwa.

Niikyangw hak oovi mihikqw put aw naawaknangwu, pam paasat tuwat waynumngwuniqw oovi. Pu' hak antsa put aw naawaknanik pay pi hak pangqawngwu, "Ta'ay, itana maasawu, pay um yephaqam tuwat inumi su'an mamkyaqw nu' yep wuuyavo qatuni. Pu' piw a'ni uuyiy'tamantani su'un'iy."

According to Hopi lore, Maasaw has existed for a long, long time. Hence, a person who desires longevity and wishes to possess strength, of the caliber Maasaw is endowed with, prays to the god for these things. And indeed, if one is fortunate one will live a long time, always healthy and never ailing. One merely needs to pray to Maasaw. Praying is be the only recourse available to the Hopi to achieve certain things.

Prayers to Maasaw must be uttered at night, for that is the time he journeys across the land. For example, one may ask him for the following favor: "Now, our father Maasaw, touch me in the right way that I may live a long life and, just as you, be blessed with an abundance of crops."

Obviously, the fertility side of the death god is also present within the Hopi ceremonial framework. Although a strict dichotomy between matters religious and secular does not exist for the Hopi as it does for western man, there definitely exist degrees of ceremonial overtones in regard to certain phenomena within Hopi society. While the above quoted passages describing Maasaw's fertility role are certainly not of a secular nature, they are nevertheless isolated instances of the Maasaw fertility complex and not integral to any specific ceremony.

The two ceremonies to which the god of germination is central are the Nevenwehekiw and Sopkyaw. Both ceremonies share an elaborate ritualistic impersonation of the deity. The Nevenwehekiw,[14] a communal

___

[14]For some etymological observations, on the meaning of Nevenwehekiw, see Malotki (1983: 467).

outing celebrated in the spring with the purpose of gathering *nepni* or "edible greens," was well integrated into the Hopi ceremonial cycle. It only took place in years preceded by a *wuwtsimnatnga*, i.e., "a manhood initiation into the Wuwtsim, Al, Kwan, or Taw fraternities," carried out during the month of Kyelmuya (approximately November) of the year before. The Sopkyaw, in turn, was a communal work party that could be organized spontaneously for both planting and harvesting; hence it was not a required part of the ritual calendar.

The impersonators, who appeared as the real Maasaw and must, therefore, not be confused with the related *masawkatsina* to be discussed later, had to be *bona fide* members of the Maasaw fraternity.[15] Some of the unusual preparatory practices, which once were customary for an impersonator of the god, are given in Texts 85 and 86.

TEXT 85

Noq pu' yaw piw hisat it hakiy mamasawniqat yaw pas as it mokqat an amyangwu. Nen pu' puma put naalös pas pan aamiy'yungngwu. Pu' puma put nopnayanik pu' puma put it hiita paaqavi'ewakw ang put it wutaqat noonopnayangwu. Pu' ason put pas pan naalös aamiy'yungwt paasat pu' puma put ahoy horoknayangwu.

They say that long ago the man who was supposed to impersonate the god Maasaw was interred much like an actual corpse. For four days he was kept buried. He was fed *wutaqa*, a "white mush," through a hollow object similar to a reed. At the end of the four days he was unearthed again.

TEXT 86

Noq pu' i' maasaw it nevenwehekiwuynit put it sopkyawmaniqat ep pitunik pam ep pay qa naap hiita yuwsiy'kyangw pitungwu. Pam it kanelsakwit pas hiitawat tuu'amiyat angqw put nasimokyaatat pu' put yuwsingwu. Pu' yaw pam oovi piw it peekyet pas

When on the occasion of a Nevenwehekiw or Sopkyaw, Maasaw is to make an appearance, he arrives wearing a special costume. He actually borrows a tattered woman's dress from a grave, and puts it on. To fit the occasion the dress must be dried stiff from pus.

---

[15]Note that my Sopkyaw accounts only speak of one Maasaw impersonator. Titiev mentions two (1944: 185). The same is true for Forde (1931: 397). Compare also Fewkes (1903: 39).

aw huur qarokiwtaqatnen pu' yaw
piw suuputningwu. Pam yaw a'ni
hovaqte' yaw pas suupamningwu.
Pu' pam oovi naalös tookilnawit
put oovi angqe' nakwsungwu. Ephaqam yaw himuwa put himuy
kyaakyawne' pam yaw put qa
maqangwu. Haktonsa yaw pam
as put langtoynaqw, pay yaw pam
put pas qa aw no'aninik pam yaw
put huur nguy'tangwu. Paasat
pu' yaw pam piw nawus sutsvoni-
ngwu. Noq pu' pay kya pi himuwa
put ookwatuwe' pu' pam pay
paasat put sumqangwu. Niiqe pam
oovi pas soosovik pang tuutu'amit
ang put oovi nakwsungwu. Pu' i'
yepeq orayveq mamasawniqa piw
yaw oovi yukiq pöqangwwawarpiy
taavangqöymiq mastupatsmiq piw
hom'oytongwunen pu' pam paasat
piw pangsoq haqami pas pakingwu.
Noq pu' pepeq himu put aw
hepninik put pam put pangsoq
uutangwu. Pu' pam tsawne'
paasat pu' pam hopit an
paklawqw, put pay paasat qa
himu hötangwu. Pas pam ason
masvaklawqw paasat pu' pam son
pi qa pas maasaw put hötangwu.

Furthermore, it must exude a
nauseating stench. For four nights
the impersonator goes about in
quest of this costume. If a dead
spirit is unwilling to give the dress
up, it will not cede it to the man.
Even if the latter tugs on it, if
the corpse does not wish to give
it up, it will cling to it tightly.
At this time the impersonator has
no choice but to go elsewhere.
But if a spirit has pity on him,
it will readily give the dress up.
In this fashion the impersonator
visits every gravesite in search of
a dress. At Orayvi, the person
chosen to assume the role of
impersonator usually goes to
Mastupatsa, a site west of Pöqangw-
wawarpi, where he deposits
some prayer feathers. In the course
of this undertaking he actually
enters this place. And if some
being then intends to test the
man's courage, it will enclose him
within this place. Should he
become frightened and weep like a
human being, nothing will open
the closure. And not before he
cries out the cry of Maasaw will
the god let him out.

One impersonator's frustrations in conjunction with this "enclosure"
experience had almost fatal consequences. Fortunately, Maasaw asserted
his role as protector and saved his protégé.

TEXT 87

Noq yaw i' hak orayve M. yan
maatsiwqa yaw put pantsakngwu-
niqw put yaw qa suus pan himu
uuta. Noq pu' pay yaw pam
itsivutiqe pu' pangqawu, "Pay nu'

M. of Orayvi, who frequently
played the role of impersonator,
experienced this enclosure more
than once. At this he became
infuriated and indicated, "I won't

paapu yaasavo it yantsakni. Nu'
as ung pa'angwantaqe nu' maqson-
lawu. Noq aasakis hak peqw
pakiqw um hakiy yantsanngwu.
Noq pay nu' oovi it qe'tini," yan
yaw pam itsivuti.

Noq pu' yaw pepeq mastupatsay
aqw tatkyaqöymiqwat hötsinii-
kyangw pu' piw pangsoq a'ni
tuupelay'ta. Pu' yaw pam oovi
pay pangsoq tso'okye' pay pi yaw
naap hiniwqat pantini. Niiqe
pu' yaw pam oovi pangsoq laho'-
makyangw pu' yaw pam pangsoq
pitut pu' yaw pam pangsoq tso'o.
Pu' yaw pam pantikyangw piw
yaw pam qa naap hin pangsoq
posto. Pas pi yaw put paas himu
pangsoq hawniy'ma. Niiqe pam
yaw oovi qa naap hin piw pepeq
yeeva.

Yanti yaw pamniiqe pu' yaw pam
put ang ahoy wuuwaqe pu' yaw
naami pangqawu, "Pay kur himu
nuy kyaakyawnaqw oovi nu' naamahin oongahaqaqw poskyangw qa
hinti. Pay pi nu' oovi paapu qa
yanhaqam hintsakni," kita yaw
pamniiqe pu' yaw pam oovi piw
put aapiy hintsaktiva.

do this any more. I'm trying to
help you but only have to endure
hardships in return. Each time I
enter this place, you do this to
me. So I'm going to quit," the
man uttered in anger.

South of Mastupatsa was a break
in the terrain featuring a sheer
drop-off. Therefore the man
decided to hurl himself down this
precipice, no matter what the
outcome. So on all fours he crept
towards the edge and upon reaching it jumped off. Much to his
amazement, however, he gently
floated down. Something trans-
ported him slowly down to the
ground. Consequently, he
reached the bottom without hitting
it hard.

When M. experienced this, he
thought things over and said to
himself, "Someone must treasure
me, for even though I fell from a
great height, I wasn't hurt in any
way. Therefore I'll cut out this
foolishness." With that he started
to enact the role of Maasaw again.

Text 88 represents the recollection of a Third Mesa informant of the
long extinct Nevenwehekiw. Supplementary and occasionally overlapping
information may be gleaned from Story 9 (ATR 10) as well as from the
Glossary.[16]

[16]The only account published is in Titiev (1944: 140-41). Titiev, in a footnote,
mistakenly refers the reader to a passage in Stephen which he considers a sketch of the
Nevenwehekiw. Actually, the latter describes aspects of the Sopkyaw. This is verified by
the fact that Stephen's entry for the event is October, a month during which the Nevenwehekiw ritual could not take place.

TEXT 88

Nevenwehekniniqw pam hapi it natngat it wuwtsimuy aapiy pu' paniwtingwu. Noq oovi wuwtsim- tuy natngay'yungqw ep pam enang tiingaviwngwu. Paapiy pu' panma- kyangw pu' yang i' tutskwavaniiqa nepni pay naat qa soosoy siy'va- yaqw, pep pu' paasat pam neven- wehekiwuy aw pitsiwiwtangwu. Niikyangw pam soosoy himu sihu pay angqe' siy'vayangwu, heesi, mansi, qatsi, tsu'öqpi.

Noq antsa it yan hisat neven- wehekniqat aw pituqw pu' pam mamasawniqa tuwat taalö' teevep puwngwu, ispi yaw pam tookyep angqe' waynumngwuniiqe oovi. Niiqe pam oovi su'aw taawat pakiqw pu' pam havivokyale' pu' suutokilnasamiq pituqw, pu' pam paasat pangqw kwankivangaqw yamakngwuniqw oovi paniqw put pangqaqwangwu, maskiva, kito- tangwu. Pu' pam paasat angqe' nakwsungwu, hom'o'oytinumngwu. Pu' piw haqe' tu'amqölpa neengem yewashepnumngwu, nasimokyaa- tinumngwu. Nen pam oovi su'aw taawat yamaktoq pu' pam piw kivay aw ahoy pitungwu. Panis ahoy pitut, nöst pu' pam pay piw puwvangwu. Pu' mihikqw piw taataye' pu' pay piw antingwu. Naalös yaw pam pantingwu.

The Nevenwehekiw, a ceremony in the spring which involves the gathering of edible greens, can only take place after the initiation of novices into the Wuwtsim, Agave, Al, and Taw societies. For this reason the ceremony is also announced at the occasion of this initiation in November. The proper time for the ritual comes when not all the greens growing on the land have bloomed yet and when the various wild flowers begin to appear: mariposa lilies, painted cups, gilias, and beard- tongues.

Long ago, when the time for this affair drew near, the man who had to portray the role of Maasaw would sleep all day long, the reason being, of course, that he had to travel around all through the night. Right at sundown, he usually became fully awake and at midnight he emerged from the kiva of the Kwan society, which is therefore also referred to as Maasaw's kiva. He then went about, depositing prayer feathers together with sacred cornmeal. In addition, he had to visit grave- sites in search of clothes he could borrow for himself. Just before sunrise he returned to his kiva. Immediately after his arrival he had breakfast whereupon he went to bed. Upon awaking in the evening, he went through the same procedure again. This he did for four consecutive days and nights.

Pu' pan nevenwehekniniqw pu'
ima tootim neeventinumyaqw, pu'
ima mamant somivikit noovalal-
wangwu. Pu' puma tootim put
nepnit, öngatokit pu' mö'öngtor-
havut, möhat pu' homimat, tumit,
puuvut hapi neeventinumyangwu.
Pu' puma piw it sihut sitkotinum-
yangwu.

Paasat pu' put nevenwehekiwuy aw
talöngvaqw, pu' i' tsa'akmongwi
puma haqami nööngantaniqat
talavay put tsaatsa'lawngwu. Noq
yep orayve pi pangso leenangw-
vami puma tsovaltingwu. Pu' ep pi
manneyangyangwuniqw oovi puma
mamant somivikit, tangu'vikit,
puuvut hiita noovay kiwiskyaa-
kyangw imuy tootimuy, taataqtuy
amumum pangso tsovaltingwu. Pu'
ima nevenwehekqam haqam
tsovaltiqw, pepeq pu' ima leelent
piw pumuy amumum tsovalte' pu'
puma pumuy amungem piw
leelenyangwu. Pu' puma pep piw
tsootsonglalwangwu. Tsootsong-
lalwakyangw yukuyaqw, paasat pu'
puma mamant pepeq soosoyam it
noovay akw it sihutnit pu' it nepnit
imuy tootimuy amumum naahoy-
ngwantotangwu. Pantsaklalwakyangw pu' soosoyam nan'ivaqw
put himuy soosokyaqw pu' paasat
imuy leelentuy taawi'am so'tingwu.
Paasat pu' pay hak pangqawngwu,
"Ta'a, pay aw pituniy. Pay paasa'ay."

Paapiy pu' puma pay kiimi ahoy
nankwusaqw pu' ima leelentsa pay
pepeq akwsingwngwu. Noq ep pi
ima maswikkatsinam ökingwu-
niqw, puma leelent hapi kur

For a Nevenwehekiw all the young
boys and unmarried men go out
into the fields gathering wild
greens while the girls cook *somiviki*, small cakes made of blue
cornmeal. The greens picked by
the boys include *öngatoki, mö'öng-
torhavu, möha, homima, tumi*,
and other such edible herbs. Wild
flowers are also picked.

On the actual morning of the
ritual the village crier announces
the location where everybody is to
gather. In Orayvi Nevenwehekiw
participants always congregated at
Leenangw Spring. Since both sexes
mixed during this ceremony, the
girls headed out to the spring
with *somiviki, tangu'viki*, and
other delectables they had prepared for the boys and men they
would meet there. By the time the
participants are all gathered, the
members of the Flute society are
also assembled alongside them and
play their flutes for them. Ritual
smoking is also performed there.
As soon as the smoking is over,
the young ladies exchange their
food for the flowers and wild
greens the young men have collected. When both sides have
finished trading, the songs of the
Flute members come to an end.
Then someone announces, "All
right, let the ceremony begin.
All the greens are distributed."

Everyone now heads back to the
village except the members of the
Flute society, who remain behind.
They impersonate the Maswik
kachinas who arrive in the course

pumayangwuniqw oovi ima maswikkatsinam pumuy su'amun
yuwsiy'yungngwu. Niikyangw
puma pepeq imuy sinmuy amumum tsovawte' puma paasat pay
naat qa kwatstangawtangwu. Noq
pu' puma pi pumuywatuy tsimon-
mamantuy tuwat manmuy'yungngwu. Noq pu' oovi puma sinom
kiimiyaqw, paasat pu' puma
kwatstangaltikyangw pu' paasat
maswikkatsinamniikyangw pu'
pangqewat kwiningyaqe tumkyaqe
kiimiye', pu' puma pep angqe'
tipkyatinumyangwu. Niiqe puma
ayaq atkyaq tipkyaveq oovi mooti
tiivat pu' pangqw piw sutsvowat-
yat, pu' paasat kiisonmiyat pu'
paasat pay aqw taatöq ninmangwu, yukiqhaqami kowaway-
mamiq. Puma kowawaymangaqw
ökingwuniiqe oovi puma pangsoq-
haqami ahoy ninmangwu.

Noq pu' puma maswikkatsinam
haqamwatyaqw pu' i' maasaw
pumuy amumi pitungwu. Niikyangw puma maswikkatsinam
naat pu' taawiy omiwayat kuyna-
yaqw, pu' pam it kukuynaqatnit
pu' it kwukwsunaqat nan'ivo
sukyaktsiyamuy aw matyawt pu'
paasat töqtingwu. Paasat pu'
puma maswikkatsinam ninmaqw
pu' paasat ima taataqt, tootim
pep kiisonve put maasawuy aw
kwekwetstiwyangwu. Noq pu' pam

of the Nevenwehekiw. This is the
reason why the attire of the
kachinas is nearly identical to that
of the Flute members. Of course,
the Flute members remain unmasked while still among the
group gathered at the spring.
Their female counterparts are the
Tsimonmamant or "Jimsonweed
girls." After the people have left
for the village, the Flute members
don their masks, whereupon they
too proceed to the village, now in
the guise of the Maswik kachinas.
They arrive along the northern
end of the mesa rim and upon
reaching the village, move from
one location to another, performing a dance at each of these stops.
They first perform at a site known
as Tipkyavi or the "Womb," after
which they go on to another spot.
After this, they dance in the plaza,
whereupon they return home to
Kowawayma, a place south of the
village. Since they entered the
village from the direction of
Kowawayma, they also return in
that direction.

While the Maswik kachinas are
still at one of their dance locations,
Maasaw comes up to them. The
very moment the kachinas have
begun to sing the first upper
portion of their song, Maasaw
places his hands on the shoulders
of the song starter, as well as on
the man behind him who "picks
up" the song, and then lets out his
cry. When the Maswik kachinas
are through dancing and have
returned home, the men and boys
begin to taunt and tease Maasaw

pumuy pep ngöynumngwunen pu' pam hiitawat wiikye' pu' pam put hotpeq maawikiy akw taatuvangwu, wuvaatangwu. Noq pu' pay pam hopi sumokye' pu' angqe' wa'ökmangwu. Pantiqw pu' pam maasaw put awnen, pu' pam put hiita yuwsiy'taqw pu' pam put aapa poswe', pu' pam put ang ahoywat tuwat pakingwu.

Pantit pu' pam pay put yuwsiy'-kyangw pu' pay piw pep pumuy ngöynumngwu. Paasat pu' imuy taataqtuy, tootimuy amungaqw pu' haqawa tuwat put maasawuy maawikiyat nawkye', pu' pam put tuwat akw taatuve', pu' paasat put maasawuy tuwat niinangwu. Noq pu' puma put aw homikmaqw pu' hak hiita himuy put maasawuy paasat nawkingwu. Noq pu' puma pantotit pu' puma pay put kiisonviy teevengewat sikwitsötsöpyakyangw pu' put pepehaq tuuvayangwu. Hisatniqw pu' pay pam piw ahoy taataye' pu' pam paasat piw ahoy angqwnen pu' paasat piw pumuy pep ngöynumngwu. Pay yan puma pep put maasawuy aw yaayalalwangwu. Pas ason hisatniqw puma piw put niinaye' pas qa atsat haqami yaavoq tuuvawisqw, pu' pam pay qa ahoy pitungwu. Paasat pam pay pas qa atsat mokqat pangqaqwangwu.

Pam pay paasat nimangwu. Pu' pam maasaw haqam yuwsiqey pam pay paasat ahoy pangsoqningwu. Pepeq pu' puma hakim put wu'yay'yungqam put ahoy powatotangwu. Yuwsiyat oyanayat pu' paahomyangwu.

at the plaza. Maasaw chases after them and each time he catches up with one of them, strikes him on the back with his *maawiki*, a club resembling a drumstick. The person struck immediately sinks to the ground unconscious. Maasaw approaches the fainted man, strips him of his entire costume and dons it himself, although the wrong way around.

In his new attire the god now once again runs about, pursuing his taunters. At one point one of the men or boys will, in turn, snatch the club away from Maasaw. Hitting Maasaw with the thrown club, he in turn now kills, or rather stuns, the god. Then everybody rushes up to Maasaw and retrieves his various costume pieces. Next, Maasaw is bodily hauled off to a place west of the plaza and dumped there. As soon as he revives, he once more returns, only to resume chasing the men. In this manner Maasaw is pestered and teased. Later he is killed once again, and the men rid themselves of him at a site further away, from which he does not return. People say that Maasaw has truly died now.

The god then returns home, back to the spot where he disguised himself. There some people who have him as their clan ancestor discharm him, remove his garb, and cleanse his body with water.

Figure 12   Figure 13

Maswikatsina with *pavayoykyasi* or "moisture tablet" on back. Photographs by E. Malotki. Courtesy Museum of Northern Arizona.

The *maswikkatsinam* or "Maasaw-fetching kachinas" were highly specialized kachinas, performing only at the occasion of the Nevenwehekiw. Text 89 furnishes a description of this kachina type.[17]

TEXT 89

Puma pi maasawuy wikvayangwu-
niiqe paniqw oovi maswikkatsinam. Pay pi pumuy tuwiy'yung-

The Maswik kachinas (*mas-wik-
katsinam* "Maasaw-take-along-
kachinas") derive their name

[17]For pictorial renditions, of both the male and female Maswik kachinas, see Wright (1973: 252-53).

qam lavaytangwuniqw pam maswikkatsina yaw it leenangwkatsinat
su'an soniwngwu. Niikyangw pam
pay qa pavayoykyasit iikwiwta-
ngwuniikyangw pu' piw qa lensit
nakway'tangwu. Pam pay panis
angaapuyawkyangw pu' pay
sakwapkuwtangwu. Pu' pam
pitkunkyangw pu' it mötsapngön-
kweway'kyangw hopikweway'-
kyangw pu' pukhaytangwu. Pu'
pam it lensit suyngaqwwat yawkyangw pu' ayangqwwat eyokinpiy'tangwu. Pu' paasat pam pay
piw panis honhokyasmiy'kyangw
pu' pam piw it sakwatnit torikiwtangwu. Pan i' maswikkatsina
yuwsiy'kyangw pu' piw soniwngwu.

Pu' i' maswikkatsinmana pay as
katsinmanananingwuniikyangw pam
yangqw putngaqwwat nasmiy aqw
it tsimonsit tsurukniy'tangwu. Pu'
pam oovat uskyangw pu' kanel-
kwasay'kyangw pu' wukokweway'-
tangwu. Pu' pam yepeq qötöveq
kwavöönakwat qa homaskuytaqat

from the fact that they take or
bring Maasaw along. People who
have seen them relate that the
Maswik kachina closely resembles
the Leenangw kachina, who
portrays a member of the Flute
society. He differs from the latter
in that he neither carries a *pavayoykyasi* or "moisture tablet" on
his back, nor wears a *lensi* or
"flute flower," fashioned from
dried cornhusks on his head. The
kachina's long hair flows freely
down his back, and the color of
his face is green. The rest of his
costume consists of the decorated
kilt, the wide embroidered sash, a
native belt, and a fox pelt sus-
pended from the kilt in the back
of the waist. In his left hand he
carries a flower fashioned from a
half gourd, which is attached to a
short stick, and in his right hand
he holds a bell. Around his ankles
he wears only anklets, while across
his torso is slung an indigo-hued
yarn bandolier. This is the way the
Maswik kachina is attired; this
is his appearance.

Maswikkatsinmana, the female
counterpart, is an exact replica of
the *katsinmana,* the regular
kachina female. Unlike the latter,
however, she has tucked into the
right whorl of her butterfly coif-
fure a jimsonweed blossom. In
addition, she has draped about
her shoulders in shawl fashion the
white bridal cape and wears the
dark colored wool dress with the
rain sash around her waist. Right
above her forehead an eagle down

yukiq momiq tsurukniy'tangwu.
Pan i' maswikkatsinmana soniwngwu.

feather without any trace of black
adorns her hair. This is what a
female Maswik kachina looks like.

Noteworthy in this context is the dramatization of Maasaw in the role of a planting god, which Fewkes witnessed in conjunction with the Powamuy ceremony in the month of February, 1900. None of my Third or Second Mesa consultants were able to confirm the existence of such a performance for their respective home villages. At this occasion the god was accompanied by an escort of men impersonating both male and female *maswikkatsinam*. His mask, resembling a large human skull, consisted of a hollow gourd daubed with black paint and punctured with round holes for eyes and mouth. During the night dance, which was staged in every kiva, the impersonator of Maasaw came down the kiva ladder and approached the fireplace "where he assumed the posture of a man planting. He held a planting-dibble and a basket-tray in his hands, while over his shoulders was thrown an old blanket. Yucca fibre garters were tied on his legs, and he was barefoot. The most striking object in his appearance was the old glistening gourd, painted black" (1902a:23). A second, unmasked impersonator followed "to take his seat by the side of Maasaw, assuming the posture of a man planting, holding one end of the planting stick to the floor as if it were soil" (1903:40).

In another account of the same event Fewkes relates that one of Maasaw's masks, which had been positioned in back of the fire place, was raised during the singing by one of the chief participants. "He talked directly to it praying for success of crops during the coming season....The songs rose and became so loud that no one could tell what was said, but the intent throughout were prayers to fertilize the fields that the corn might germinate and grow....The two personators manipulating their planting sticks in rhythm kept time to the songs" (1917:227).[18]

Tyler attributes a phallic element to this symbolic planting stance (1964:21), as he also does to the overall appearance of the god with "the sightly enlarged size, the head shaped like a squash" (1964:21).[19]

---

[18]Fewkes has published two additional summaries of this event, (1902a: 21-24) and (1903: 38-40). In the latter he refers to it as "The Advent of Maasaw."

Titiev describes a rite closely resembling Fewkes' *maswikkatsina* dance during the Orayvi Soyal ceremony (1944: 139-40).

[19]For the close relationship between fire and sexuality see Chapter 5. Here it is especially the twirling fire-drill which is interpreted as a symbol of phallic powers, and hence of fertility.

The materials submitted in Texts 90 and 91 represent insights recollected by several of my resource persons in regard to the long extinct practice of the Sopkyaw. In both cases a communal harvest is described, though working parties characterized by the ritual appearance of Maasaw were once also customary during the planting season.[20] Text 90 is a summary of Third Mesa Sopkyaw traditions.

TEXT 90

Put sopkyawmaniqat pi pay himuwa tunatyay'taniqa pam put pay aw naap pan wuuwat pay qa pas pas hakiy aw maqaptsitat pay put pantingwu. Pam put tuwat haalaypit tunatyawte' pam put sopkyawmaniqat tunatyay'tangwu. Pu' pam put pan tunatuytaqw pu' paasat antsa pi pantotingwu, sopkyawmangwu. Niikyangw mi' tunatyay'taniqa pay naat uuyit tukwsiwmaqw pay pan tsa'lawngwu. Pu' ima sinom oovi soosovik put tokilat paas enang navotiy'yungngwu. Pu' aw pituqw hakim oovi antsa pi piw naap noovatotat pu' hakim put pangsoq kiwiskyaakyangwyangwu. Pu' hakim hiita tutsayat'ewakw inpiy'- wisngwu. Put aw hak somivikiy mokyaatangwu. Pu' paasat hakim haqami pantsanwisniqey epeq ökiqw, paasat pu' ima taataqt

The person who intends to sponsor a Sopkyaw initiates this ritual on his own; that is, he is not required to ask permission to carry it out. On the sponsor's mind is the desire to provide enjoyment for the people. As soon as he announces his intentions, the communal harvest becomes a reality. The corn plants, however, are still not fully mature when he publicly announces the event from a roof top. Now people all over are aware of the date on which the Sopkyaw will take place. When the time for the Sopkyaw is at hand, the young women prepare food and take it out to the field. They take along a receptacle such as a sifter basket in which to place the harvested corn. Into the same sifter they also put their *somiviki* and wrap everything into a bun-

---

[20] Accounts of a ceremonial planting Sopkyaw are found in Forde (1931: 396-97) and Curtis (1922: 177-79). Though sketchy, they reveal a host of insights typical for the behavior of Maasaw. Term-wise, Forde's White informant confuses the Maasaw impersonators, of whom there are two, with the *masawkatsinam* when they are described as "corpse or skeleton katcinas" (1931: 396). While many of the accompanying features are reminiscent of the harvest Sopkyaw, one of Forde's impersonators is equipped with a planting stick and goes through the motions of actually planting "four holes of corn" (1931: 397). According to Curtis, the "Maasaw men," as he refers to them, "plant a few hills of each kind of seed" (1922: 178).

haqam tsovawtaqw pu' hakim
pangsoyaqw, pu' puma pep pösaa-
lay puhiknayaqw pu' hakim
pangso somivikiy oo'oyayangwu.
Pangso hakim put pangalayangwu.
Pu' paasat puma pepeq hakimuy
put nopnayangwu.

Paasat pu' hakimuy oo'oyaqw pu'
paasat aw pitungwu. "Ta'ay, uma
kya öö'öyay," höq'ayay'taqa,
sopkyaw'ayay'taqa kitangwu. "Uma
kya öö'öya. Uma aw nankwuse'
ang höhöqyaniy," kitangwu.

Paasat pu' hakim awye' pu' ang
uuyit wa'öminnumyangwu. Pu'
mamant pi pay oovi piw amumum
höhöqyangwu. Hak put tutsayay
aw yawme' hak put aw qaa'öt
inlawngwu. Paasat pu' hak put
inpiy aw qaa'öt mo'ole' pu' haqami
put pangalantotaqw pu' hak
pangsosa put kimangwu. Hakim
put suuvo pangalantotaqw pam
qaa'ö pep wukovangawtangwu. Pu'
pam maasaw pangsonen pu' pam
put akw naatupkyangwu. Noq oovi
hakim kur put maasawuy aw put
qaa'öt pangalantotangwu. Paasat
pu' puma taataqt hin'ur kwano-
notangwu. Puma paasat hapi kur
mit maasawuy pangqwniiqat
nanvotnayangwuniiqe oovi hin'ur
kwanokmantangwu. Put atpipaqw
hapi kur pam aamiwtangwu.

Pu' yaw pam oovi paasat qa'ötso-
valnit angqw yamakngwu. Pam
pep son pi qa naakwaptangwuniqw
oovi hakim put qa tuway'yungngwu. Pu' pam pangqw yamakye'
pu' pep tuungöylawngwu. Pu' pam

dle. When the women arrive at the
field where the men are assembled,
they spread out their blankets,
put down their *somiviki* and feed
this dish to those who have congregated there.

When everyone is satiated, the
actual harvesting can begin. "All
right, I guess you're full," the
sponsor of the harvest party calls
out. "You've probably eaten your
fill. Go to the field now and reap
the corn!"

The workers do as bidden and go
about treading the stalks down.
The girls also participate. They
use their sifter baskets to heap the
corn on. After a basket is loaded
to its fullest, it is taken to the site
where the maize is being dumped.
Since it is all deposited at one
single location, it grows into an
immense pile. At one point Maasaw goes to this pile and hides
himself underneath the corn. The
harvesters are therefore now un-
loading their corn on top of the
god. At this time there is boister-
ous shouting and laughing among
the men, for evidently they are
aware of Maasaw's presence.
Ostensibly, he is buried underneath the heap of corn.

The time then comes for Maasaw
to emerge from the pile. He must
have been covering himself with a
blanket so that no one was able
to spot him. Immediately upon
coming out from his hiding place,
he chases people around. With

put maawikiy piw enang yawnumngwuniiqe oovi himuwa awniqw
pam pay putakw hakiy wuvaatangwu. Pay pan pam hiitawat
niinangwu.

Pu' hiitu piw kawaymuy akw ökye'
pu' puma pumuy höhöqyaqamuy
ngöynumya. "Uma mamant kiisit
aqwye' pangsoq yungniy," kitotaqw
pu' hakim pangsoq yuutukye' pu'
kiisit aqw yungngwu. Pu' puma
kawaymuy akwyaqam pu' hakimuy
aqwye' pu' hakimuy aw ö'qal-
yangwu. Pu' puma peetu pumuy
ayo' laayintote' naanan'i'voq
kawaymuy ayo' hoonantotangwu.

Pu' pam tunatyay'taqahiisa'haqam
tsatsakwmötsaput, sowiy'ngwat
sööngöntangwu. Pu' paasat pay
hak hiita engem kwayaniy'te' pu'
pay put pa'angwaninik pu' pay piw
put söngnaqw pu' put piw enang-
yangwu. Noq pu' suukya put yawkyangw waayaqw pu' puma piw
put ngöynumyangwu. Pu' himuwa
wiikye' pu' su'an ngu'e' pu' put
nawkingwu. Pu' piw sukwat-
yangwu. Qa suukya put pan-
numngwu. Pantsakkyaakyangw
puma pang yuyuttinumyangwu.
Pu' mima pay qa kawaymuy
akwyaqam pay moomorotuy
akwyangwu. Pu' peetu tis pas
naapyangwu. Pu' puma kur
mamantuy hapi kwaptotaniqam
pay puuvumuy moomorotuy,
kawaymuy akwyangwu.

him he carries his *maawiki*, a
drumstick-like club with which he
strikes any person who comes near
him. In this manner he "kills" a
person, that is, he renders him
unconscious.

Next some men arrive on horseback and chase after the workers
doing the harvesting. "You young
women run to the field shelter and
go inside!" they shout, whereupon
the girls dash to the shelter and
enter it. The riders are approaching the girls now, trying to get to
them. The others, however, are
warding them off and attempting
to scatter the horses in every
direction.

The sponsor of the Sopkyaw now
ties several pieces of cloth or whole
buckskins to the end of a shaft.
Anyone else who has saved a prize
of this type to help the sponsor on
this occasion may also attach it to
the tip of a pole. Someone on
horseback then takes the pole and
dashes off with everybody else
giving chase. The pursuer who
catches up with him must grab
him in a special way to take the
prize on the pole away from him.
Then the chase starts all over.
This procedure is repeated by a
number of men who carry the
shaft. Of course, all of this happens with people scurrying here
and there. Those who are not on
horseback use burros for mounts.
Some even participate on foot.
Obviously, the men who will pick
up the girls ride on the horses or
burros.

Pu' oovi tapkiqw yukuyaqw, "Ta'a, pay uma yukuya. Itam maatavet ninmaniy," kitaqw pu' paasat oovi hakim put mongwit angk pangqw leetsiltingwu. Pu' hak ngas'ew naalöqhaqam qaa'öt tutsayay aw intat put mokyaatat paasat pu' hak put pantaqat pangqw yawmangwu. Put soosoyam mamant angqw pantotingwu. Pu' hak hakiy mööyiy awniqw pu' pam hakiy naakwayngyavo pookoy aqw tsokyangwu. Pu' hak pi pay qa kwanawkyangw angqw tsokiwmangwuniiqe oovi hak yukyiq suuvoq hokyay wilakniy'mangwu aqw wuuve'. Hak oovi okiw sutsange' piw tsokiwmangwu. Puma piw panhaqam mamantuy tsokiy'wisngwu.

Noq ephaqam naat hakim höhöqyaqw pay hiitu kwanokmangwu. A'ni töqtotiqw pu' haqaqw qö-'akuytingwu. Paasat pu' puma songyawnen tuwqam pangqw yuutukkyangw pu' hakimuy amumiqye' pu' töqkyaakyangw hakimuy qöqönyangwu. Pu' hakim pumuy amuupa yuutukye' pu' hakim pumuy amumum pay atsananaywakyangw pu' hiitawat tuuvayaqw, pu' pam pay paasat hakimuy amumum höhöqtivangwu. Naanangk puma hakimuy amumi pan kikiipokyangwu.

Noq hiituwat kur put maasawuy enang tsokiy'numyangwu. Panmakyangw pu' hakimuy höqyukuyaniqat aqw haykyalniy'wisqw, paasat pu' puma put wikkyaakyangw hakimuy amumi ökingwu. Paasat pu' puma pangso pumuy

By late afternoon the work is done. "All right, I suppose you're all done. Let's quit and go home," the sponsor yells out, whereupon everyone falls in line, following the man in charge of the Sopkyaw homeward. Every female worker helps herself to at least four ears of corn, which she puts into a tray, bundles up and takes home. All the girls do the same. A girl then approaches a nephew, who places her on his mount behind himself. She must not ride along straddling the animal though, so upon mounting, the poor girl sits with her legs dangling to one side. In this manner the girls are given a ride.

Occasionally, while the harvest work is going on, all of a sudden there is yelling. As the shouts are heard, a cloud of dust is seen rising. What then happens may be likened to enemies rushing towards you. Upon reaching you, they encircle you giving out war whoops. The men within the work party, in turn, now rush at the intruders. What follows is a mock fight, and the moment a horseman is thrown off his mount, he joins in on the gathering of the corn. Several groups in a row make raids on the harvesters in this fashion.

One of these groups apparently has Maasaw riding with it. The men in that group arrive with him just as the reaping of the corn is about to draw to a close. As they

höhöqyaqamuy amumi put maasawuy tuuvayangwu, tso'okna-
yangwu. Pep pu' pam hakimuy
ngöylawngwu, pam pep hakimuy
amumi kwekwetstiwngwu.

Noq pam naat tuungöynumqw pu'
mi' kookopwungwmana put maasawuy awnen pu' pam put ngu'e'
pu' paasat pam put pepeq wik-
numngwu. Noq pu' pam maana
put maasawuy pangso haqam pam
pok'amniqw pam put pangso
wikngwu. Pam oovi pay piw kur
paas pumuy amungem maskya'iwtangwu. Noq pu' puma taataqt
put maanat pokyat aqw tsokya-
yaqw, pu' paasat pam maasaw
put angk aqw wupqw pu' pam
maana put kiimi ahoy tsokiy'-
kyangwningwu.

Pu' hakim ninme' pu' haqam
hakiy engem sopkyawmaqat kiy'-
taqw pangsoq pu' hakim ökiwis-
ngwu. Paasat pu' pepeq hakimuy
tsotso'nayaqw paasat pu' hak put
qaa'öt pangqw kiy aw kimangwu.
Noq pu' pam kookopwungwmana
put maasawuy paasat kiy aqw wikngwu. Kiy aqw wikqw pu' puma
put pepeq son pi qa hintsatsnangwu. Wu'yay pitsinaye' pu' pephaqam puma son pi qa put aw
tuwat tsovawkyangw tsootsongyangwu. Pu' puma pepeq yukuyaqw paasat pu' pam maana put
maasawuy angqw pangso kiisonmi
wikngwu, pam put wikvaqa. Pu'
aw pangqawu, "Ta'a, yep um
tuutiitaplawni. Pu' ason pi pay um
son aqw qa itamumiqnit pu'
nimani," aw kitat pu' pam pep
put maatapngwu.

arrive, they simply throw Maasaw
down amidst the workers. The
god then falls to chasing the men
about and harassing them.

While he is still pursuing the men,
a girl of the Kookop clan goes up
to him, grabs him and leads him
about. Eventually she takes Maasaw to the site where a horse is
waiting. This would indicate that
the animal is readied for the two
beforehand. The men now place
the girl upon the animal, Maasaw
mounts the beast after her, and
the girl guides the god to the
village on horseback.

After returning home, everyone
congregates at the home of the
man who has inilited the Sopkyaw.
There the girls are taken off the
mounts and return home with the
four ears of corn they received for
their participation. The Kookop
clan girl now takes Maasaw to her
home where some sort of ritual
probably takes place. Since the
clan members have their clan
ancestor in their midst, they most
likely gather about him and perform some ritual smoking. As
soon as this ritual is concluded,
the girl who brought in Maasaw
from the field leads him to the
plaza. There she instructs the god,
"Now, entertain the people here.
When done with that, make sure,
though, to stop in at our clan
house before you go home." With
these instructions she leaves him
there.

Paasat pu' pam maasaw pay pangso tuupelmo matyawe' pu' pam pay pep pankyangw pay yantangwu. Noq pam pi kanelsakwit torikiwtangwu. Pam hapi pas qa atsat tuu'amit angqw put kanelmötsaput horokne' pu' put yuwsingwu. Nuutsel'ewayningwu pam himu maasaw.

Pu' haqaqwwat kivapt yuuyahe' pu' puma put aw kwekwetstiwwisngwu. Pu' himuwa put aw pite' pu' pam put aw töqtikyangw pu' mo'ay palalaykwinangwu. Pu' pam maasaw put ngöyvangwu. Pu' pay ephaqam qa wiikingwu. Pu' piw suukyawa awnen pu' pamwa piw warikqw, paasat pu' pam maasaw piw putwat ngöyvangwu. Pu' pam pep pumuy pantsakngwu. Pu' hiituwat kivapt hisatniqw yuuyaat pu' awye' pu' piw tuwatyangwu. Pu' pam hiitawat amum warikye' pu' put wiikye' pu' pam put maawikiy akw wuvaataqw, pu' pam mokqey an angqe' pusumtingwu. Paasat pu' maasaw put awnen pu' put hiita yuwsiy'taqat put soosok aapa poswangwu. Pu' pam put yuwsiyat soosok nawkye' pu' pam put ahoywat yuwsingwu. Pu' pam taaqa put hiita votontorikit'ewakw torikiwtaqw pu' pam put tuwat putvoqwat torikngwu. Pitkunte' pu' pay piw soq suyvoqwat hötsit pitkuntangwu. Pu' piw tootsiyat

Maasaw now places his hands on one of the house walls there and stands in that position. He is garbed in a Hopi woman's dress, all torn to shreds, which is slung about his left shoulder and fastened under his right arm. He actually has taken this dress from a grave site. He is always a hideous being, this Maasaw.

Next, a particular kiva group gets ready to go and tease Maasaw. Usually, a man appproaches him and gives out a yell, slapping his mouth with his hand at the same time. Maasaw immediately pursues him, but may at times fail to catch up with him. Then another man nears him, only to scamper off as Maasaw sets out to chase him. This is what Maasaw keeps doing with his taunters. Soon another kiva group will costume itself and have its turn at the plaza. Each time the god competes in a race with a man and actually overtakes him, he strikes him with his club, whereupon the person hits the ground with a thud as if he were dead. Maasaw then falls on his victim and takes every bit of clothing he is wearing. These clothes he now dons himself, contrary however to how they should be worn. For instance, if the man happens to be wearing a coin-studded pouch, Maasaw will sling it over his shoulder, but over the left rather than the right. If it is a kilt, he will wrap it around himself, but with the opening on the left side. And if he takes a

nawkye' pu' pam piw ahoytotsvak-
ngwu. Paavantsakngwu pami'.
Hakim oovi piw put maasawuy
aw tsutsuyngwu.

Pu' pam mokqa ahoy taataye',
pu' pam haqam laaputnen pu'
put sisngit pu' put taqtsokye', pu'
pam put angqw yawkyangw awnen
pu' pam paasat put mo'ami iita-
ngwu. Mo'ami iitaqw pu' pam
tuwat angqe' pusumtingwu. Pu'
pay pam tuwat pan put niine' pu'
pam paasat put yuwsiy nawkingwu. Pu' puma paasat put awyaqw pu' haqawat put maasawuy
hokyaveqniqw pu' piw lööyöm
matpikyaqewat ngu'aqw, pu' puma
paasat soosoyam put haqami
sikwitsötsöptiwiskyaakyangw put
tuuvawisngwu. Pu' puma put
haqam kwayngyaveq maatatvet pu'
paasat aw kwanokmaqw, pay pam
piw pangqaqw pumuy ahoy
ngöyvangwu. Pu' paasat puma put
piw kiisonmi ahoy pitsinaye' pu'
piw pep put aw kwekwetstiwyangwu. Pantsaklalwakyangw pu'
puma tapkinaye' pu' pay paasat
qe'totingwu. Qe'tote' pu' pay
maasawuy ninmaniqat aw pang-
qaqwat pu' pay put maatatve-
ngwu.

Pu' pam maasaw pay paasat ayoq
kookopngyamuy kiiyamuy aqwnen
pu' epeq pituqw pu' puma put
yuwsinayangwu, paahot maqayangwu. Nakwakwusit maqayat pu'
engem piw hiita yungyaput aw
piikit intotangwu. Pangqw pu'
pam put yawkyangw haawe' pu'
ayoq mastupatsmiqhaqami nimangwu, orayviy taavangqöyvaqe.

man's moccasins, he puts them on,
but on the wrong feet. Things of
this nature Maasaw does. No
wonder people are amused, and
as a result laugh at the god.

When the taunter who had passed
out regains consciousness and
finds some cedar bark, he will
shred it and then light it. With it
he may approach Maasaw and
then hold it out to his mouth.
With the bark burning in his face
it will now be Maasaw who plops
over dead. The man who slays the
god in this manner can now
retrieve his costume. All of Maasaw's taunters then come up to
him and, with some of them
grabbing him by the ankles, and
with two other taking him by the
wrists, they cart him off bodily
to dispose of him. At a dumpsite
along the edge of the village they
let him loose, yet, as they mock-
ingly yell at him, he chases after
them anew. Back at the plaza the
teasing starts all over again.
Eventually, as evening rolls around,
the whole business comes to an
end. The men bid Maasaw to
return home whereupon they leave
him.

Maasaw now goes to the home of
the Kookop clan where he is
presented with *paaho* and *nakwakwusi*. In addition to these prayer
feathers, a trayful of piiki is
prepared for him. With these gifts
the god descends from the Kookop
clan house and proceeds home to
Mastupatsa on the west side of
Orayvi. Mastupatsa is the place

Pepeq puma mamsam kiy'yungwa.
Yantotingwu piw puma.

where the dead reside. And all
this is what people usually do
during a Sopkyaw.

Beaglehole confirms the custom of using a bundle of ignited juniper
bark as a ploy to get rid of the god at the end of the *kwekwetstiwya*
drama. "One [of the men] lights a piece of this and advances with it
towards Maasaw, who, being afraid of light and fire, falls as if dead"
(1937:47). I do not believe, however, that Maasaw dies here because of
the fire—after all, the entire Sopkyaw is staged during daylight hours.
Rather, I suggest that the smoke and fumes are offensive to him. This is
in keeping with the Hopi post-funerary practice of employing juniper
smoke as an agent, to purify a survivor from the contagion of death.

Why Maasaw should display such an abhorrence of the burning
cedar brand is also seen as a puzzle by the Hopi nowadays. After all, the
god himself carries a cedar bark torch during his nightly rounds.

TEXT 91

Pam yaw piw it laaput töövu'iwtaqat mamqasngwuniiqat pay it
tsaatsayom yan yu'a'atotangwu nuy
naat tsayniqw. Noq hin pi it pay
nu' qa hisat hakiy wuukoq angqw
navota.

When I was still a yong boy,
children used to say that Maasaw
was afraid of glowing cedar bark.
I don't know if this was true.
I never heard this from an adult.

Text 92 gives details of a harvest Sopkyaw at the Second Mesa village
of Songoopavi.[21]

TEXT 92

Sopkyawmaniqat ep hapi soosoyam
sinom höqwisngwuniqw oovi pam
sopkyawma yan natngwaniy'ta.

At a Sopkyaw all the people
participate in a harvest, hence
its name, which in English ap-

[21]Additional information may be gathered from Sopkyaw material preserved for
First Mesa by Stephen (1936: 994-95) and Curtis (1922: 179), for Second Mesa by
Beaglehole (1937: 46-47) and for Third Mesa by Titiev (1944: 184-87). Bradfield gives a
composite picture taken from the majority of these sources in (1973: 252).

Noq himuwa pas a'ni uuyiy'te'
pam kur hin put naala höqninik,
paasat pu' pam put sopkyawmaniqat tunatyay'tangwu.

Noq pam hapi sopkyaw son kya
pi piw qa maasawuy'te' pu' su'an
yukiltingwuniqw oovi ep i' maasaw
pas sonqa pitungwu. Noq ima
masngyam tuwat put wu'yay'-
yungqw oovi hak put maasawuy
yuwsinangwu. Pu' pam put it
qötsvit akw pölölat pu' it kanelsakwit toriknakyangw qa it hopi-
wuutit ani'. Pam tuwat put suyvoq
hötsit ang pakiwtangwu. Pu'
kwaatsi'atniqa pam pay it lakput
sowivukyat angqw yukiwtangwunii-
kyangw aasonmiqwat pöhöy'tangwu. Pankyangw pu' pam maasaw hokyavaqeniikyangw pu' piw
matpikyaqe moohot akw somiw-
tangwu. Pankyangw pu' pam it
kokomqa'öt kwewtangwu. Pu' pam
it kwaatsiy ang pakiqw paasat pu'
put yuuyuwsinaqa it sowit ungwayat qötömi wuutangwu. Pu'
pam put qötömi wuutaqw pu' pam
put aapa munvakyangw pu' put
atkyamiq enang aatsavalngwu.

Pu' ima paasay'yungqam pay
mooti awyaqw pu' puma masngyam put pookoy pasmiq wi-
kyangwu. Pu' puma sopkyawmaqam haqam höhöqye' puma
put qaa'öt suuvo haqami pangalantotangwu. Pu' puma höhöq-

proximately denotes "everyone is
going." A Sopkyaw or "communal
harvest" is held whenever a person
has an abundance of corn that he
cannot reap by himself.

To complete a Sopkyaw successfully, Maasaw's presence is essential; thus, he never fails to
make an appearance. Since the
people of the Maasaw clan regard
the god as their ancestor, a member of that clan prepares him for
this role. Having smeared the
Maasaw impersonator's entire body
with ashes, the clan member
drapes a tattered Hopi woman's
dress about his shoulder. Unlike
a woman, who normally leaves her
right shoulder exposed, Maasaw
wears the dress with his left shoulder exposed and joined together
below the armpit of the same
side. The mask is fashioned from
dried jack rabbit skins with the fur
on the inside. Tied around the
impersonator's calves directly
below his knees, and tied around
his wrists, are strips of yucca.
Girding his waist is a belt of
purple corn. As soon as he dons
his mask, the person dressing him
pours jack rabbit blood on his
head, which streams down over his
entire body and combines with
the ashes.

The owners of the field where the
harvest is to take place are the
first to head out to the field,
followed by the people of the
Maasaw clan who bring their deity
along. At the location of the
communal harvest all the corn

yaqam kur put qaa'öt maasawuy
atsmi pangalantotangwu. Noq qa
hak navotiy'ta pam put qa'ötsoval-
nit atpipaqw pakiwtaqw.

Noq pu' yaw puma pepeq höhöq-
lalwaqw pu' pay pam sopkyaw-
'ayay'taqa pay taqatskiy epeq
qatungwu. Pu' pangsoq yaw
höhöqyaqam qaa'öt oo'oyaya-
kyangw pay yaw pephaqam aqlap
put qaa'öt pangalantotangwu. Pu'
kya pi puma oovi pantsatskya-
kyangw pu' tapkiqw yukuyangwu.
Noq paasat pu' i' tunatyay'taqa
pangqawngwu, "Ta'ay, uma
soosoyam pew tsovaltiniy," yaw
kitangwu. Noq pu' puma soosoyam
mamant, tootim pangso qa'ötsoval-
nit aw tsovaltiqw pu' pep hakim
piw tsootsongyangwu. Noq pu'
puma yukuyaqw pu' yaw pam
mong'iwtaqa amumi pangqawngwu, "Ta'ay," yaw kitangwu,
"itam kya yukuya. Uma sopkyawat
sinom inumi unangwtatveqw oovi
nu' yaasa'haqam höqqe nu' haalayti. Oovi itam yaapiy soosoyam
hopiit itaaqatsiy ö'qalyaniy. Oovi
uma tuwat haalaykyaakyangw
ahoy umuukikiy ang ahoyyaniy,"
yaw kitat pu' pumuy amungem
pöötapngwu.

Noq naat pangqaqwa, "Ta'ay,
itamyaniy," yaw kitotaqe pu' yaw
puma nankwusaniqw pu' yaw pam
pep qaa'ö pangawtaqa soosoy
poniniyku. Noq puma yaw aw
taayungqe wuuwantota hintiqw
piw pam poniniykuqw. Noq naat
yaw puma aw taayungqw pay yaw
angqaqw himu amumi suymakqw
yaw kur pam i' maasaw.

ears are piled into one mass.
Apparently they are dumped on
top of Maasaw, but no one is
aware that he is underneath the
heap.

While the people are gathering the
corn, the man sponsoring the
Sopkyaw party stays in the field
hut. This is actually the place to
which the corn is taken by the
workers; they pile it up adjacent
to the hut. Generally, their task is
completed as evening approaches.
At that time the sponsor says,
"All right, all of you gather
around me." When all the girls
and boys are congregated by the
corn pile, a ritual smoking is held.
When that is over, the person in
charge addresses the harvesters as
follows: "Well, I guess we're
finished. All of you have lent me
a hand, therefore I've reaped a
large amount and I'm pleased.
So, from this day on, let each and
every one of us Hopis strive for a
long life. Now go back to your
homes, being happy in your
hearts." After making this speech
the sponsor lays out a path of
cornmeal on the ground in the
direction of home.

And no sooner have the workers
agreed and replied with "All right,
let us go!" and are about to de-
part, when the entire pile of corn
begins to stir. The people are
staring at it, puzzled why it should
be moving. Suddenly a creature
jumps out at them from amidst
the heap, and they all realize that
this being is Maasaw.

Pu' yaw pam pepeq pumuy ngöynumngwu, mamantuy, momoy-
muy, tootimuy, taataqtuy. Pu' pay
yaw tootim, taataqt tsaatsawnaqe
pu' yaw puma kawayvokmuy ang
yayvangwu. Pu' yaw puma waytiw-
numyaqw pu' yaw pam pumuy
pep ngöylawngwu. A'ni yaw pam
himu maasaw wartaqe yaw hiitawat kawayot amum warikye' pu'
yaw angk pite' pu' yaw pam put
kawayot suruyat langakne' pu' aqw
kwangwasutskikngwu. Niikyangw
pam yaw tuwat su'ahoywat taykyangw akw tsokiwnumngwu. Pu'
yaw pam pookoy'taqa mashuruute'
pay paasat angqw posngwu. Pantsakngwu yaw pam pep pumuy
amumum.

Pangqw pu' yaw pam pumuy
kiimi ngöytangwu. Pay kya pi pam
piw pangqw pumuy tuwalniy'ma-
ngwuniiqe oovi pam pay pumuy
yuumosa amungk panmangwu.
Pangqw yaw pam pumuy lay-
mangwu. Noq himuwa yaw hihin
hoytaqw pu' yaw pam piw aw
warikqw pu' yaw pam nawus piw
hihin nahalayvitangwu. Pu' kya pi
pam hakiy maanat kyay'te' pu'
put maamatse' pu' yaw pam put
awnen pu' put naakwayngyavo tsokyangwu. Paasat pu' yaw pam
aakwayngyap tsokiwmaqw, pu' yaw
maasaw tuwat su'ahoywat taykyangw put maanat tsokiy'mangwu. Panmakyangw pu' yaw pam
pumuy soosokmuy pangsoq tupoq
tsovalat pu' pay yaw qa amungk-
ningwu.

Noq pu' yaw puma kawaymuy
akwyaqam pangqw yayvangwu.

Immediately Maasaw falls to
chasing the males and females
present. Frightened, the men and
the young boys mount their horses.
As they scurry about to elude the
god, he continues his pursuit.
Being endowed with great swift-
ness, he races with a horse and,
upon catching up with it, tugs on
its tail, quickly and easily mounting it. As a rule, however, he
lands on it backwards, so that he
rides along facing the rear. This
scares the rider of the horse so
much that he tumbles off his
mount. This is how Maasaw
carries on with the people there.

From the field Maasaw then gives
chase to the harvesters bearing
towards the village. I suppose the
purpose of following the people
in this manner is to guard them
on their way home. As Maasaw
drives them onward, if one person
lags behind he dashes towards
that person, who has no choice
but to increase his pace. If the
person portraying the god then
recognizes a girl who is a paternal
aunt of his, that is, his father's
sister or niece, he will approach
her and mount her on his horse
behind himself. Giving the girl a
lift in this manner, he rides along
facing backwards. Having driven
all the people to the base of the
mesa, Maasaw finally desists from
his pursuit.

Those who are on horseback now
ascend to the mesa top. When all

Pu' piw naapyaqam soosoyam yayvaqw, pu' yaw mi' mong'iwtaqa kawayot aqw wuuve' hiita söngniy'kyangw warikqw pu' yaw puma put ngööngöyangwu, put himuyat nawkiyaniqey oovi. Noq pam pantsakye' pam ephaqam pösaalat söngniy'mangwu. Noq angqe' pi himu sowiy'ngwa haqningwuniqw oovi pam kya pi put nuutungk horokne' pu' put piw söngniy'-kyangw waayaqw pu' puma put angk yuutukngwu. Pu' puma kya pi pep pannumyakyangw pu' hisatniqw kya pi yukuyangwu.

Yukuyaqw pu' puma sopkyawmaqam nöönösangwu. Nöönösaqw paasat pu' yaw piw kiisonve hintsatskyaniqw pu' yaw oovi puma awyaqw paasat pu' yaw maasaw pep kiisonve waynumngwu. Pu' pep yaw ima tootim, taataqt pay himuwa pan naawaknaqa pay naap hin yuwsiy'kyangw pu' put maasawuy awnen pu' pep put aw kwekwetstiwngwu. Noq yaw hisat i' hak yootat an yuwsiy'taqa mooti kwiningyaqw aw kiisonmi paki. Aw pakiiqe pu' yaw pam maasawuy awniiqe pu' yaw aw a'ni töqtit pu' waayaqw pu' yaw pam maawaw put ngöyva. Noq hak yaw put maasawuy aw kwekwetstiwqw, pam hakiy amum warikye' pu' wiikye' pu' maawikiy hakiy akw wuvaataqw pu' pay hak sumokngwu. Pu' yaw pam put niine' pu' pam put yuwsiyat nawkye' pu' yaw tuwat ahoywat ang pakingwu. Oovi pi yaw yootat panti. Put

those on foot have also reached the top, the sponsor of the Sopkyaw climbs on a horse with a pole in his hand, to the end of which something is tied. The instant he takes off the others chase after him, the objective being to snatch away the object tied to the pole. Occasionally, the sponsor rides along with a blanket fastened to a pole. And because in those days buckskins were scarce, that was the last item he would use in this chase game. Finally this entertainment ceases.

Now all the Sopkyaw participants have a feast. When the feast is over, the action continues at the plaza and everybody heads there, where Maasaw is going about. There those boys and men, who so desire, tease Maasaw in all sorts of disguises. On one such occasion a man dressed in the attire of a Plains Indian entered the plaza from the north. Upon his entrance he walked up to the god, yelled a war whoop in his face and then took to his heels. Right away Maasaw dashed after him. When the god is taunted like this, he usually races with his taunter and upon catching up with him, strikes him with his club, as a result of which the taunter immediately faints. Having knocked his taunter out cold, Maasaw disrobes him and garbs himself in his costume. He puts it on backwards, however. In this manner Maasaw also dealt with the man disguised as a Plains Indian. He caught him, knocked

ngu'aaqe niinaqe pu' yaw kwaa-
tupatsayat ang pakiqw, tuwat yaw
kwaatupatsat kwasru'at suumo-
miqwat haayiwyungwa. Pan-
kyangw yaw pam pep wawarti-
numa.

Pan kya pi pam hintsakqw pu'
paasat yukiltiniqat aqw haykyal-
tiqw, pu' paasathaqam kya pi pay
ima maswikkatsinam kiisonmi
yungngwu. Nen pu' puma pep
tiivangwu, put maasawuy engem.
Noq pep pu' pam pumuy tiimayt
pangqw pu' pam kiisonngaqw
yamakye' pu' yaw pam pep tuwat
haqaqw kiingaqw mamasawlawe'
put kiihut qöqönngwu. Yaw naalös
put qöniltit pu' yaw pam pangso
wuuve' pu' pangso pakingwu. Pep
pu' yaw pam kwaatsiy tavingwu.
Nit pu' yaw pam pep nöst pu'
yaw pam pep naasungwnangwu,
puwvangwu.

Pu' ason yaw suutokilnasaveq pu'
yaw pam piw maasawuy an yuwsit
paasat pu' yaw pam kitsokit piw
qöqönngwu. Pam yaw naalös put
qöniltingwu. Pantsakkyangw pu'
yaw pam taalawne' pu' yaw pam
haqami put kwaatsiy naat taawat
qa yamakqw tavitongwu. Pu' pam
oovi haqam put kwaatsiy tavit pu'
yaw ahoy kiy awnen pu' paasavo
pam put hintsakngwu. Pangso
pam sopkyawma yukiltingwu pam
maasaw kwaatsiy taviqw'ö.

him out, and donned his war-
bonnet, but the feathers of this
headdress dangled down in front
of his face. Wearing it in this
fashion, the god scurried about in
the plaza.

When the time to cease performing antics of this kind draws near,
the Maswik kachinas enter the
plaza. They dance there in honor
of Maasaw. After the god has
watched them perform, he makes
his exit from the dance court and
goes back to the house where he
prepared for this event. He makes
four circuits around this house
before he ascends to its top and
enters. Inside he takes off his
mask, rests, and finally goes to
sleep.

At midnight the impersonator
once again takes on the guise of
Maasaw and circulates around the
village. Altogether he makes four
rounds. Eventually, as daybreak
comes, but still before sunrise, he
goes somewhere to put away his
mask. Having done this, the god's
performance terminates, and the
impersonator can return home.
With this act also the entire
Sopkyaw ritual comes to an end.

Obviously, the complex Maasaw impersonation, as practiced during
the Sopkyaw, contains a multitude of symbolic acts which refer to the
essence of the god. Not all of these can be interpreted here in detail. One
activity shall be selected. This activity, termed *kwekwetstiwya*, pertains to

the ritual "teasing" in which Maasaw kills his offenders by the touch of his club and strips them of their costumes. Tyler suggests that "on one level this is a mime depicting the life cycle of the corn plant—the ear is stripped of its seeds... but he, as a corn symbol, rises again" (1964:33). The Hopi view of this mock battle merely points to the defensive might of the god.[22]

TEXT 93

Ima pi pay put maasawuy aw kwekwetstiwyaqam pay tuwat tuwqamuy akw aw ökiwtangwu. Pam pi a'ni himuniqw kur hisat hiitu tuwqam ökiqw, pam maasaw hapi pumuy pay hikwsiy akw qöyani. Noq oovi himuwa aw pan kwekwetstiwqw pam put aw hikwsuqw pam antsa sumokngwu. Noq pam put tutu'awnaqe oovi paniqw himuwa put aw kwekwetstiwe' pam hiita tuwqat akw aw pitungwu. It yootat sen yotsi'et, tasavut, pay puuvumuy himusinmuy akw puma put maasawuy aw pantsatskyaqw, pu' pam pumuy qöyantangwu. Hisat puma tuwqam hopiituy amumi ökiqw, puma hopiit hapi qa pas kyaananaptaniqw oovi paniqw puma piw pep kiisonve pantsatskyangwu.

The men who tease and taunt Maasaw at the plaza come in various guises, representing typical enemies of the Hopi. Since Maasaw is a powerful being, he will slay any arriving foes by breathing on them. He merely breathes on the man who comes to harass him, and the latter immediately sinks to the ground unconscious. This is what is symbolically represented here: the person who intends to annoy the god comes as an enemy. Maasaw is thus taunted by men dressed as Plains Indians, Apaches, Navajos, and members of various other tribes. He kills them all. If ever these enemies should confront the Hopi, the Hopi will not have a hard time dealing with them, and this is what the drama at the plaza portrays.

[22]Compare the didactic explanation of the same episode in a story collected by Stephen: "Maasaw... shows us by his pantomime how he used to treat his enemies and teaches us that he would treat us in the same way if we grew lazy and refused to plant his corn" (1929: 57).

7

Slayer of Enemies

Although only sparsely documented in Hopi ethnographic literature, war lore at one time constituted a sizable part of the Hopi cultural fabric.[1] To be sure, the warfare the Hopi engaged in was often forced upon them by predatory intruders such as Navajos, Apaches, Chemehuevis, Utes, and other non-sedentary Indians who devastated their

---

[1]For specifics on Hopi war practices compare Stephen (1936: 96-100), Titiev (1944: 16), and Beaglehole (1935: 17-24).

fields, raided their livestock, and even attacked their villages. On the other hand, the Hopi certainly have not lived up to the utopian image of an entirely pacifist people which has been ascribed to them. This is borne out not only by the numerous references to violence, aggression, and feuding which lie scattered throughout their folktales but also by historic events such as the fratricidal destruction of Awat'ovi. The epithet "peaceful,"[2] so frequently used in descriptions of the Hopi, turns out to be untenable as a valid interpretation of the tribal name. Indeed, the entire Hopi lexicon contains no semantic equivalent of our concept of "peace". By contrast, the whole realm of war, with its tangible as well as intangible aspects, is conceptualized to a highly sophisticated degree and, for that matter, lexicalized in great detail in the Hopi language.

It comes as no surprise, therefore, that at least five personages are encountered in Hopi mythology who have strong war affiliations: Kookyangwso'wuuti, Pöqangwhoya, Palöngwhoya, Sootukwnangw,[3] and Maasaw. While the two Pööqangw brothers are recognized as war gods *par excellence*, from the beginning of Hopi time, Maasaw's original function appears to have been more that of a caretaker of Hopi ways and a protector of the land which he entrusted to the Hopi. His guardianship of life and land is substantiated in Texts 94 and 95.

TEXT 94

I' maasaw pay qa orayvituysa mihikqw tuuwalangwu. Pam pay pas soosovik kitsokinawit pan tuwalannakwsungwu. Noq pam pay naap tutskway pi angqe aasakis mihikqw nakwsungwu. Pam pay panis itamuy tuuwala, qa himu hapi itamuy yuuyuynaniqat oovi. Pam tutskway qalavaqe tookyep wawarngwu, tuuwalangwu. Qa hak hopit yuuyuynaniqw oovi pam pantsakngwu. Niiqe pam oovi pangqe tuuwaqalpaqe qöniltingwu.

Maasaw does not guard only Orayvi at night. He acts as a watchman among all the villages. Each night he traverses his own land. His sole task is to protect us so that nothing will molest us. Throughout the period of darkness he runs along the edges of his territory and guards us. He does this to make sure no one bothers the Hopi. This is his reason for making a circuit around the edges of the earth.

[2]Fewkes may have been the first proponent of this notion: "The Hopi Indians, as their name indicates, are preeminently people of peace" (1902b: 482).

[3]For war associations in conjunction with Sootukwnangw see Stephen (1936: 84 and 96). A comprehensive portrait of the god Sootukwnangw, based on the available literature, has been compiled by Hartmann (1976).

TEXT 95

I' maasaw hapi pay itamuy tuuwalangwu. Pu' pangqaqwangwuniqw pam sinmuy tokvaqw pu'
pam paasat tuwat nakwsungwu.
Pu' pam angqe' haqe' pootangwu-
niiqey pangningwu. Noq pu' oovi
itam peqwhaqami pu' itaatimuy
put meewantota, hakim mihikqw
qa yaktangwu. Hakim as paasat
pay tokngwu. Ispi pam sinot aw
maqaptsiy'tangwuniiqe oovi ason
pas soosovik tookiwqw paasat pu'
pam nakwsungwu. Pu' sinom naat
qa soosoyam tookye' puma hapi
put sööwuy'toynayangwu. Niiqe
pam oovi kur hin pas pay paasat
nakwsuni, ispi naat qa soosoyam
tokngwuniqw oovi.

Ii'i' hapi put tuwat aw nukushimu.
I' put qatsiyat tumalayat hapi
nukushintsaatsanngwu. Pu' pam
hisat puutsemokye' itamuy maa-
tapqw pep pu' pay itam hintaqat
pi aqw ökini. Itamuy ÖÖnate'
itsivute' pam hapi itamuy tatamtani.

Maasaw definitely provides protection for us. He is said to set
out on his journey after all the
people have fallen asleep. At that
time he embarks on the route
where he normally does his guarding. This is the reason that up to
the present we have been dis-
suading our children from roaming
about at night. People are supposed to sleep at that time. After
all, Maasaw waits until people
everywhere have gone to bed; only
then does he start out. Those who
fail to go to bed delay his journey.
He cannot commence his trek
then, because not everybody is
asleep.

These things are not pleasant for
him, for they interfere with his
work as caretaker of life. If ever he
should become disgusted with us
and abandon us, it is hard to say
what sort of fate will be in store
for us. One thing is clear, though:
if ever he should tire of tending
to us and become angry with us,
he will desert us.

Rooted in his role as guardian of the land, Maasaw's more direct
association with war may have grown out of the dread-afflicting and
death-dealing qualities attributed to him. He attained the stature of a
full-fledged war deity when, as a strongman and clan ancestor of the
aggressive Kookop clan, he manifested his war powers in a legendary
victory for the Orayvians.[4]

[4]See Story 6 in ATR 10. Also compare Titiev (1944: 155-56).

From a ceremonial point of view Maasaw must certainly be regarded as one of the principal Hopi war gods.[5] This is evidenced, for example, by the fact that Maasaw's effigy was displayed alongside those of Kookyangwso'wuuti "Old Spider Woman" and her war-like grandsons, the Pööqangw brothers, Pöqangwhoya and Palöngawhoya, on the altar of the *momtsit* or *moomotst,* "initiates" of the once prominent *"motswimi."* This "warrior society" used to celebrate its annual rites in the fall after the close of the women's Maraw ritual (Titiev 1944:156). As a rule, the *momtsit* were joined by members of the *nakyawimi* society, whose affiliates, the *naanakyat,* who distinguished themselves by stick-swallowing feats (*naasotanta*), were also known as *nasotanwiwimkyam.* Fewkes, in an account of a war festival staged at the First Mesa village of Walpi, reports that Maasaw is said to have been impersonated in the course of the ritual (1902b:990). However, the impersonation was never witnessed by him personally.

While in the context of these war ceremonies the god's aid may have been invoked in a rather general way, quite specific prayers were addressed to him prior to the actual setting out of a war party. Texts 96 through 98, below, indicate that prayers were customarily accompanied by the fashioning of prayer feathers in the form of *paaho* or *nakwakwusi.* Obviously, these demanded adherence to certain ritualistic details in order to assure the desired results. Interesting in this connection are the facts, that the prayer must only be uttered at night (Text 96),[6] that the god is addressed as *itana* "our father" (Text 97), and that the supplicant who deposits the prayer feathers is not permitted to face the shrine of the deity (Text 98).[7]

---

[5] Parsons suggests that Maasaw is "undoubtedly to be equated with *masawi* of the Keres, who is the younger of the two war gods, although sometimes appearing as among the Hopi as a single figure" (1923: 173). Given Maasaw's encompassing status within Hopi culture, I consider it highly unlikely that his name and function as war god represent a linguistic and conceptual borrowing from Keresan.

[6] The formulaic address form *itana* "our father" typically also occurs in prayers to Taawa, the Sun god.

[7] Note that generally it is Maasaw who behaves contrariwise. In this case it is the supplicant who displays a pattern reversed of the usual norm.

TEXT 96

Hak maasawuy engem nakwakwuste' hak sukw tsa'akmongwit aw tavingwu. Pu' hak sukw ayoq maasawuy kiiyat aqw hom'oytongwu, put maasawuy engem. Niikyangw hak pan tunatyawte' hak mihikqw, qa taalö', pan naawaknangwu hakim tuwqamuy suuqöqyaniqat. Noq maasaw pumuy tuwqamuy hintsanqw, pay hakim qa pas pas pumuy tuwqamuy amumum naanaywat pay pumuy qöqyamantaniqat oovi.

Yaniqw oovi hak put maasawuy antsa engem nakwakwustangwu. Pam maasaw a'ni himuningwuniiqe oovi hakiy suninangwu.

The person who fashions prayer feathers for Maasaw gives one to the town crier. Another he takes to the shrine of Maasaw and places it there, along with sacred cornmeal. Next he utters his prayer. The prayer, which is spoken only at night, expresses the wish that the enemy may be killed off easily. Maasaw is asked to affect the enemy in such a way that no battle is necessary to destroy him.

For this reason prayer feathers are fashioned for Maasaw. The god is such a powerful being that he can quickly slay one's enemies.

TEXT 97

Pay pi pangqaqwangwuniqw antsa pam a'ni öqala, a'ni himu, nuutsel'eway. Noq yaniqw oovi hopiit put engem paahototangwu haqami tuwvöötotanik. Noq oovi puma haqami tuwvööte' puma pan put aw maasawuy aw naanawaknangwu: "Ta'ay, itanay, um itamuy pa'angwani. Um imuy itaatuwqamuy mashuruutapnaqw puma yephaqam qa hohongvit akw yaktaqw itam yep pumuy qa pas kyaananaptat, suuqöqyat qa hinkyaakyangw ahoy ökiniy." Angqaqw itam put sutsep oovi aw yan naawakinwisa.

In addition to being extremely hideous, Maasaw is reputed to be very strong and endowed with greater than human powers. On account of this, Hopi men make prayer feathers for him before they go on the warpath. Thus, when they intend to carry out a raid, they pray to Maasaw: "Our father, please help us. Let our enemies be so petrified with fear that they will walk around on weak legs so that we can slay them quickly and easily and return home unharmed." For ages we have been praying to Maasaw in this manner.

TEXT 98

Pay hopiit antsa haqami tuwvööto- tanik puma yaw antsa it maasawuy aw naanawaknangwu. Niiqe puma oovi put engem it nakwakwusit yukuyangwu. Pu' pay yaw koo- kyangwso'wuutit piw enang puma hiita engem yuwsiyangwu.

Noq hopi tuwqat niine' paasat pu' pam yaw pas qaleetaqtingwu. Noq oovi i' qaleetaqa piw maasawuy awningwu. Sen pi pas aw pitu- ngwu, sen pi kiiyat awningwu. Niiqe pam oovi pumuy hopiituy amungem put maasawuy aw naawaknangwu. Pu' son pi piw qa engem nakwakwustangwu, paaho- tangwu. Nen pu' antsa yaw pam haqami put it maasawuy engem oyate', pam yaw aqw pite', pam yaw put qa aqwwat taykyangw pephaqam put tavingwu. Pam yaw put ahoywat aw tavingwu. Pu' pam it maasawuy aw naanawak- nangwu. Pam pumuy amungem imuy tuwqamuy mashuruutap- naqw, puma hopiit qa kyaa- nanaptat qa hiniwqat akw pumuy suuqöqyamantani. Pu' pam piw qa ahoy taatayt pu' pay pam pangqw ahoy kivay aqwningwu.

Pu' pam pumuy amungem pan- tiqw pu' kur antsa i' maasaw put hu'wanaqw, pu' yaw kur puma hopiit kiipokye' pu' pumuy tuwqa- muy naat qa tokqamuy amumi ökiqw, paasat pu' yaw i' maasaw it kookyangwso'wuutit amum yaw pumuy tuwqamuy hintsanngwu. Paasat pay yaw puma pumuy qa hiniwqat akw qöqyangwu. Ima

It is true, indeed, that the Hopi pray to Maasaw when they plan to go on the warpath. In such an event they fashion prayer feathers for him. They also make prayer feathers for Old Spider Woman.

Upon slaying an enemy, a Hopi becomes a warrior. As a warrior he then has the right to approach Maasaw. He may really encounter him face to face or perhaps visit his shrine. During any rite, it is he who prays to Maasaw on behalf of the Hopi. He usually also prepares for him *nakwakwusi* and *paaho,* which represent different types of prayer feathers. When the warrior goes to offer these prayer feathers to the god, he avoids facing the shrine as he deposits them. Then he prays to Maasaw. The god is to frighten the enemies stiff, so that the Hopi can quickly destroy them without suffering and without too much effort. Then the warrior returns to his kiva, without looking over his shoulder.

This the warrior does for the Hopi. If Maasaw grants his wishes he, along with Old Spider Woman, will cast a spell on the foe in case the Hopi come to raid while their enemies are not yet asleep. Now they can kill off their enemies without much effort, for they do

tuwqam yaw qa rohomtotingwu.
Puma yaw pas qa atsat mashuruu-
totiqw paasat pu' yaw puma
pumuy su'angwutotangwu. Qa
nanaptangwu yaw hopiit pumuy
amumi ökiqw.

not retaliate. They are truly
petrified with fright so that the
Hopi can easily overcome them,
or they are not even aware that
the Hopi come upon them.

The express expectation, which emanates from the prayer passages above, is that the god's intervention has a stunning or paralyzing effect on the enemy. Maasaw is thus not appealed to as a slayer of enemies but rather as a preparatory agent for easy dispatch of them. He is to cripple the foe by reducing him to a state of fright, helplessness, or confusion so that he can fall easy prey to the Hopi. This role of the god is in keeping with the Hopi belief, that the mere revelation of his horrifying appearance is usually sufficient to frighten a mortal out of his wits. To bring about the desired effect among the enemy, the god can draw on several options. Thus, Maasaw's club, known as *maawiki*, is believed to render any mortal unconscious when only touched by it.[8] Bradfield states that, prior to their departure, warriors "prayed to ancient deceased warriors and to Maasaw, who was asked to move in spirit among the enemy and to touch them with his club so that they might be easy victims for the Hopi" (1973:249).

Curtis has preserved a story in which the people of Orayvi, resentful for constantly losing their races to a running star from Kiqötsmo, a once-upon-a-time village on the mesa overlooking Sikyatki, challenged the rival villagers to a life-and-death kick ball race. The winners were not only to behead their male losers but also to acquire their wives, children, and other possessions. During the actual race, in which each side was allowed to use magic, the people of Kiqötsmo were aided by Maasaw, among other deities, who "kept throwing his club at their [opponents'] legs, and thus made them heavy" (1922:195). Another formidable weapon is Maasaw's breath.

---

[8]The practice of "killing" his opponent by means of the club was a prime ingredient during the ceremonial mock battles staged at the occasions of the Nevenwehekiw and Sopkyaw (see Chapter 6).

TEXT 99

Maasaw yaw hakiy aw hikwse' yaw hakiy pas sonqa hintsanngwuqat pangqaqwangwu. Noq pam pay pi a'ni lay'taqat hikwsiy'tangwuniqw oovi. Pu' pam hakiy qa öqawiy'taniqat oovi hakiy pantsanngwu. Pu' pam hakiy aw hikwsuqw hak soosoy tsakwngwu. Pay tuwqamuy tis pi oovi pay pi pantsanngwu. Pay puma tuwqam qa hongvitotiniqat oovi pam maasaw pumuy pantsanqw, pu' puma hopiit pumuy su'angwutotangwu.

It is said that when Maasaw's breath falls on a person, it seriously affects that person. After all, his breath is very potent. He breathes on a person so that he will not have any strength. His breath simply drains a person of all his energy. He especially uses this weapon against his enemies. He wants them to lose their strength so that the Hopi can easily conquer them.

Story 6 (ATR 10), the legend of "How Maasaw Destroyed the Enemies for the Orayvi People," portrays the god as the supernatural strongman and clan ancient of the Kookop clan; it also demonstrates the use of this breath weapon. Here, the action of breathing on the enemy is reinforced by an additional scattering of magic ashes while circling the foe. In Story 4, (ATR 10), "The Youth Who Was Turned into a Maasaw," the breathing act has been substituted for by the use of a magic medicine, which the two Maasaw impersonators chew and then spurt on the enemy. Again, use of the medicine occurs subsequent to a circling of the enemy. Rather than merely sapping the enemy's strength and his will to fight, though, as is achieved in the first narrative by the combined power of breath and ashes, the use of the magic medicine in the latter story throws them into such a state of disarray that they direct their weapons against themselves.

The most potent device attributed to Maasaw's arsenal of weapons is the qöötsaptanga, a sort of "anti-personnel" weapon, as can be gathered from its effect in Story 6 (ATR 10).[9] The Hopi term, which literally translates as "container of ashes," has popularly come to be known as

---

[9]Titiev's abridged version of the Kookop clan myth differs from mine in that two Maasaw impersonators intervene with their devastating jars of ashes on behalf of the Orayvians. "The Kookop chief instructed the two Maasaw actors to run in opposite directions, describing wide arcs in back of the enemy lines.... This they did, and as their paths crossed they threw down their gourds of ashes. Immediately the contents flew up like flames, covering the attackers and making them faint and sluggish" (1944: 155).

"gourd of ashes."[10] I have no explanation for the origin of the English concept. One of Courlander's informants, though, speaks of "a pumpkin filled with ashes [used] in the Maasaw ceremony." Unfortunately he fails to identify the ceremonial event he alludes to (1982:100). The following folk definition implies, however, that the container was fashioned out of clay.

TEXT 100

I' maasaw pi it qöötsaptangat tuwat hinwat yep sinot akw yuku-nangwuniiqe oovi pam put tuwat himuy'ta. Niiqe oovi pam naa-qöyiwuy ep tuwqamuy amuupew wunupte' pu' pam pumuy putakw hintsanngwu.

Pam qöötsaptanga yaw pas himu sus'a'ni öqala. Noq pam qötsvi it kuysiphoyat tsöqat angqw yukiw-taqat angqw tangawkyangw pay son pi qa hiita enang neengaw-taqw, oovi pam umukngwu pam put tuuvaqw.

Maasaw owns a container filled with ashes which he uses to afflict people. In a battle he positions himself before the opponent and overcomes him by means of this device.

The container is said to constitute a most powerful weapon. Inside the jar, which is made of clay, are ashes.[11] Most likely they are mixed with some other ingredient because the container explodes when Maasaw hurls it.

The use of clay as construction material for the container is confirmed in Story 6 (ATR 10), in which Maasaw as the clan progenitor of the Kookop clan wins the day for the Orayvians. There, the *qöötsaptanga* is actually described as a *kuywikoro* or "water canteen." Hopi vessels of

---

[10]This version was apparently first introduced by Titiev (1944: 78 and 155). It is also found in a joint letter to President Nixon by the Hopi Traditional Village Leaders in 1970 (Katchongva 1975: ii).

[11]The formidable power, believed to be inherent in the ashes employed by Maasaw, is also confirmed by Nequatewa. In discussing Yukiwma, the leader of the "hostile" faction that was forced to leave Orayvi and subsequently founded Hotvela, he says about the latter: "He belonged to the Fire or Maasaw Clan. This gave him the idea that his clan ancestor had the power to do anything, almost. This clan has the idea that Maasaw can hypnotize people, so he always has said that if any expedition is sent against him all he has to do is to take out a handful of ashes and blow them on the army and they would fall to pieces" (1973: 65).

this function have been manufactured out of clay since prehistoric times. Additional evidence, that the receptacle for the ashes was not a gourd, can be gleaned from an episode in Crane's version of the Hopi emergence.[12] Here, his informant states that "the bravest of the warriors... put explosives in pottery, and threw these bombs among the enemy, and scattered them" (1926:165).

Whether the *qöötsaptanga* actually contained ingredients in addition to the ashes, must remain speculative; after all, the device constituted a ceremonial weapon. All available sources are in agreement, however, that the vessel exploded after being hurled and impacting the ground.[13]

The *qöötsaptanga* was actually used by the Hopi in historic times when, by means of ceremonial warfare, they attempted to intimidate a unit of the U.S. cavalry. The latter had arrived in Orayvi to arrest several of the leading men of the village. The confrontation was brought about by the United States government's intention to force-educate Hopi children at boarding schools, away from the reservation. This intention was bitterly opposed by a section of Hopi known as *qa pahannanawaknaqam*, "ones who do not want the white man's way," who later came to be labeled "hostiles" in English. The event, which took place in the summer of 1891, has been described by both Fewkes and Titiev. Fewkes, however, makes no mention of the jar of ashes. According to him, the personification representing the god of death "carried various objects, among which was a bowl filled with a liquid medicine... and as he passed along the line of soldiers he sprinkled them all with this medicine, using for this purpose a feather" (Parsons 1922:275-6).

Titiev, on the other hand, reports that after Maasaw's appearance "a woman named Sinimka was supposed to come out with a gourd full of ashes. This she was to dash on the ground, scattering the ashes and so weakening the enemy that they would be helpless to resist being clubbed to death" (1944:78).

My own accounts in Texts 101 and 102 concerning this matter were obtained from two resource persons who, of course, received their information only second-hand. Both concur, however, in the observation

---

[12]This episode alludes to the same event that is also narrated in Story 6 (ATR 10), where Maasaw, the *wu'ya* or "clan ancestor" of the Kookop clan, prepared the annihilation of the hostile forces by employing his *qöötsaptanga*.

[13]Courlander's informant, who characterizes the *qöötsaptanga* as "a pumpkin full of ashes," also has a plausible explanantion for its inherent potential to explode. "One time I had a pumpkin in the stove. I didn't put a hole in it [for steam to escape]. I just left it there. And all at once the thing exploded and knocked everything around. See how powerful it is?" (1982: 100).

that Maasaw did make his appearance with his jar of ashes. It should be noted that Text 102 wrongly places the occurence at the time of the Orayvi split, which did not take place until 1906.

TEXT 101

Yaw antsa yep orayve i' maasaw imuy solaawamuy amumi pituqw put antsa itaaso hisat inumi lalvaya. Noq antsa yaw puma solaawam hisat pep pumuy amumi öki. Pay pumuy kya pi son pi qa hintsatsnaniqe oovi. Pay pi angqe' ima peetu imuy timuy amungem it tutuqayiwuy qa naanawaknaqw, pu' oovi puma solaawam pep ökiqw pu' puma it maasawuy yaw yuwsinaya. Pay niikyangw yaw qa putsa. Yaw ima hakim piw imuy pöqangwhoyatuy yuwsi. Noq pu' yaw i' haqawa piw tuwat itwat kookyangwso'wuutit yuwsiqw, pu' it kwaatokot piw yaw hak yuwsi. Pam yaw hak kwaawungwtaqa, qötsngöyva yan maatsiwqa, pam yaw it kwaatokot yuwsi.

Noq pu' yaw puma solaawam pep ökiqw, pu' yaw pam maasaw pep haqam puma kookopngyam

Once my grandmother told me that Maasaw really confronted a party of soldiers at Orayvi. One day, many years ago, these soldiers came to the people of Orayvi, probably with the intention of harming the people. At that time a number of Hopis did not want their children to be educated in an Anglo school. Thus, when the soldiers appeared, the villagers dressed a man to impersonate Maasaw. But he was not the only one they costumed. Two men also garbed themselves in the guise of the Pööqangw brothers, while yet another dressed as Old Spider Woman, and a fourth did an impersonation of Kwaatoko.[14] The person who portrayed Kwaatoko was of the Eagle clan and known by the name of Qötsngöyva.

When the soldiers arrived, the Maasaw impersonator donned his costume at the home of the Koo-

[14]Titiev defines the *kwaatoko* as a powerful war bird that lives in the sky. According to Hopi lore, Kwaatoko is supposed to come out after the slaughter and feast of the dead. The fact that the bird was impersonated by a *kwaawungwa* or "member of the Eagle clan," leads me to assume that Kwaatoko once designated the now extinct condor in Arizona, since members of this clan consider the eagle and other powerful birds as their *wu'yam* or "clan totems."

In a story recorded by Voth, in which the mockingbird is assisted by Kwaatoko, the latter "spreads his large wings across the eastern sky, completely covering up the dawn" (1905a: 179).

kiy'yungqw pep yaw pam yuwsi.
Noq pu' yaw i' yukiwma imuy qa
pahannanawaknaqamuy amu-
ngaqw pu' yaw pam put maasawuy
pangso pumuy solaawamuy amumi
wiiki. Noq pu' yaw pam maasaw
pep pumuy amumi pitukyangw
pu' pam pi pay qa yu'a'ata kya
piniiqe pay yaw pam panis pumuy
amumi maasanta. Niiqe yaw pam
pan ayo' may iitat pu' paasat
angqw naami tawitsqay aw yan-
tingwu. Pam yaw yang it tutskwat
himuy'taqey yaw pam pumuy
aawintaqe paniqw yaw pam
pumuy amumi pan maasanta.
Pantit pu' yaw pam pep pumuy
amumi it qöötsaptangay tuuva.

Noq pay pi puma put hiita maasawuy qa tuwiy'yungkyangw pu'
piw pay qa itamuy hopiituy amun
put mamqasyaqe paysoq yaw okiw
aw tsutsuya. Niikyangw pay yaw
pam pumuy pö'aaqey yan kya pi
put yukiwmat aa'awna, ispi pay
yaw puma solaawam put qa hin-
tsatsnaqw oovi.

Yan pay yaw pam pumuy pö'at
paasat pu' yaw pam pay pangqw
pumuy kookopngyamuy kiiyamuy
awniqw, pu' puma pep son pi put
qa hin tumaltota. Pay pi son hin
qa powatota. Noq paasat pu' pay
yaw pam pangqw ahoy yamakt pu'
pay yaw haqami. Pay pangsoq-
haqami i' hak hisat mamasaw-
ngwuqa yukye' pangsoq ahoynen
pu' pepeq put hiita yuwsiy'taqey
put oyangwuniqw pay pangsoq.
Pu' pepeq pam son pi qa hin
naavootsiwa.

kop clan. Then Yukiwma, who
sided with the group that did not
care for the ways of the White
man, led Maasaw to the troops.
Upon approaching them at their
location Maasaw only motioned to
them since he is incapable of
speaking. He repeatedly held out
his arms, whereupon he placed the
palms of his hands on his chest.
In this fashion he attempted to
tell the soldiers by gesture that he
was the owner of the land. In
the end he threw his container of
ashes at them.

The soldiers, of course, who were
unfamiliar with Maasaw did not
dread him as we Hopis do, only
sneered at the poor soul. Maasaw,
however, informed Yukiwma that
he had defeated the soldiers since
they had not harmed him.

Convinced that he had gained the
upper hand over the troops, Maasaw returned to the Kookop clan
house where he must have undergone some sort of treatment. Most
likely he was purified; then he
went to the site where the Maasaw
impersonator usually goes to take
off his costume after completing
the portrayal of the god. He
probably also went through some
sort of discharming ritual there.

Noq pu' yaw imawat hakim
mimuywatuy hiituy yuwsiyaqam
puma yaw pay pumuy solaawamuy
qa aw naamataqtotat pu' pay
yuwsiy o'yat pu' yaw pay naavoo-
tsiwya.

Meanwhile, those who had dressed
to impersonate the other beings
did not make their appearance
before the troops but discarded
their costumes and discharmed
themselves.

TEXT 102

Antsa yaw pepeq orayveq ep puma
naatsikqw, ep yaw ima solaawam
pepeq ökikyangw pu' imuy peetuy
qömapsolaawamuy enang tsam-
vaya. Puma hapi peetu orayvit
pay yaw timuy amungem qa
tutuqayyaniqat naanawakna. Noq
puma yaw hapi pumuy tsaatsakwmuy oovi pepeq öki. Niiqe pu'
yaw puma solaawam kya pi pepeq
pumuy sinmuy amumi may'yungkyangw pu' amumi umtoynayaqw,
pu' yaw ima hakim tuwat maasawuy wu'yay'yungqam yaw put
maasawuy wangwayya. Pam yaw
as pumuy solaawamuy amuminen
pu' pumuy mashuruutapnani. Pu'
pam yaw as pumuy qöyaqw pu'
puma paasavo pumuy amumi
umtoynayani.

Pu' yaw puma oovi put maasawuy
yuwsinayat pu' yaw solaawamuy
aw put maatatve. Pu' yaw pam
pitukyangw put yaw antsa qöötsaptangay yawkyangw yaw ep pituuqe
pu' put solaawamuy amumi
tsalakna. Noq puma solaawam
put maasawuy pi pay qa tuwiy'-
yungqe tuwat yaw aw tsutsuya.
Pas yaw himu nanan'ewaynii-
kyangw pu' piw okiwyuwsiy'taqw,
paysoq yaw solaawam put maasawuy aw tsutsuya. Niiqe yaw
oovi maasaw qa hin solaawamuy
tsaawina.

It is true, they say, that during
the split of Orayvi a troop of
soldiers, among whom also were
some blacks, arrived at the village.
Since some Orayvi inhabitants did
not want their children educated
in the White man's school,
the reason for the soldiers'
arrival was to carry off the children by force. When the soldiers
molested the people and fired
their guns at them, those who
possessed Maasaw as a clan ancestor called upon the god. He was
to approach the troops and petrify
them. He was to kill them so that
they would cease their shooting.

Consequently, someone was costumed as Maasaw and let loose
upon the soldiers. He arrived,
bringing along a container of
ashes, which he hurled at the
troops. But since the latter had no
concept of what Maasaw represented, they merely mocked him.
In their eyes the god appeared
ridiculous. They also laughed at
him because he was garbed in
such shabby clothes. Thus Maasaw
completely failed to frighten the
soldiers.

8

Disease and Health

The paradoxical nature of Maasaw, which is reflected in his embodiment of the phenomena of death as well as life,[1] finds a "logical" extension in his association with sickness and health. Thus, parallel to prayers for a good life and longevity (see Chapter 6, Text 84), the deity

---

[1]Regarding this dualistic aspect of the god, Titiev suggests a parallelism between Christianity and Hopi beliefs: "Maasaw, like the Lord, giveth and taketh away" (1972: 167).

is also supplicated for physical well-being and soundness of health.[2] Warding off diseases is, of course, compatible for a tutelary spirit who fends off enemies. Tradition has it that Maasaw already had committed himself to this task in mythological times when he promised to Matsito, the legendary founder of Orayvi, "to guard the village by night with a firebrand and to keep off enemies, disease, and pestilence" (Talayesva 1942:421).

Interesting in this context is Stephen's remark that, in the case of an ailing child, Maasaw is expressly asked to visit the child but to refrain from touching it with his death-dealing club. "When his child is sick, the Moki [i.e., Hopi] prays Maasaw to come and look upon it and pass by without touching it" (1940:103). Text 103 confirms that Maasaw is beseeched for good health.

TEXT 103

I' maasaw yep it soosok tutskwat himuy'ta. Itam hopiit put tutskwa- yat ep paysoq naat yeese. Paniqw oovi hopi put aw naawakne' pam pangqawngwu, "Ta'ay, pay nu' qa hinkyangw yep uututskway ep nuutum waynumni," himuwa yan naawaknangwu.

Maasaw owns all the land of this earth. We Hopis live on his land only as tenants. Thus, when a Hopi prays to the god, he usually says, "All right, let me live in good health as I walk upon your ground along with the others." This is the prayer one utters.

In keeping with the Hopi belief that the god is about at night, Maasaw is expected to shield people from disease particularly during the hours of darkness. He is relieved in this role by Taawa, the Sun god, during daytime. Hence, Maasaw and Taawa complement each other in their care for the Hopi.

---

[2]The Hopi custom of addressing Maasaw in prayer, after the construction of a new house, must probably be seen in this context. Simpson reports that "when the home was completed, the man would place prayer-plumes and food-offerings among the rafters. Some of these were to Maasaw and were accompanied by a prayer that Death would long spare the occupants of the house" (1953: 59).

TEXT 104

Antsa pi maasaw yep soosokmuy itamuupa popta. Pam yan too-kilnawit itamuupa waynumngwu-niqw yan mihikqw hakim put aw naanawaknangwu. Pu' pay qa hin-kyaakyangw tokvaniqey pay put hakim aw naanawaknangwu. Pu' piw itamuy sopkyawatuy sinmuy paas tumalay'maniqat, paas itamuy tsaamiy'maniqat.

Pu' yan taalawvaqw pu' itam itwat taawat aw pan piw naaqavo naanawaknangwu. Niiqe pay itam pumuy nan'ivo amumi itaaqatsiy sutsep tuuvinglalwa, itaatimuy amungem, qa nenngemsa. Pu' pay hak yan hakiy tuwiy've' pay hak put piw engem enang aw naawak-nangwu, pu' piw timuyatuy amu-ngem. Pu' hiita itam noonovaniqat put piw hakim enang pumuy amumi tuuvinglalwangwuniiqe pay itam oovi qa qatsitsa put aw tuuvinglalwa, pay sopkyawatuy sinmuy amungem, itaatimuy, itaa-tuwimuy, itaakwatsmuy amungem.

Maasaw truly looks out for all of us. He travels about among us during the night, so it is at night that we address him in prayer. We pray to him that we may fall asleep without experiencing any illness. In addition, we ask him to provide for all of the people in the world and to lead us along with care.

As soon as the day breaks, we turn to the Sun in prayer. We do this regularly each day. So we con-stantly petition both Maasaw and the Sun god for a good life, and not only for ourselves but for our children as well. And when one makes another's acquaintance, one also prays in behalf of him and his family. In addition, we request of these gods the food with which to sustain ourselves. Therefore, it is not only life that we pray for. For these things we beg on behalf of all people, our families, our acquaintances, and our friends.

Prayers to Maasaw typically incorporate also a wish for physical wholeness. All acts of Hopi praying, which generally are utterances in silence, feature concomitant offerings. These offerings, which in the case of Maasaw comprise *piiki*, tobacco, and the ever-present cornmeal, are deposited at the shrine of the deity. Due to the god's close link with darkness, offerings to him must be deposited at night.

TEXT 105

Pu' paasat pay sen hak piw hiita ep pay qa pas pas kwangwahin-

At times when one is unwell, due to some ailment, or also when tangwu. Pu' sen himuwa hakiy ti'at piw haqam pay hiita akw nawawataqw, hak kur hintsanninik pay hak okiw it orayve maasawuy qatuuqat pangsohaqami wuuwankyangw hak mihikqw kiy iipoq hiita oyangwu, ayo' pay qalavo. Pay himuwa hiita akw qa kwangwahintaqa qalaptuniqat put hak aw naawaknangwu. Pu' hak qa tuutuyniqey oovi it piivat, piklakvutnit pu' it hoomat yep pööpavehaqam oyangwu. Pay hak put aw naawakne' pay yanhaqam hintingwu.

one's child is suffering pain and there is nothing one can do about it, one thinks of the Maasaw who resides in Orayvi. This is done by setting some food outdoors at night at a place away from the house. Then one prays to Maasaw that the person who is ill will overcome his malady. In order not to become ill oneself, one deposits some tobacco, crushed dried piiki, and cornmeal somewhere on a trail. This is more or less the procedure adhered to when praying to Maasaw.

In addition to individual offerings which are being placed at the god's shrine, certain ceremonies require the fashioning of special prayer objects, such as *paaho* "prayer sticks" and *nakwakwusi* "prayer feathers." Stephen mentions Maasaw prayer feathers which are adorned with pine needles (1936:91). They are "to send plenty of earthly blessings, that sickness may not come" (1936:94). The proper way of depositing a *nakwakwusi* for Maasaw may be gathered from Text 106.

TEXT 106

Pu' hakim put engem nakwakwustotanik hakim put it kwaahut pas hongvit pöhöyat angqw put yukuyangwu. Hak put engem nakwakwuste' pu' hom'oyte' pu' hak put tuwat ahoywat haqam put engem tavingwu, maasawuy pi yaw ahoywatsa hiita hintingwuniqw oovi.

When fashioning a *nakwakwusi* for Maasaw, the stiff down feather of the eagle is used. The prayer feather is then deposited backwards for him, because it is believed that Maasaw does things in an order reverse to the normal procedure.

Paaho for Maasaw are always made during Soyalangw, the "Winter Solstice ceremony."

TEXT 107

Hisat soyalangwuy aw pituqw put
maasawuy engem it paahot mooti
yukuyat pu' ason pay mimuywatuy
hiituy soosokmuy, itam amumi
enang tatqa'nangwyakyangw
yesqw, pumuy amungem piw put
yukuutotangwu. Pay pam son piw
tuwat put paahot itamumi qa
tunglay'taqw, oovi hakim aw
maqayaqw, pay pam tuwat haa-
layte' pu' piw aapiy itamuy qa
tatamiy'mangwu. Noq pu' pam
put ömaate' pay pi son pi qa
yanhaqam tuwat lavaytingwu:
"Kwakwha, kur nuy u'niy'yungqe
oovi inungem paahotota."

When the time for the Soyal
ceremony comes, the first *paaho*
is always fashioned for Maasaw.
After that more prayer feathers
and prayer sticks are made for
the other deities on whom we rely
in our daily life. Maasaw must
crave for this prayer feather from
us, for when we bestow it on him,
he is so grateful that he continues
to help us. Upon accepting the
paaho he probably says, "Thanks!
Evidently they still remember me
because they made this prayer
feather for me."

In addition to the ingredients mentioned in Text 105, Talayesva,
who once had occasion to take *paaho* out to Maasaw's shrine during the
Soyal ritual, also included raw rabbit with the offering. On reaching the
shrine of Maasaw, on a moonless night, he first sprinkled the meal and
then prayed as follows: "Great Maasaw, I have been sent over here to
ask your help in our lives. Give us moisture and protect us; let the people
increase, live to old age, and die without suffering" (1942:287).

Text 108 constitutes an actual Hopi prayer to Maasaw. It confirms
the custom of having *piiki*, tobacco, and cornmeal as the three essential
ingredients in the offering which is to accompany the Maasaw prayer.

TEXT 108

"Ta'ay, itana'ay, um yep itamuy
tumalay'maqa, um itamuy qa
haqami tatamtani. Qavomi imuy
itupkomuy, ivavamuy, ingumuy,
itiw'aymuy, itimuy, sopkyawatuy
sinmuy amungem piw um it
lolmat qatsit tunatyaltini. Um
itamuy it lolmat ang tsaamiy'-
maqw, itam piw qaavohaqam

"Now, our father, you who tend
to our needs, never forsake us.
For the coming day plan a good
life for my younger and elder
brothers, my parents, my nieces
and nephews, my children and
all the other people in the world.
Guide us in goodness so that
tomorrow we will rise healthy and

suphelawkyaakyangw talöngnayani.
Yep'e," hak aw kitat paasat pu'
hak it hoomatnit piikitnit hopivivat
put hak sumiqrilat pu' hak put
haqami oyangwu, put hakiy qataymataq qatuuqat engem.

sound. Here, I have this for you."
Upon uttering these words one
takes some cornmeal, piiki, as
well as some wild tobacco, mixes
them together and then places the
mixture somewhere for the god
who lives unseen.

While Maasaw is, as a rule, implored for a general absence of illness, *tsawintuya* or "anxiety sickness" is a particular disorder he is beseeched to heal. This disorder, which represents an extraordinary fear of sudden noises, darkness and nighttime, constitutes a phobia which may actually stem from an excessive dread of meeting the god at night. Note that the disease, of which symptoms are outlined in Text 109, can be cured not only by Maasaw but by members of the Kookop clan. Text 110 outlines in detail the proper procedure for placing a *nakwakwusi* at Maasaw's shrine when suffering from such anxiety sickness.

TEXT 109

Hak hiita ep tsawne' hak putakw
tsawintutuytingwu. Nen pu' hak
nalmamqasngwu. Noq oovi pam
piw pan maatsiwa, nalmaqtuya.
Pay as hak taalö' haalayngwunii-
kyangw pu' taawa atvelmo sirokq,
paasat pu' mihikmi pitutoq hak
iipoq yamakninik hak pay tsawi-
niwtangwu. Pu' hak son hakiy
aqlap hiita yanhaqam suqlakin-
tangwu.

Pu' hak paas tsaakwikiwmangwu,
hak hin unangway'tangwu. Pas
himu haqaqw hakiy aw hinti-
niqat hak yan wuuwankyangw hak
mihikniy'mangwu. Pu' hak mihikqw pas soosoy tururutangwu.
Pas hak tsawiniwtaqey su'antangwu. Pu' hak pangsoq kookop-

A person who gets frightened by something suffers from *tsawintuya,* or "anxiety illness." He is then basically afraid to be left alone. Hence this disorder is also called *nalmaqtuya* or "afraid-to-be-alone-ailment." During the daylight hours, the person is generally happy but as soon as the sun begins to set and night falls, he is scared to leave the house. Also, one cannot make any banging noises near that person.

The person suffering from anxiety illness becomes very frail. He is always nervous and keeps im-agining that something will grab him as darkness approaches. During the night he shivers all over. He behaves exactly like one who is frightened. At this point

ngyamuy awniqw, pu' puma hakiy naavootsiwnayaqw pu' hak put qalaptungwu.

members of the Kookop clan who discharm the patient are usually consulted, whereupon he recovers from this malady.

TEXT 110

Ima peetu hopiit maasawuy aw naanawaknangwu tsawintutuytote'. Noq himuwa tsawintutuytiqw pay i' taaha'at, na'at, kwaa'at, pam himuwa put engem nakwakwus- taqw, paasat pu' haqawa put engem maasawuy kiiyat aqw hom'oytongwu. Niikyangw pam pas mihikqw tookilnasaveq put pangsoq hom'oytongwu. Pu' pam qa put maasawuy kiiyat aqw taykyangw put oyangwu. Nii- kyangw pam put mooti aw naa- waknat, oyat pu' pay ahoy angqw nimangwu. Pu' pam piw angqw ahoynen qa ahoy yorikngwu. Pantiqw pu' pam put aw lay'vaqw pu' pay himuwa put tsawintuyat qalaptungwu.

Some Hopis pray to Maasaw when they come down with anxiety illness. As a rule, upon contracting this ailment, the patient's uncle, father, or grandfather fashions prayer feathers for him which someone takes then to the shrine of Maasaw where they are placed, together with some cornmeal. This task needs to be undertaken in the middle of the night. While the prayer feathers are deposited, one must avoid facing the god's shrine. Before leaving for home, the supplicant utters a prayer over the feathers. On his way back he must not look over his shoulder. As soon as this rite has been carried out, the remedy becomes effective and the patient will be cured of the anxiety disease.

After the same manner in which believers in Maasaw are shielded by the god, from disease and sickness, so also are those who "transgress into his sphere," as I will refer to this phenomenon, expected to be affected by illness. When such a "transgression" takes place the god, generally, afflicts the "transgressor" with an ailment that is said to be Maasaw's *tunipi* "weapon" or *wuvaapi* "whip." The three major diseases most frequently inflicted by Maasaw are listed in Text 111.

TEXT 111

I' maasaw tuwat tuuyat tunipiy'- taqw pam tuuya paypwa. Noq

Maasaw possesses three types of diseases which he employs as

sukw hak akw masna'paliwtangwu.
Pu' sukw hak akw maslakiw-
tangwuniikyangw pu' mitwat hak
akw hinte' yaw masvakiwtangwu.

weapons. The first, generally
referred to as *masna'paliwta*,
causes ulcers on a person's body.
The second, *maslakiwta*, leads to
atrophy. The last is known as
masvakiwta.

Diseases believed to be caused by Maasaw occur for a number of reasons. Normally, the violator of ceremonial secrets that pertain to a Maasaw ritual can expect to be punished by the god. However, transgression into the god's sphere may also come about in a ceremonially legitimate way. Thus, Titiev cites the case of a man, who in a race for wives' clans[3] "dressed as Maasaw, club and all." Shortly after, when the man's baby "broke out with sores called *masna'pala*, it was decided that the 'power' of Maasaw had got into it" (1972:228).

Then again, the god may be beseeched by a clan member, from among those who venerate him as their *wu'ya* or "totem," to strike with his diseases a person who has harmed this clan member. Also, it is held that the disease can be sent by the god on behalf of the Kwan society, of which he is the patron. "Each secret society," as Titiev points out, "has an ailment which it inflicts on those who betray its secret or break its rules" (1944:79). Conversely, it is believed that a sufferer from an ailment which is controlled by a society can only be relieved or cured of the malady by an affiliate of that society or clan. This practice, of consulting either a Kookop clan man or a Kwan society member, is mentioned in conjunction with a description of *masna'paliwta*, in Text 112. The disease consists primarily of ulcerous sores which erupt and discharge pus. Pus-filled ulcers, and their associated odor, are typically believed to represent a stage in the decomposition process of a dead body. This accounts for the Hopi term, a stative verb which literally translates "to have contracted corpse."

TEXT 112

Himuwa masna'palqa pam soosovik u'yay'vangwu. Niikyangw
hakiy kwaapi'at mooti pöstingwu.
Pay pi hakiy antsa maasawuy an

A person afflicted with a disorder
referred to as *masna'paliwta*,
develops ulcers all over his body.
At first the area around the neck

[3] The Hopi expression for this type of race is *nömananamunwa* "they are wife-racing."

yangqe kwapkyaqe wilalaykungwu.
It maasawuy pangqe kwapkyaqe
wilalata. Pu' hakiy qötöva u'yay'vangwu. Noq pu' ephaqam pay
hiitawat qa qötöva uya'iwte' paasat
pay put mapqölpa sen kukva
uyay'vangwu. Pu' pay himuwa akw
qa puuvuwngwu. Pu' pam hakiy
aasal'iwmaqw hak tapkiwmaqw
soq havivokyal'iwmangwu, qa
puwniqey antangwu. Pu' hak
mihikqw soq tuwat havivokyal'iwkyangw taalö' puwmokiwtangwu.

Pu' pam piw lööpwaniiqat pangqaqwangwu. Peetuy yaw ang tuutuyngwu, pu' peetuy pay piw ang
qa tuutuykyangw pay pam panis
mumkilngwu. Noq put piw ang
hin'ur hovaqtungwu. Pu' pay
himuwa tsay piw pante' pu' pam
piw tuvatsoningwu. Pakmumuye'
pam ngasta posvalay'tangwu.
Posngaqw posvala'at qa mumun-
ngwu pam pakmumuyqw. Pantsakkyangw pu' pam nuwu pay laakiw-
maqw, nuwu sikwi'at ang sulaw'iwmangwu.

Paasat pu' pam maswungwa hakiy
naavootsiwnangwu. Pam kookopwungwa hakiy qötöyat ang ngömaapit akw paahomnangwu. Pu'
kur i' kookopwungwa put powata-
niqey qa nakwhaqw, paasat pu' i'
kwaaniy'taqa put powatangwu. I'
kwaaniy'taqa soosok put hiita
pavasiwtawit tuwiy'taqe oovi put
powatangwu. Noq pu' piw himuwa

will swell up, and the skin there
will become saggy like Maasaw's.
The god's skin is really slack
around this part of his body. Next,
sores break out all over the head.
Once in a while, however, when
there are no sores on the head,
they show up at the palms or the
feet. The person suffering from
this disease cannot sleep. As the
disease spreads he, paradoxically,
gets wide awake in the evening
and feels no urge to go to bed.
And since at night he is fully
alert, he is sleepy during the
daylight hours.

The illness is said to take on two
forms. Some people experience it
with aches. Others do not suffer
any pain, but are feverish instead.
Their bodies then give off a
terrible stench. If a child suffers
from this sickness, it cries constantly. It cries without actually
shedding any tears. There are
simply no tears emited from the
child's eyes while it is crying. As
the illness progresses, the child
becomes thin and its flesh withers
away.

It is at this point that a member
of the Maasaw clan will discharm
the patient. The Kookop clan
member usually cleanses the head
with the liquid of boiled juniper
sprigs. In case the Kookop man
or woman refuses to carry out this
purification, a member of the
Kwan society will take on the task,
for he is familiar with all the songs
associated with the ritual. If the
patient is to recover, he will then

qalaptunik qalaptungwu. Pu' pay
himuwa qa qalapte' pay akw
sulawtingwu.

do just that. One who does not
regain his health after the purification, however, will die.

Curtis, in conjunction with reporting a cure for "swelling of the
neck," which is described as an early symptom of *masna'paliwta* in Text
112, above, indicates that a *maswimkya*[4] or "initiate of the *maswimi*"[5] is
the privileged healer of such a disease. "Swelling of the neck is believed
to be caused by the god Maasaw, and when such a case arises, one of
the men who personate this deity is summoned. He opens the affected
part and sucks out the pus, and the person thus cured becomes em-
powered to personate Maasaw" (1922:177).

In this connection Curtis also cites an interesting example of an act
illustrating what I have called "transgressing into Maasaw's sphere."
"Momi, a priest of Maasaw, in the course of his ceremonial duties had to
make a circuit of the mesa on four consecutive nights, and as he was a
very old man, partially blind, and the nights were very dark, his task was
a difficult one. Heya, meditating on the old man's blindness, thought
that he would like to take the place of Momi and relieve him of his task.
Of course, he was not able to do this, but the mere thought was immediately known to Maasaw, who therefore sent the swelling of the neck
as a sign that Heya was to be one of his priests" (1922:177).

Failure to undergo a discharming rite after contagion with death
constitutes another transgression into Maasaw's sphere. The god avenges
it by striking a person with the ailment of *maslakiwta*. The English
equivalent of this term, which denotes "a state of being dried out/
withered like a corpse," is severe atrophy, as may be gathered form
Texts 113 and 114. Titiev characterizes the disease as "loss of weight,"
implying "that the body is wasting away to a skeleton" (1944:241).

[4]According to Beaglehole, at Second Mesa the chief of the "*maswimkya* society," as
he puts it, "came from the Eagle clan and it specialized in curing swelling in the head,
and head pains. Those cured... join the society" (1937: 46).

[5]For a Hopi definition of *maswimi* see the Glossary in ATR 10. Additional information on the Maasaw fraternity may be gleaned from Curtis: "Those who have personated
Maasaw compose *Maswimi* ('Maasaw fraternity') ; but it seems that this society never held
meetings nor performed a ceremony. On account of the arduous duties of this office in
travelling among the rocks and along the edge of the cliffs in darkness, men are usually
loathe to fill it. The people are very careful, when the personators of Maasaw are
dressing, not to approach them, for, if any one were to observe them at such a time, he
would be seized and required to act in the character of the god. The Crier Chief issues a
warning to pass on the other side of that locality while the Maasaw men are dressing"
(1922: 179).

TEXT 113

Hak maslakqw pu' pay hakiy
sikwi'at ang paa'iwmangwu. Hakiy
toko'at ang paa'iwmaqw hak
ööqasa peetingwu. Pu' pam hakiy
ang soosoy paatiqw pu' put pangqaqwangwu, "Pam pas tsootso'a,"
kitotangwu. Paasat pu' pay hak
pelvoqsa hoyte' pu' hak hisat pay
mokngwu.

A person stricken with *maslakiwta*
becomes emaciated. The patient's
flesh withers away to the point
that he is nothing but skin and
bones. When no flesh remains
anymore, people say, "He is going
out like fire." Then one becomes
progressively worse and finally
dies.

TEXT 114

Hopiit pi pangqaqwangwuniqw
hak yaw it mokput aw hintsakye'
pu' piw nuutum put tavite', pu'
hak ahoy pitukyangw qa naavootsiwe', hak yaw put na'palngwu,
maasawuy. Nen pu' hak suytsepngwat laakiwmangwu. Pu' pas
hakiy qa naavootsiwnayaqw, pu'
hak pan maslakye' pu' hak putakw
pay mokngwu. Pu' piw himuwa
kiive mokq pu' it tsayhoyat, tiposit
yu'at iikwiwkyangw piw pangso
pakingwu naat put qa taviyaqw.
Pu' pam pep pakiwtaqa put
awniwtiqw pu' pay pam tsayhoya
maslakye' pu' pay piw putakw
tuutuylawngwu. Pu' piw ephaqam
akw mokngwu. Pu' put pantaqat
qalaptsinayanik put naavootsiwnayangwu. Niikyangw hisat pi pas
mimayangwu, maswiwimkyam, pu'
piw ima kookopngyam put qööhit
himuy'yungqam, puma hakiy
naavootsiwnayangwu. Noq pu' pi
hinta. Pu' pay hak aspirin sowa-
ngwu.

According to the Hopi, a person
who fails to purify himself after
returning home from handling a
corpse and from accompanying
others on a burial, will contract
the disease *maslakiwta*. As a
result, the person becomes increas-
ingly scrawny. If he does not
undergo a discharming rite after
being struck by this illness, he
will die. The same holds true
when a person dies inside a home
and a mother enters with an
infant or little child on her back
before the dead person has been
buried. If this happens, the child
will contract the sickness *maslakiwta*. At times the ailment may
lead to death. To cure a child in
this condition a discharming ritual
is necessary. Long ago only men
entitled to impersonate Maasaw,
and the members of the Kookop
clan, who own the fire, were
qualified to carry out the task of
purification. I don't know what
the procedure is at present. Now,
one simply takes aspirin.

Proper fumigation with smoke from juniper branches or resin, after contact with the dead, is considered an effective means to prevent contraction of the disease.

TEXT 115

I' maasaw yaw it ngömaapit kwiitsingwuyat yaw qa himuningwu. Noq oovi hakim it mokqat tuu'amye' pu' hakim ahoy pangqw tu'amqölngaqw ökye' pu' hakim kiy ep it ngömaapitnit pu' saanat enang uwiknayangwu. Pu' hakim put kwiitsingwuyat aw naakwitantotangwu. Hakim qa maslakyaniqey oovi, pu' piw qa masna'palyaniqey oovi hakim putakw naakwikwitayangwu. Pu' hakim it hiita akw tuu'amqölöt hangwantotaqey hakim put soosok enang kwiikwitayangwu. Noq pu' itam piw pu' pay pas imuy sikisvemuysa piw pu' akw hiitawat mokqat pangsoq tu'amqölmiq paniy'wisngwuniqw, oovi hakim piw pu' pas pokmuy enang pan kwiikwitayangwu.

Pu' haqawa piw kiy ep mokq pep kiihut aasonve piw put kwiikwitayangwu. Paasat pu' hakim yukuyakyangw pu' hakim piw naakwikwitayangwu. Pu' ephaqam pay hakim saanatsa akw naakwikwitayangwu. Yan hopiit mokiwuy ep naavootsiwyangwu, putakw hakim put maasawuy qa na'palyaniqey oovi. Noq oovi hisat hiitawat mokq hakim nanapte', hakim pay paasat kiikiy ang tangalte', pu' pay panaptsava huur hiita tsatsakwmötsapu'ewakw akw utatotangwu. Hakim hisat tuu'amwisqamuy son tiitimayyangwu.

The smoke from burning juniper leaves is said to irritate Maasaw. Hence, when people have interred a deceased and returned from the burial ground, they burn in their home sprigs of juniper together with sap from the same tree. Then they fumigate themselves with the resulting smoke. This custom is practiced so that they will not be afflicted with diseases that are caused by the handling of the corpse. Every tool which was used to excavate the grave is also purified with smoke. And since, nowadays, we utilize only motor vehicles to transport the corpse to the graveyard, people now also purify cars or trucks with smoke.

This ritual also applies when a person dies at his home; the interior of the house is then treated in the same fashion. Once the smoking is completed, people in turn fumigate themselves. Occasionally, juniper resin alone is used. In this manner a Hopi purifies himself so as not to contract the disease of the dead. Thus, in times past, when people became aware of a death, they retreated into their homes and tightly shaded their windows with something like fine cloth. It used to be that people never watched a burial procession.

Unauthorized imitation of the god also results in contracting *masla-kiwta*, "the condition of atrophy."

Hak yaw oovi piw maasawuy qa tututskyaynangwu. Yaw hak pantsakye' maslakngwu.

One should never imitate Maasaw. If one does so, one will contract a disease caused by the god as a result of which one becomes very emaciated.

To prove one's sincerity in a matter a person may, occasionally, wish the state of atrophy upon himself. Since this act of invoking the terrible disease is thought to actually trigger its contraction, Hopis are warned against using this invocation. A similiar phrase, less frequently heard than the one cited in Text 117, is *maasawtinik* signifying "I'd rather become a dead person."

TEXT 117

I' wuuti pi ephaqam koongyay'-tangwu. Put pam aw lööqökqe pu' pam put amum qatungwu. Noq pu' put koongya'at sukw taaqat ismamqasqe pu' pam put taaqat put nöömay kongtotoyna. Noq pu' nööma'at put taaqat qa naawakne' pu' put qa koongyay'taqey aw pangqawu. Pu' pam pas put akw aw qa pevewmaqw, pu' pam pas kya pi itsivutiqe pu' pam koongyay aw pangqawu, "Maslaknik pi put koongyay'ta," aw kitangwu.

Pu' pay pam maasaw kur hin put qa navotngwuniiqe pu' pam put pantsanngwu. Paasat pu' pam okiw paas laakiwma. Hakiy pang-qawqw maasaw hapi yaw navote'

Every so often it happens that a woman takes a mate. After going through the marriage ritual with him, she lives with him. Should her husband then suspect another man of having an affair with his wife, he will accuse that man of being her lover. But if she does not care for him, she will deny that. If her husband continues making these accusations, she may really get angered and say to him, "Rather than having him as my mate I'd like to get as withered as a corpse."

Maasaw is bound to learn of this wish and will strike the woman with the malady of *maslakiwta*. She then begins to dry up like a corpse. People claim that when Maasaw hears someone uttering

pam yaw hakiy qa maatapngwu.
Hak yaw oovi qa pangqawlaw-
ngwu.

this self-malediction, he will not
let that person be. Therefore, one
should not say something like this.

Masvakiwta is a disease which leads to a sickly discoloration of the
patient's skin. It is attributed to Maasaw because the resulting yellowish
tint of the skin appears to match the skin color of a deceased person. The
symptoms of the ailment, for which I have no English identification, are
described in Texts 118 and 119.

TEXT 118

Masvakiwtaqa pay maasawuy
na'paliwme' pam pay suytsepngwat
laakiwmangwu. Pu' piw ephaqam
himuwa mokput aw hintsakqa
pam pay piw masvakngwu, qa
naavootsiwe'.

A person who suffers from *masvakiwta* is afflicted by a Maasaw
disease, and as a result becomes
progressively more emaciated. The
same illness will be contracted by
one who has handled a corpse and
has failed to discharm himself.

TEXT 119

Hak masvakiwte' hak qa suyan
soniwngwu. Hak paasat paas
sikyangpu'iwtangwu. Noq pu'
tiposhoya masvakiwtaqw, put
mapqölngaqw mooti hin'ur mukiitikyangw haqaapiy pu' pam angqw
sikyangputingwu.

When affected by the disease
known as *masvakiwta,* one's entire
appearance is sickly. The person's
skin in particular takes on a
yellowish color. In an infant
suffering from this illness, the
symptoms begin with the palms of
its hands becoming very hot; later
its body begins to turn yellow.

Masawsiiki in Text 120, finally, is a relatively minor skin disease
which is not mentioned in Text 111. It affects the corners of the mouth
in the form of sores and is blamed on Maasaw. The disease, which
literally denotes "Maasaw farted on someone," is triggered by breaking a
taboo which forbids the consumption of food at night, the time when
the god is about. The folk remedy which is also described below calls
for *püki,* one of the offertory ingredients placed at the god's shrine
(see Text 105).

TEXT 120

Hak yaw as hiita qa talpuve qa tuumoytangwu. Hak yaw mihikqw qa talpuve hiita tuumoyte' hak yaw masawsiikikngwu. Pu' hak pantiqw hakiy mo'ayat tupaq ephaqam pas nan'ivaq uyay'vangwu. Pu' hak put powataninik hak piikit angqw hiisakw tuumoytat pu' hak put moykyangw kiy iipoq haqamiwat susyavoqniiqat tuyqayat aqwnen pu' hak ayoqwat paayis kuyvangwu. Paasat pu' hak put tuumoyiy pangso uyay aw tongongoykinangwu. Pantit pu' hak put tuumoyiy pangso tuupelmo piitaknangwu. Pu' sen pang put kiihut tuukwa'at susmataqniqw, pay hak pangso haqami put tuukwat amuutsami tsuruknangwu. Pantit pu' hak pay hiisavo maqaptsiy'tat pu' hak piw ayoqwat suukuyvat pu' hak paasat kiy aapami ahoy supkingwu.

One is not supposed to eat anything during darkness. When one eats things in the dark of the night, Maasaw farts at one. As a result, a person develops sores at both corners of his mouth. To remedy these sores, one chews a small amount of piiki and then, with the piiki still in one's mouth, goes outdoors to the farthest corner of the house. Around that corner one peeps three times. Next one takes the chewed piiki, touches the sores with it, and then one sticks it on the wall. Or, if the mortar beds of the wall are visible, it is inserted between the layers of the building stones. One now waits for a little while, and at some point quickly peeps around the corner once more and rushes back into the house.

9

The Hunting Connection

As Parsons has pointed out, "among all Pueblos there is a close conceptual relationship between killing men and killing prey animals, between hunting and warring organizations" (1939:134). Although not very prominent, traces of such a conceptual link are also observable for Maasaw. Underlying the god's primary aspects centering on a mortuary complex (death, war) and an agricultural one (land, fertility, fire) there exists a faint yet definite substratum of earlier associations with hunting.

Evidence for Maasaw's connection with hunting and, in a broader sense, with game animals, is rather sparse. A marginal link with hunting

185

can perhaps be traced to the fact that the Maasaw-Kookop phratry includes clans with such totemic animals as the coyote, the fox, and the wolf, all of which are known for their crafty hunting skills (Stephen 1936:1071).

One Hopi emergence myth credits Maasaw with teaching to the newly-arrived people "the habits of wild animals" (Stephen 1929:55). According to another tradition the goddess Tiikuywuuti[1] created all the game animals by turning effigies fashioned by the Hopi into living beings.[2] This Mistress of Animals professed to the Hopi that Maasaw "had consented to be the father of the animals."[3] For this reason, "whoever among the young men wished to kill game, would always succeed through offerings made in the morning. That is why young men in former times always went early in the morning to make offerings to Tihkuyi [i.e., Tiikuywuuti] and to Maasaw" (Curtis 1922:191). In yet another narrative Maasaw is found "surrounded by deer and antelope" (Curtis 1922:193).

Personally, I have not been able to collect any new or even confirmatory insights into Maasaw's linkage with Tiikuywuuti. Nor was it possible to get his association with big game animals confirmed. As a rule, the god is linked with rabbits, both jack rabbits and cottontails. This linkage is not insignificant inasmuch as rabbits have ranked among the most important food animals of the Hopi, in prehistoric as well as historic times. Maasaw's special relation to rabbits is manifest from the very fact that he constantly pours their blood over his masked head in order to protect his face from the intensive heat of the fire by which he

---

[1]At Third Mesa *Tii-kuy-wuuti* "Child-sticking-out-woman" is also known as *Tuwapong-tumasi* "Sand-spread-out-clanswoman" or *Tuwapongtumsi,* showing contraction in the final lexeme. The tradition that *Tiikuywuuti* is the wife of Maasaw seems to be primarily established on First Mesa, as a statement of Stephen indicates (1936: 356). Compare also the tales recorded by Curtis (1922: 190-93).

[2]For comparative materials on Tiikuywuuti, mythical mother of all the game animals, see Malotki (1978: 69) and Curtis (1922: 103).

[3]"To a Hopi all the game animals are people, the offspring of Tiikuywuuti, a goddess, the spirit of a woman who was cast out of the tribe at the time of the legendary migration and Maasaw, the earth god" (Nequatewa 1946: 61).

sits (see Text 14). In this context the god is actually characterized as a *maakya*, the Hopi term for "a successful hunter."[4]

TEXT 121

Noq pu' pam yaw piw pas maakya. Pu' yaw pam oovi sowit niine' pu' yaw pam put ungwayat tuwat qötömi wuutangwu.	The god, who is reputed to be a very capable hunter, makes it a habit to pour the blood of his prey on his head whenever he slays a jack rabbit.

Maasaw's intimate relationship with rabbits is also attested in Hopi narratives. While in one story Maasaw, together with Tiikuywuuti, instructs Hopi hunters in the art of reading the tracks of the jack rabbit (Curtis 1922:192), he takes in another tale a quantity of rabbit meat to the girl he is wooing (Voth 1905a:122).

Ceremonially, Maasaw's connection with hunting comes from the fact that he was one of the Hopi gods who were implored for success in hunting by means of prayer offerings. Thus, Beaglehole reports that prior to an antelope or deer hunt a prayer stick was made for the god (1936:6). The same was true in the case of a mountain sheep hunt (1936:9). Stephen notes that "on the night before a rabbit hunt, the young men make eight prayer-feathers for Maasaw, and four for his wife, and deposit them during the night, four for each Maski [i.e., the shrines belonging to Maasaw], and the four for his wife [Tiikuywuuti] on the stairway leading down to Tihkuyiki [correctly *Tiikuyki*, ...the shrine belonging to Tiikuywuuti]. These prayer-feathers are all alike, a single feather from under the eagle's wing and a short cotton string" (1936:1006).

That *nakwakwusi* or "prayer feathers" were fashioned for Maasaw prior to a communal rabbit drive is confirmed in Text 122. This passage is the only authentic Hopi folk text I have been able to record concerning Maasaw's affiliation with the domain of hunting. It is noteworthy, that the prayer feather is made by the *maktunatyay'taqa* or "sponsor of the hunt."

[4]As to Maasaw's expertise in hunting, my own recorded narratives are contradictory on this point. Story 2 (ATR 10) portrays him as a *mapsi*, "a dead shot" who kills a cottontail with his *murikho* or "throwing stick" at first strike. In Story 10 (ATR 10), on the other hand, he hurls his *maawiki* or "club" at a fleeing prairie dog and misses.

TEXT 122

Hak maakiwqw maktunatyay'te'
hak lööqmuy nakwakwustangwu.
Sukw hak it tsa'akmongwit engem
yukungwu, pu' sukwat maasawuy
engem. Pu' hak put sukw tsa'akmongwit aw yawmangwu. Pu' hak
pep put aw pangqawngwu haqe'
maakiwniqat. Pu' hin hakim
mamaqaniqat hak put paas aw
yukungwu. "Ta'ay, yanhaqam oovi
um imuy tootimuy, taataqtuy
aa'awnani," hak kitat pu' put
sukw nakwakwusit tsa'akmongwit
aw tavingwu. Pu' hak mitwat
yawkyangw pu' maasawuy kiiyat
aqw put hom'oytongwu. Pepeq
pu' hak put aw naawaknat pu'
pepeq put nakwakwusit tavit pu'
hak angqw nimangwu.

When a person sponsors a communal hunt he readies two prayer
feathers, one for the town crier,
the other for Maasaw. After
delivering the first to the town
crier, the sponsor informs him
what area is to be covered during
the hunt. He also relates to him,
in detail, how the hunt is to be
carried out. "All right, make it
known in this manner to the young
boys and the men," he declares,
whereupon he presents the town
crier with the prayer feather.
With the second *nakwakwusi* the
sponsor proceeds to the shrine of
Maasaw where he deposits it,
together with some cornmeal.
Having prayed over it he sets it
down and then returns home.

10

Clan Ancestor

The most prominent clans claiming Maasaw as their *wu'ya* or "clan ancient" are the *masngyam,* "Maasaw clan," *kookopngyam,* "Kookop clan," and *isngyam,* "Coyote clan." Totemic connections with the deity are rooted in Maasaw's close affiliation with death, war, and fire. The unnamed phratry to which these three clans belong includes also the *kwanngyam,* "Agave clan people," *paa'isngyam,* "Water coyote clan people," *hovaqapngyam,* "Sagebrush clan people,"[1] *hongyam,* "Juniper

---

[1]Compare Courlander (1982: 14).

clan people," *leengyam*, "Indian millet clan people," and *letayngyam*, "Fox clan people." The intricate relations that exist between some of these clans are alluded to in Texts 123 through 126.

TEXT 123

Ima masngyam pay imuy kookop-ngyamuy amumumyakyangw puma tuwat it maasawuy wu'yay'-yungwa. Put puma tuwat aw naanawaknangwu. Pay kya pi itam haqaqw nöngakkyangw hoyoyoy-kuqw pay pam maasaw pangqw itamum nakwsuqw, pu' puma sinom mooti put haqam aw ökiiqe puma put wu'yay'vayaqe oovi puma masngyam. Noq pu' ima masngyamniqw pu' ima kookop-ngyam pay as pi suukw put hiita maasawuy wu'yay'kyaakyangw puma pay piw tuwat qa pas suuvo toonavit. Noq imuy pas masngya-muy amungaqw pu' pay kya qa hak pas peeti. Pu' imuy pay kookop-ngyamuy amungaqw yepeq hotvel-peq pay naat qa suukya qatu.

The members of the Maasaw clan are associated with the Kookop clan, and both claim Maasaw as their clan deity or ancestor. They, too, pray to him for their needs. When we set forth from the site of our emergence, Maasaw jour-neyed along. The group who first encountered him made him its clan totem and for this reason is the Maasaw clan. But although both the Maasaw and the Kookop clan regard Maasaw as their clan ancestor, they do not constitute a single group. While the Maasaw clan seems to be extinct today, several members of the Kookop clan still live at the village of Hotvela.

TEXT 124

Puma hapi kookopngyam pay piw masngyam, put hapi maasawuy puma wu'yay'yungqe oovi'o. Nii-kyangw pamwa maasaw, pumuy wu'ya'am, pam yaw pay nukpana.

Pu' puma kookopngyam it uuwi-ngwuy, töövut himuy'yungwa. Noq i' maasaw pay piw puuvut enang himuy'kyangw pam tuwat mihikqw put qööhiy'numngwu. Niiqe puma kookopngyam oovi put wu'yay

The people of the Kookop clan are also considered Maasaw clan people, due to the fact that Maasaw is their clan ancestor. Their Maasaw, however, is said to be evil.

The Kookop clan people also own fire and embers. Maasaw, too, is the possessor of these things and lights his way with them on his nightly treks. Thus, the Kookop group and their clan ancestor have

peep su'anyungwa. Noq pam maasaw son pi qa imuy masngyamuy sen kwanngyamuy sen imuy kookopngyamuy hin hak qööngwuniqw pumuy tutuwnaqw oovi pumangyam pu' put himuy'yungwa.

a great deal in common. Most likely, Maasaw taught the members of the Maasaw clan, the Agave clan, and the Kookop clan the knowledge of making fire, which accounts for the fact that they own it now.

TEXT 125

Ima kookopngyam tuwat it maasawuy wu'yay'yungwa. Pu' pumuy amungaqw piw ima qaqleetaqtyangwu. Pu' puma piw it kwanwimit himuy'yungwa. Pu' puma piw tuwat imuy masngyamuynit imuy isngyamuy amumumyangwu.

The members of the Kookop clan, who have Maasaw as their totem, used to supply warriors in the past. They also own the Kwan society and share a phratry with the Maasaw and Coyote clans.

TEXT 126

Pu' ima hiitu hongyam as piw naatyangwuniiqe puma as imuy kookopngyamuy, masngyamuy amumumyangwu. Noq pay pi hintiqw puma tuwat suupyangwu. Sen pi i' kookopngyamuy, masngyamuy wu'ya'am maasaw put hohut laapuyat kopitsokiy'tangwuniqw oovi.

When the *hongyam* or "Juniper clan" still existed, it was together in one phratry with the Kookop clan and the Maasaw clan. Why they were grouped with the latter is uncertain. Perhaps because Maasaw, their clan ancestor, uses the bark of the juniper tree for his torch.

Within the phratry, close ties seem to have existed especially between *masngyam* and *kookopngyam*. While this fact is already clear from Text 124, it must be added that members of the two clans dressed identically in competitive races. In these races the participants formerly represented their clans. To indicate their clan affiliation, the runners of the Maasaw and Kookop clans wore the costume "of [the] Maasaw impersonator, with red cloth on [their] head to represent his bloody head, rabbit-skin garment draped across the body with the left shoulder bare, and sometimes a cedar-bark torch" (Titiev 1939:38). On the other hand, Coyote clan members, who also regard Maasaw as their *wu'ya*, wore "cornhusks fashioned into long coyote ears and attached to the head."

Furthermore, in their name-giving practices both clans draw from attributes and characteristics which are associated with the god. The names *Maasaw* and *Masawhoya*, "Little Maasaw," were thus reserved for name donors whose clan affiliation was *maswungwa* or "Maasaw clan member." Two names transmitted in this context by Voth are *Moto'ma*, "going along with head bent down," and *Nasiwaytiwa*. While the former alludes to a typical posture of the deity, *nasi*, denoting "adornment anywhere on one's body," the latter is supposed to refer to the *kokoma* or "dark purple corn ear" carried by Maasaw as decoration on his back (1905b:93).

Among names attributed to name donors of the Kookop clan we find *Kopitsoki*, "cedar bark torch," *Maawiki*, "Maasaw's club," *Tsiptima*, "to be shuffling along," the characteristic gait of Maasaw, *Na'uywayma*, "to be walking along stealthily and without making a noise," as Maasaw who might approach a person in this fashion to scare him, *Tuuwala*, "to guard," an allusion to one of the god's primary functions. A number of names display fire references. *Qööhi* simply denotes "fire," *Uwtima*, "to go along flaming up," has to do with his torch. Both *Kookosi*, "to get embers" and *Kookosto*, "to go and fetch hot embers," relate to the practice of borrowing fire from a neighbor if an unattended fire happens to go out. *Tövuhoyta*, "glowing coals are moving along," probably alludes to Maasaw's glowing eyes at night. *Tövuhoyiwma*, captures the motion of "sparks flying" from his firebrand. *Taatalawva*, which means "a light is going on and off," also points to the erratic behavior of the god's fiery torch.

The warlike behavior of the *kookopngyam*, or "Kookop clan members," is emphasized throughout the literature. Held to be the most aggressive of all Hopi clans, its people, according to one legend, deliberately persuaded a group of *Tsimwaawam*, the Hopi term for the "Chemehuevis," "huge men with gigantic feet, supposedly the worst enemies of the Hopi" (Titiiev 1944:155), to attack the village of Orayvi in order to compel Matsito, the village leader, to use their services as defenders. After their repulsion of the invasion, and their admittance into the community of Orayvi, the Kookop clan re-established the *motswimi*, "Warrior society," that had been extinct for nearly three generations.

The etymology of Kookop has long puzzled Hopi ethnographers. As an eponymous clan label it is, invariably, linked to the group's strong associations with fire and wood. Hence, one finds translations such as "fire" (Waters 1963:44), "firewood" (Courlander 1972:23), "cedarwood" (Parsons in Stephen 1936:1067), and "charcoal" (Lowie 1929:

309). Whiting assigns to the Second Mesa form *Kokof-* [correctly *Kookov-*] the value "juniper." Hopis themselves connect the term with *koho* "wood" or *kopitsoki* "cedar bark torch." Linguistically, none of these interpretations are tenable.

While the etymon of Kookop- must thus be left to remain obscure, the clan is also said to own the bird *kokophoya* as a *wu'ya* or "clan totem." The bird, which according to Hopi ornithological lore sleeps during the day — a probable allusion to Maasaw's antithetical behavior of sleeping during daylight hours — is identified as "black-throated sparrow" by Bradfield (1974:74). However, the above-mentioned trait of the bird's sleeping during the day seems to be much more in tune with *koko*, "the burrowing owl." Interestingly enough, Crane, in an episode involving the Kookop clan, calls the latter "Ghost-and-Bird clan" (1926: 165). This binomial label obviously refers to the two clan ancestors of the group, with "ghost" alluding to Maasaw and "bird" relating to *kokophoya*.

TEXT 127

Kookopngyam pi antsa tuwat it maasawuy wu'yay'yungwa. Niiqe puma oovi tuwat put enang aw yankyaakyangw yeese. Puma pay piw put hiisakwhoyat tsirot, kokophoyat, enang wu'yay'yungqe oovi kookopngyam yan maamatsiwya. Pam piw pay pumuy himu'amniqw oovi puma put pookoy'yungwa. Puma kya put hongvi'ayay'yungwa sonqeniiqe oovi tuwat put piw enang naatoylay'yungwa.

It is well known that the members of the Kookop clan claim Maasaw as their clan ancestor and look to him for aid in their daily lives. In addition, they consider the black-throated sparrow as their clan totem. From this small bird, whose Hopi term is *kokophoya*, they also derive their name. Since it belongs to them, they possess him as a pet. He is probably their guardian and, for that reason, they use his name to designate their clan group.

Within Hopi society, the overall importance of the Kookop clan, which is based on its special relationship with Maasaw, is further strengthened by the fact that the clan is said to be entrusted with the Pööqangw brothers, Pöqangwhoya and Palöngawhoya, as well as with *kookyangwso'wuuti*, "Old Spider Woman." Kookop ownership of these powerful deities is manifest from Texts 128 and 129.

TEXT 128

Hotvelpe puma kookopngyam pumuy pöqangwhoyatuy taviy'yungwa. Pu' pay pep pumuy kookopngyamuy kiiyamuy ep pam maasaw piw qatu. Niikyangw pam pay piw suukyawa maasaw. Pam hapi pay songyawnen pöqangwhoyatuy taaha'am. Noq oovi pay qa suukya pep hotvelpe put yorikiy'ta. Pas yaw pam qööhi kwangwahoyoyotangwu, hiihintsakmangwu. Niikyangw pam yaw sutsep pangsoq put maasawuy kivayat aw pakingwu. Pu' pangqw piw ahoy yamakye' pu' piw pangso kookopngyamuy kiiyamuy awhaqaminingwu. Pu' pay qa qööhininik pay yaw himu silaqvuningwu.

Pu' soyalangwuy ep puma pas suyan pangqw yamakngwu, lööyöm. Pu' mi' qööhi'am yang ayoq hoopoqhaqami nangkningwu. Puma kivanawit nakwsungwu.

The Kookop clan at Hotvela houses the two Pööqangw brothers. Maasaw also resides in the same house, but this is another Maasaw. His relationship to the two brothers is more or less that of an uncle. Quite a few Hotvela villagers have seen a fire there. It is said to move along nicely, doing all sorts of things. It never fails to enter the kiva belonging to Maasaw, and after emerging from it (the fire) proceeds to the home of the Kookop clan. And if the god does not manifest himself by fire, he uses cornhusk instead.

During the Soyal ceremony assuredly two Maasaw personages emerge from this place. Their fires then move eastward, one following the other. They go from kiva to kiva.

TEXT 129

Niikyangw pu' puma kookkopngyam piw pumuy pöqangwhoyatuy enang taviy'yungwa. Suupan as puma pay pumuy paysoq haqamyaqe oovi pumuy taviy'yungqw, kur puma kya pi piw pas pumuy makiwa'am. Niiqe oovi puma son suupan qa pumuy soyamuy, it kookyangwso'wuutit, piw enang taviy'yungwni. Noq pam kur pas piw pumuyngyamuy himu'am. Pu' pay puma naa-

The Kookop clan also owns the two Pööqangw brothers, Pöqangwhoya and Palöngawhoya. One might have thought that they keep them only because they found them somewhere, but apparently they were entrusted with them. Thus it seems probable that they would also have in their charge Old Spider Woman, grandmother of the Pööqangw boys. Evidently she truly belongs to them. The two brothers are quite mischievous.

tupkom pi tuwat panta, qahop-
hoyat. Noq pay naamahin puma
pantaqw, pay hiitawat ti'at mööö-
yi'at hiita akw tuutuye' okiwhin-
taqw pu' himuwa pangso pumuy
amumi put tuutuyqat wikqw, pu'
pam kookopwungwa put tuumoy-
toynaqw pu' pam piw öqawtangwu.

In spite of this character trait of
theirs, a child or grandchild who
is ailing, or is in some other sad
state, will be taken to them,
whereupon a Kookop clan member
will take a piece of food from his
mouth and feed it to the child.
Thereafter the child will gain its
strength again.

Because of their special ties with Maasaw, the Kookop people are
said to have been the first allowed to enter the bamboo in their climb to
the upper world. "We are the ones who are entitled to go first, for
Maasaw is our special benefactor. We shall take the lead" (Courlander
1972:30). After the emergence, however, when requested by the other
Hopi to assume the leadership role also during the upcoming migrations,
they declined and declared, "We shall be responsible only for ourselves"
(Courlander 1972:39). This early mythological incident is possibly the
origin for the widely-held view that Kookop affiliates have always been
troublemakers. More important in this connection, however, seems to be
a statement in Text 124 which brands their clan *wu'ya* Maasaw as a
nukpana or "evil being." Text 130 actually speaks of two Maasaw personages. Since the existence of two Maasaws, with radically different
character profiles, is still quite prevalent among older consultants at
Third Mesa today, and since this belief has never been attested to in
the literature before, I will document it as broadly as practical below. It
is noteworthy that Text 130 identifies the benevolent Maasaw as *wuko-
maasaw*, "big or great Maasaw."

TEXT 130

Pay pi it tuutuwutsit ang pan
lavaytangwuniqw pam maasaw yep
tuuwaqatsit ep kiy'ta. Noq itam
hopiit tuwat pan navotiy'yungqw
pam mooti yep tuuwaqatsit ep
qatuqw itam hopiit pew nönga.
Niikyangw pam maasaw pay
orayve huruutiqe pam orayviy
taavangqöyveq kiy'ta. Noq put
wukomaasaw kitotangwu. Pam pas

Hopi folk narratives relate that
Maasaw lives on this earth. Tradition also has it that he was the
first inhabitant of the earth when
we Hopi made our emergence.
He permanently stationed himself
at Orayvi where he resides on the
southwest side of the village. This
Maasaw is referred to as *Wuko-
maasaw* or "Great Maasaw." He

wukomongwi. Noq pu' oovi i'
wukomaasaw pi pay sinmuy tumalay'kyangw qatu. Pam sinmuy
amungem nukngwat qatsitniqat
pay putsa tuwat tunatyawta. Pam
pay pas nu'okwa. Pam qa hisat
hakiy yuuyuyna.

Noq pu' ayaqwat piw orayviy
hopqöyveq piw suukya maasaw
kiy'ta. Pumawat kookopngyam
pepeq put wu'yay'yungwa, maa-
sawuyu. Pu' puma piw it kookyangwso'wuutit pöqangwhoyatuy
piw amumum soy'yungwa. Noq
ima kookopngyam puma pan qa
nun'okwat, puma soq sinmuy
yuuyuynayangwu. Yan hisat sinom
put yu'a'atota. Puma qa hopiitniiqe sinmuy soq yuuyuynayangwu-
niqw oovi kookopngyam panyungwa hotvelpeq.

holds an extremely high position,
and he lives tending to the needs
of the people. His only desire is
to provide a good life for the
people. He is very compassionate
and has never molested anyone.

Another Maasaw resides on the
northeast side of Orayvi. The
Kookop clan has him as its clan
ancestor there. This clan also
claims Old Spider Woman as its
grandmother, together with the
two Pööqangw brothers. The
Kookop people are without heart
because they do bad things to
people. This is what was said
about them long ago. They are
evil and harm other people,
characteristics which also apply to
members of the Kookop clan in
Hotvela.

The Kookop clan members, who were characterized in Text 130 as
evil people without compassion, are also reputed to use their malevolent
wu'ya to achieve their means. This may be gathered from Texts 131 and
132.

TEXT 131

Pay nu' pan navotiy'taqw ima
kookopngyam it hiita maasawuy
wu'yay'yungqw pumuy wu'ya'am
yaw tootsiy'ta. Pu' pamwa pumuy
wu'ya'am yaw piw nukpanmaa-
sawu. Pay ephaqam yaw puma put
aw hin nunu'ingyaqw, pay yaw
pam pumuy nakwhane' pu' pay
hakiy hintsanngwuniiqat pay
kitotangwu. Pam yaw pay nukpananiiqe pay yaw soq sinot
hintsanngwu.

To my knowledge, the members of
the Kookop clan consider Maasaw
as their clan ancestor. This Maasaw is said to wear shoes and is
characterized as a malevolent
being. At times, Kookop clan
members may ask him to perform
certain tasks for them. If he grants
their wishes, he can bring harm to
a person. Because he is wicked,
he will abuse people.

TEXT 132

Pamwa pumuy kookopngyamuy wu'ya'am, maasaw, pam pay nukpana. Pam yaw soq ephaqam hiitawat pay aw nukpantingwu. Pam yaw hakiy tuukyayanik pay hakiy pantingwu. Pam qa nu'okwaniiqe pam oovi paniqw nukpana. Pam it hiita nukpantawit himuy'taqe oovi pam hakiy putakw maslaknangwu.

Pu' mi'wa maasaw orayve qatuuqa pam pay qa nukpananiiqe oovi pam pay son hakiy pantsanmantani. Pam pay pas soosokmuy sinmuy paas. Ispi pam pumuy sinmuy atkyaqw pew nöngaknaqe oovi pam qa hakiy iingyala.

The Maasaw, who is regarded as the clan ancestor of the Kookop people, is considered to be an evil being. Every so often he does wicked things to someone. For instance, if he so desires, he will place a bewitched object in a person's body which will cause that person to become ill. He is without mercy and consequently malevolent. He knows a song by means of which he can make a person as emaciated as the dead.

The Maasaw who resides at Orayvi, on the other hand, is not evil and would never treat anyone this way. He is gentle to everybody, and because he permitted those living in the underworld to emerge into this world, he has no animosity against anyone.

A comprehensive view of how the "good" Maasaw differs from his "evil" counterpart is given in Text 133. Twice it points to the fact that the "good" Maasaw walks barefoot, whereas the "evil" one wears shoes (see also Text 131). In addition, the latter will reveal himself to man. He will harm people when so requested by his clan proteges. This point may be a reference to the weapons and diseases the god is believed to own.

TEXT 133

Niiqe oovi lööyöm maasawt'u. Suukyawa kookopngyamuy wu'ya-'am, pam hapi nukpana, pam tootsiy'ta. Pu' mi'wa kwaakwantuy amumumningwuqa, qa totstaqa, pamwa itamuy paas tumalay'ta, pam hapi lomamaasaw. I' maasaw hapi pas qa atsat

Consequently there are two Maasaws. One of them, the clan ancestor of the Kookop clan, is evil. He also wears shoes. The other, who is affiliated with the Kwan society, walks barefoot and really sees to our needs. He is the good Maasaw. He truly exists, but

qatuqw put hakiy itam pay qa
tuwiy'yungwa. Pam tookilnawit
sopkyawatuy sinmuy pu' piw aqwhaqami hiituy yesqamuy, hiihiituy
tutskwava poninitotaqamuy tumalay'ta. Nuy navotiy'taqw pam
orayve qatu.

Noq pu' i'wa sungwa'at piw suukya
maasaw, pam imuywatuy kookopngyamuy wu'ya'amniikyangw
pamwa yaw pay nukpana. Pam
yaw pay hakiy aw naamataqtangwu. Pam imuy kookopngyamuy
wu'ya'am pay yaw pan nukpanat
makiway'ta. Pu' putwat piw pangqaqwangwu pam tootsiy'taqat. Pu'
i'wa qa totstaqa pam yep itamuy
tumalay'ta.

I'wa nukpananiiqa pam hakiy hiita
akw hintsanniqey paniqw oovi pam
tunipit himuy'ta. Putakw pam
sinmuy okiwsaasantima. Pu' ima
kookopngyam put aw yanyungqe
paniqw oovi puma hakiy putakw
aw rohomtotingwu. Pu' oovi
haqawa hinwat put hakiy aqw
hingqawqw, pu' pam put navote'
pu' pam wu'yay aw taqa'nangwti-
ngwu. "Ta'ay, um it yantsanni.
Um it inungem yantiqw pay pam
tatam qa qalaptuni." Puma hiita
ep hintsaniwye', kur put ep naa-
tuhotote', puma hapi putakw
wu'yay tuwiyat akw sinot tuwat
tuuwayaniqey, amyaniqey it yan
tunatyaltotingwu.

Noq pu' i' itamuy tumalay'maqa
pas qa atsat maasaw. Pam itamuy
hin lolmat qatsiyesniqat, qa
haqam hiita akw ö'öpul'kyaa-

we are unfamiliar with him.
Throughout the night he watches
over all the people wherever they
may live, and takes care of all
living things that roam the earth.
According to my knowledge he
lives at Orayvi.

His associate, on the other hand,
a different Maasaw, is the clan
ancestor of the Kookop group and
one who is thought to be malevolent. He, it is claimed, will
reveal himself to a person. The
clan deity of the Kookop group is
endowed with evil. While he is
said to be wearing shoes, the
barefooted Maasaw is the one who
takes care of us.

The evil Maasaw possesses a
weapon with which he can harm
people. He uses it to make people
suffer. Since the Kookop people
rely on him for assistance, they
resist others by drawing on his
powers. Hence, if a Kookop man
is criticized by an outsider and
becomes aware of it, he calls upon
his clan ancestor for help. "All
right, you bring harm upon this
person. Having done that for me,
I hope that he will never get well
again." In instances where Kookop
members have been harmed to the
extent that they hurt, they strive
to do away or strike dead the
offender by using the knowhow of
their clan ancestor.

The one taking care of us is the
true Maasaw. His concern is for
us to live a good life, to go through

kyangw wuyomiq itaaqatsiy naavo-
kyawintiwisniqat, yan pam tuwat
tunatyawkyangw itamuy tumalay'ma.

life without suffering, and to enjoy
a full life into old age.

Figure 14.—Maasaw petroglyph at Tutuventiwngwu (Willow Springs, AZ).
According to a member of the Maasaw clan, the glyph specifically portrays
the *nukpanmaasaw* or "evil Maasaw." This interpretation is based on the
bow associated with it on the right, linking the figure with fighting and war.
For some Hopis this association only applies to the "evil" Maasaw, never to
the "good" one. Photograph by E. Malotki.

Whether the tradition of two Maasaw figures is of long standing, and whether it can be traced back to trouble with the Kookop clan that the Hopi already experienced in mythic times, must remain speculative. I tend to think that it may already have been established prior to the Orayvi schism in 1906—the Yukiwma speech in Text 134 implies that. I also believe that the general idea was reinforced parallel with Maasaw's rise to the near-monotheistic position of "Great Spirit" (see Chapter 14). When a new, positive Maasaw took shape in the form of the "Great Spirit," the old Maasaw with all his negative connotations was simply left behind, or rather consigned exclusively to the Kookop clan that had claimed the god since time immemorial anyway.

The final Text in regard to this subject matter constitutes a speech. It was—allegedly—given by Yukiwma, one of the most important figures among the conservative Hopis who, in 1906, emigrated from Orayvi to found the village of Hotvela. [2]

TEXT 134

I' hak wuutaqa, yukiwma, pam piw kookopwungwa. Niiqe pam piw put maasawuy pi wu'yay'taqe pam it itamumi yu'a'atangwu: "Uma hapi qa iwu'yay amumyani. Uma hapi qa itamumyani. Uma hapi pas itaatimu. Uma hapi hakiy pas itaatahay as timatnii-kyangw uma hapi qa inumumyani. Uma pay imuy kwaakwantuy amumyani. Itam kookopngyam hapi maasawuy piw amumya. Nii-kyangw puma kwaakwant pay piw yep maasawuy amumyaqw oovi uma pay pumuywatuy amumyani. Puma kwaakwant hapi pas qa hakiy ii'ingyalya. Puma soosokmuy sinmuy paasya. Uma hapi pumuy amum pew mooti ökiiqe pay oovi uma pumuy amumyani. Uma oovi

The old man Yukiwma happened to be a Kookop clan member. Naturally, his clan ancestor was Maasaw and he used to say to us, "Don't you follow my ancestor, don't be a part of our group! Granted, you are our children by blood; you are the children of our uncle, but don't go along with us. Rather follow the members of the Kwan society. We Kookop clan people go with one Maasaw, the Kwan members with another, so unite with them. They don't push anyone aside and are kind to all people. When you first came upon this earth, you were accompanied by them, so team up with them. Don't even think of joining us. For if you associate with them,

[2] See Titiev (1944: 83 and 86).

qa itamumyaniqey anyungwni. Pay
uma pumuywatuy oovi amumye'
pay uma qenit ang hinwisni,"
kitangwu itamumi pam yukiwma.
"Noq itam oovi hapi pas qa
nun'okwat. Niikyangw itam kyaa-
hakit wu'yay'yungwa. Pam kyaa-
hakiniikyangw pam pay nukpana.
Pam qa hakiy engem hiita lolmat
wuuwanta. Pam pay piw qa yep
tutskwat himuy'ta. Pay i' yep
mooti qatuuqa pam hapi put
himuy'ta. Noq oovi uma putwat
amumyani. Kwaakwant put
amumya. Niiqe puma kwaakwant
hapi put maasawuy amum tutskwat himuy'yungqw oovi uma
hapi pay pumuy amumyani. Nen
uma qenit angyani. Itam hapi
pay qa qenivayani. Itam pay
nukpanat, pay hakiy niinangwuqat
wu'yay'yungqe oovi itam qa hakiy
engem hiita nukngwat, lolmat
wuuwantota. Niiqe oovi itam
paniqw a'ni i'tsivut'u. Itam hakiy
pay hintsatsnangwu. Noq oovi
uma qa itamumyani," kitalaw-
ngwu itamumi.

you'll be on the right path. We
aren't merciful in the least. Our
clan ancestor is rich and evil at
the same time. He doesn't consider
doing anything good for anyone,
nor does he own this land. It's
true owner is the first inhabitant
of this earth. He, therefore, is the
one you should associate with.
The Kwan members are together
with him and own the land jointly
with Maasaw. So by all means,
go with them. If you do, you will
follow the correct path. We
Kookop people will stray away
from what is right. We have a
clan ancestor who is evil and will
kill, therefore we are not bent on
doing good and nice things for
others. That's why we are very
hostile and do unkind things to
people. For this reason you must
not join us." Yukiwma would say
this over and over to us.

11

The Trickster

The concept that Maasaw should be associated with trickery is at first difficult to accept. Yet it is a trait of the god which in Hopi folklore becomes manifest again and again. "Maasaw is a thief, a liar, and very jealous, also a persistent practical joker. He made trees grow gnarly and crooked and twists men's faces into ridiculous shapes so that he could laugh at them. He not only played tricks upon men and inanimate things, but upon the other gods also" (Stephen 1929:56).

Most of Maasaw's tricks involve some change of appearance. The device which is symbolic of the god's control over his own appearance is, of course, his mask. The mask, which stands for death and decay, can be removed and allows the god to transform himself into the shape of a handsome man embodying life and growth. If we consider Maasaw's power to cause fundamental changes, including the ultimate change from life to death, the trickster concept does not appear as detached from the god's essence anymore. For an essentially supernatural being, capable "of the metamorphosis of life in nature," as Stephen has characterized him (Wade 1980:17), transformational ability of this caliber can be regarded as trickery on a very "high level."

It is not too surprising if the god, in addition to "high level trickery," stoops to "low level" pranks in the medium of entertaining folktales. Thus, Maasaw scares a dance visitor out of his wits by first appearing to him as a normal person, and then changing into a repulsive creature (Story 3, ATR 10). To gain entrance to a maiden's grinding chamber, on the other hand, he turns himself into an attractive youth (Story 1, ATR 10), and to satisfy his lecherous inclinations toward the Hopi womanfolk he mingles with them in the guise of a Navajo meat trader (Story 8, ATR 10). Titiev has passed down a "true story" in which Maasaw, in the guise of the chief's son from Songoopavi, decided to call on an Orayvi girl who had rejected all her suitors (1972:188).

Hand in hand with trickery, of course, go deception and lying. Maasaw engages in both. In Story 5, (ATR 10), to obtain the girl's consent to have intercourse with him, he not only approached her in the shape of her grandmother but came up with the fantastic excuse that women in their old age do grow a penis. In Story 15 (ATR 10), while calling on a beautiful maiden, Maasaw uttered a downright lie when giving the reason why he happened to be in the area.

One unmarried girl, whose heart was set on rings and bracelets, was deceived into marriage by means of fake jewelry. Fashioned from giant dropseed and yucca leaves, the rings and bracelets exist as jewelry during the night, but change back into their original plant materials during the day (Story 14, ATR 10). To another girl who is grinding corn, Maasaw offered entertainment in the form of a song to lighten her chore, only to sing a ditty with horror lyrics and "shout her to death" at the end of his performance (Story 1, ATR 10).

The arch-trickster Coyote is led on by the god to believe that he might succeed in outfrightening him, only to be tricked into perdition by Maasaw when he failed to remove the mask fashioned in the god's image.

As is borne out in one Hopi folk account, not even the other Hopi gods were safe from the tricks of Maasaw. In a tale collected by Stephen, the god employed the device of singing, to play a prank on them (1929: 55-57). The pertinent episode is summarized by Stephen in another location as follows: "One day the gods were assembled in council to sing and dance, as is their custom at certain seasons, and Maasaw also came carrying a bundle under his arm. The gods looked askance at him, but with the plausible manners he assumed he won their permission to join them. Toward the close of the festival each one sang a song, and when it came Maasaw's turn, so soothing an influence did his song possess that all the gods became drowsy and were soon fast asleep. Maasaw, still continuing his song, opened his bundle and, producing an effigy of himself, arranged it in a posture similar to the others, with head on knees fast asleep. He then ran to the mountain top and began rolling great stones down upon them. The gods thus rudely wakened by the crashing noise were at a loss to account for it, for there sat the mischievous one, fast asleep. One of them, presently trying to wake him, disclosed the effigy and their anger was increased when they perceived Maasaw mocking them upon the mountain top. After a lengthy chase... the gods overtook him and administered a severe punishment" (Wade 1980:17).

Archetypal tricksters, as Carr points out, are almost universally and forever presented as giving in to one of their baser appetites, "excessive sexuality" (1979:20). This trickster attribute, so prevalent in several of the stories, can, in the case of Maasaw, also be connected to his fertility aspect. Maasaw, as a lecher, is vividly portrayed in Stories 5 and 8 (ATR 10). His sexual intentions are obvious, too, in Story 2 (ATR 10). Not only does he suggest to the protagonist, a little boy, that indeed he would like to visit his mother, he also displays a great deal of curiosity about her thighs, especially their degree of whiteness.[1] In return, the boy's mother calls Maasaw a *nuvötaqa*, which in this context approximates the notion of our "dirty old man" counterpart.

In story 3 (ATR 10), Maasaw professes to an Orayvi man that "he gets to see the thighs and vulvas of women all the time." This is confirmed in the story by a Hopi from Walpi who regards the god as his clan ancestor. He explains to the Orayvi visitor that Maasaw "actually grabs hold of women, which makes him so familiar with them."

While a number of Maasaw's tricks and pranks may be termed childish, he once in a while displays behavior that actually is that of a child or dupe. Thus, in the context of Story 3 (ATR 10), Maasaw is berated by the Walpi man as one who must have "the brain of a child" to indulge in practical jokes of the kind he has just performed.

Obviously, such a characterization of Maasaw is rather incongruent in the light of the powerful god he is. In Story 12 (ATR 10), this portrayal of the god goes even one step further. There, he is cast in the role of a fear-stricken, fleeing imbecile who in his ignorance, is horrified

---

[1]Compare the Glossary in ATR 10 under "White Thigh."

by something which later turns out to be feathers in the Hopis' hair.
Here, Maasaw comes pretty close to one folk dimension of Coyote, in
which he is depicted as a gullible dupe and buffoon. I do not think,
though, that this is the intention of the story. Rather, I believe that
Hopi folklore, in this instance, tries to cope psychologically with a figure
most dreaded in real life. Just as in German folktales the devil, abhorred
and feared in real life, is outtricked again and again, so Maasaw, whose
very name strikes horror in the hearts of the living Hopi, is occasionally
reduced to the level of a childish, laughable fool.

Patron of the Kwan Society

The *kwaakwant* (singular form *kwaaniy'taqa*) as the "members of the *kwanwimi*," commonly rendered "Kwan, Agave, or One Horn society," enjoy some most intimate relationships with Maasaw, the god of death. Like the god himself, who sometimes is seen in the role of a psychopomp escorting the dead souls on their journey to Maski, the "Home of the dead," Kwan men also are charged with this duty. And since they act as Maasaw's servants in the netherworld, "the One Horn society is the most powerful of all Hopi sacred societies or fraternities and is regarded with great awe by the Hopi" (Nequatewa 1936:126).

Deriving their name from *kwaani*, the Hopi botanical label for our
"agave," "mescal," or "century plant," they were originally controlled by
the *masngyam* or "Maasaw clan." Because Maasaw is considered the *wu'ya*,
the "clan ancestor or progenitor" of the Maasaw clan, the leader of this
clan normally acts as *kwanmongwi* or "Kwan society head." In keeping
with their close affiliation with Maasaw, and with the latter's death-
dealing powers, the members of this society are supposed to fear neither
death nor the dead. It is quite fitting, therefore, if they and their patron
are distinguished by a number of antithetical traits. "Whereas all other
officers apply chiefs' markings under their right eyes and on their left
shoulders, arms, and legs, the Kwan men apply their chiefs' markings in
reverse fashion" (Titiev 1944:175). Voth has pointed out a significant
deviation in their practice of drawing cornmeal lines to represent the
six directions. In the case of marking the Below direction, instead of
sprinkling the meal from the southwest, as is customary, it was done from
the northwest (1912b:116). Nequatewa, finally, indicates that when
initiates of the One Horn society die, "their spirits cannot return to visit
the living in the form of white clouds, as is the privilege of most spirits,
but must forever remain in the underworld" (1936:126).[1]

Because the *kwaakwant* worship Maasaw as their "father," they are
referred to as *maskwakwant*. This nickname is slightly derogatory. By the
same token, the *kwankiva* or "Agave kiva" is also known as *maskiva*,
"Maasaw kiva." The Kwan society has long ceased to be a viable entity
within the ceremonial framework of the Third Mesa culture complex.
What indigenous information I have been able to obtain concerning the
perception of the society, as well as its crucial role during the Wuwtsim
ceremony, which now is also defunct at Third Mesa, is recorded in full
below.[2]

TEXT 135

Pu' ima kookopngyam antsa it
kwanwimit epya asa'. Niikyangw
pu' peqwhaqami puma put qa-
hiitatota. Noq pu' puma kwaa-

The Kookop clan was once in
charge of the Kwan society but
now has no respect for it anymore.
Because the Wuwtsim ceremony

[1] With the demise of the *masngyam* or Maasaw clan, control of the Kwan fraternity
was passed on to the *kookopngyam* or Kookop clan.

[2] For additional data on the Kwan fraternity the following works should be consulted:
Fewkes (1895 and 1900), Fewkes and Stephen (1892), Parsons (1923) and Stephen
(1936:957-93).

kwant tuwat put maasawuy nay'-
yungwa. Pay pi i' wuwtsim it
maasawuy pi himu'atniqw oovi
pam maasaw pay pi son as qa
sutsep pumuy kwaakwantuy
amumumningwu. Noq pu' oovi
pam kwaaniy'taqa piw mit qööhit
pay piw maasawuy himuyat enang
tumaltangwu. Pu' paasat i' maasaw
pumuy kwaakwantuy yungyiwtaqw,
pay as pi pam sonqa amumum
epeqningwuniqw put pay
puma qa tuway'numyangwu.
Puma pi pay piw put maasawuy
kivayat epyangwu. Pu' pumuy
kwaakwantuy oovi piw amumiq
pangqaqwangwu, kori'voskwa-
kwant. Songyawnen pi puma yaw
maamastniqw oovi pumuy amumiq
pangqaqwangwu. Noq maasaw pi
kori'voningwu. Pu' puma hapi
kwaakwant maasawuy nay'yungqe
oovi pay put maasawuy qa mam-
qasya.

Noq pu' pam maasaw piw pep
kwankivaape kiy'ta. Pu' himuwa
yaw pep puwqw pu' yaw pam
hiitawat pep aw pitungwu, aqw
pakingwu. Niikyangw pam yaw
mit silaqvut akw piw waynumngwuniiqe oovi pam pangsoq
pakye' pam yaw putakw pangqe
hoyoyotimangwu. Niiqe himuwa
oovi pay putsa tuwangwu. Pam
pay hakiy qa pas aw naamataqtanik pay putakwningwu.

Angvut yaw mihikqw haqe' hoyo-
yotinumqw pam yaw pay maasaw-
ningwu. Oovi kwankivaape puwni-

belongs to Maasaw, he is probably
always together with the Kwan
society. For this reason the Kwan
members also involve fire in their
functions, which is the property of
Maasaw. Whenever they are
assembled for their rituals, Maasaw is most likely there among
them although they are unable
to see him. They are gathered,
of course, within the kiva that is
owned by Maasaw. Due to their
close association with the god the
initiates of the Kwan society are
derogatorily nicknamed "hollow-
eyed Kwan members." People refer
to them by this name just as if
they were a lot of Maasaw creatures or "dead beings." Obviously,
the above appellation has its origin
in the hollow eye sockets, which
are one of Maasaw's facial features,
Because the Kwan society members
have Maasaw as their father, they
never fear him.

The Kwan kiva itself is one of
Maasaw's abodes. There are stories
which relate, that when a man
spends the night in that kiva,
Maasaw usually enters and reveals
his existence to him. He is said to
walk about by means of a dried
cornhusk. That is his mode of
transportation whenever he enters.
That is all that one finds, for he
uses the piece of husk only when
he does not wish to reveal his
true being.

People insist that any piece of
cornhusk seen moving along at
night represents Maasaw. Therefore, it is a frightening experience

niqw is uti. Kur pi himuwa pep
puwngwu. Pi maasaw pangsoni-
ngwu.

to sleep inside the Kwan kiva.
How anyone can sleep there at all
is beyond my comprehension, since
the place is visited by the god.

The belief that Maasaw leaves behind dried cornhusks as tell-tale
evidence of his existence is still widely held among the Hopi. The following Text constitutes a detailed folk testimonial to this extent. The account
neatly illustrates how a personal encounter with Maasaw is "coped with"
in Hopi society. At the same time, it underlines the intricate position
which the god occupies in the Hopis' view of themselves and their world.

TEXT 136

Pay pi antsa lavaytangwuniqw pay
yaw i' himu hak qataymataq
qatuuqa, maasaw, pam yaw antsa
yep imuy kwaakwantuy amumum
yannumngwu. Pay pi puma tuwat
put aw enang yankyaakyangw
wiimiy hintsatskyaqw oovi pam
songyawnen pumuy mongwi'am.
Noq pam yaw pep kwankivaape
kiy'ta. Niiqe pay pi antsa pam aw
mihikqw pakingwu. Pay pam put
kiva'atniqw pam oovi pangso pi
hintiqw piw pas sonqa pakingwu.

Noq pay antsa pi nu' navotiy'taqw
yaw hakim tootim piw hisat pep
kivaape kya pi tokni. Noq naat
yaw oovi puma qa tokqe yaw
puma nanaptaqw yaw antsa saaqa
paroskikiyku. Noq piw yaw ang
himu hintsaktima. Yaw silaqvu
ang tsipipitimaqat puma lavayta.
Niiqe pu' yaw pam himu pangqw
oongaqw hawkyangw pu' yaw
tuwat saaqat suyvaqewat aw
atkyami haawi. Pu' yaw pam pang
saaqat teevenge' aw atkyami haw-

Again and again people say that
Maasaw, the being that exists
unseen, goes about accompanying
the members of the Kwan society.
He is like their leader because they
depend on him while conducting
their ceremony. He is said to dwell
at the Kwan kiva and, therefore,
frequents this place during his
nightly round. Why he always
comes into the kiva is a mystery.

The following account I have truly
heard. Some young men once
wanted to spend the night in the
Kwan kiva. They had not yet
fallen asleep when they heard the
kiva ladder make a creaking noise.
No doubt, something was moving
down the ladder. The men agreed
that a piece of husk was shuffling
noisily along. After its descent,
whatever the thing was, it continued on down to the lower
portion of the kiva. In doing so
it chose to go around the left or
western side of the ladder which
is not the proper side to step down

kyangw pu' angqe pan tsipipitima-
kyangw yaw aqw tuwakimiq. Niiqe
son pi pangsoq hiita piw qa
pasiwna.

Noq pam maasaw pangso papkiqa
piw yaw antsa putakw waynumngwu, silaqvut akwa'. Noq yaw
puma tootim pan put yoyrikyaqw,
antsa yaw pam hiita aqw pan oyat
pu' aqw pasiwna. Niiqe pu' yaw
pam ahoyniikyangw pu' yaw pam
put pookoy pephaqam aw qöp-
qömi yeskyaakyangw tsootsong-
yangwuniqw pangso yaw kur pam
put maatapt pu' yamakma. Pu'
son pi qa ang haqe'ningwuniiqey
pang nakwsu.

Pu' pam maasaw pan pumuy
tootimuy amumi naamaataknaqe
amumi pan songyawnen lavayti,
"Pay nu' qatuqw uma nuy peevewnaya. Uma nuy peevewnayaqw
oovi nu' yep umumi namtakna.
Niikyangw uma pay qa pas pas
inumi yorikya."

Noq pu' ima pep tokqam qavongvaqw yesvakyangw pu' antsa put
silaqvut tutwa. Noq naat yaw
antsa pam pangsoq qopqomiq
qaatsi. Pu' yaw puma aw pan
wuuwaya. Pay kur pam pas antsa
putakw waynumngwu. Noq pu'
puma yan it pep kivaape hakiy
wukw'ayay aw it yan lavaytaqw,
pu' yaw pam amumi pangqawu,
"Owi, pay pam pew papki. Noq
uma peevewnaya. Pay pam yang
itamuy tumalay'ma. Niikyangw
pay pam hakiy qa hintsanngwu.

to the lower floor. It then shuffled
over to the niche at the north end
of the kiva, which is considered a
shrine. The men assumed that the
being transferred its intentions into
this shrine.

The being who frequents this
place is Maasaw, of course, and he
is said to travel about by means of
a cornhusk. The young men truly
witnessed the god place some
things into the niche and transfer
his intentions into the shrine. On
his way back he abandoned the
husk, his transportation device, by
the firepit, where the men generally sit and smoke their pipes. Then
he made his exit and continued on
his usual route.

Revealing himself to these young
men was like telling them, "Yes,
I exist. You, however, doubt my
existence. Because you don't
believe in me, I showed myself to
you. But you did not see my true
appearance."

When the men who slept there
that night rose the following
morning, they really discovered the
cornhusk. It still lay by the firepit.
As the men pondered the evidence,
they really had to admit that
Maasaw used the husk as a mode
of travel. They then related their
experience to an elder of that
Kiva who said to them, "Of course
he keeps entering this kiva. You
were skeptical. Day after day he
looks after us, yet he never harms
anyone. The only thing that can
happen to a person is that he

Pay panissa hak pantingwu,
mashuruutingwu. Pu' piw hak
put peevewnaqw pam hapi hakiy
pantsanngwu. Pu' meh himuwa
a'ni unangway'te' paavan hingqawlawngwu, "Piw pakiqw nu' ngu-
'ani. Pay nu' amum naayawvani,"
yaayan hingqawlawngwu himuwa.
Pu' antsa pam piw pay put navotngwuniiqe oovi piw aw pite' paasat
pu' pam put hintsanngwu. Niiqe
oovi pam hakiy mashuruutapna-
ngwu. Pu' himuwa as a'ni hingqawlawngwu. Hak aw unangwtap-
niqat oovi töötöqngwu. Niikyangw
pam pi mashuru'iwtangwuniiqe
oovi qa suyan hingqawlawngwu,
paysoq naawalawngwu. A'ni as
töötöqqey wuuwantangwu. Niikyangw naat qa hak aw unangw-
tapqw pay pam put maatapngwu.
Pam hak a'ni tunatyawtaqa
lavayiy, tunatyay naat qa aw
antiqw, pay pam yamakye' pu' piw
angqe' nakwsungwu. Noq pay pam
pas antsa pangso papki."

Pu' yukwat piw imuy kookopngyamuy kiiyamuy pam piw aw wup-
ngwu. Pu' pam pangso papkiqe
pam piw oovi sonyawnen tumsimuy
awningwu. Imuy kookopngyamuy
kiiyamuy ep piw pam suukyawa
maasaw, pumuy wu'ya'am, pi
qatu. Noq pay son pi puma naami
piw hin qa pavasiwnaqw oovi
pamwa pangso piw pootat pu' piw
angqe' nakwsungwu.

Noq pay pam maasaw pi pangso
kwankivami pootangwuniqw oovi
himuwa haqam aw pitungwu,

freezes from fright at the sight of
the god. He may also affect a
disbeliever in this manner. For
example, a bold and headstrong
man may brag, 'When he enters
once more, I'll grab him. I'll
fight him.' Maasaw, of course,
hears the man boasting, and the
next time he approaches him he
frightens him out of his wits and
throws him into a state of shock.
The man now tries to shout something. Because he wants help, he
attempts to scream. But because
he is frozen stiff from fear, he does
not make himself clear. All he can
do is moan, yet, he thinks he's
yelling loudly. Before anyone
comes to his aid, Maasaw lets go
of him. This boaster who had
such great plans, never has a
chance to realize them because
Maasaw already has departed from
the kiva and continues on his
nightly patrol. It is really true
that he enters that place on a
regular basis."

The god also ascends to the home
of the Kookop clan. Since he
frequently enters that location, he
goes to the house of his female
clan relatives as it were. There,
at the home of the Kookop clan
another Maasaw resides. I'm
almost positive that the two make
some sort of arrangement whereby
the great Maasaw simply looks in
and then continues on his nightly
round.

When checking in on the Kwan
kiva, someone may cross Maasaw's
path or bypass him. The person

aasawvangwu. Pu' himuwa kya
pi aw yorikye' pu' pangqawngwu,
pay pam pas antsa qatuuqat.
Niikyangw pam yaw it hiita
suqömvösaalat son pi qa pas
hopivöqniwtaqat usnumngwu.

Pankyangw pu' yaw hak piw
wupataqa. Pu' pay pi qa kwatsva-
kiwkyangw put haqawat aw nam-
taknangwuniqw oovi angaapuyaw-
tangwuqat aw yortotaqam pangqaqwangwu. A'ni yaw hak angay'-
ta. Pay kya pi qa suukya aw yori.
Noq pay pam kya pi hiitawat aw
pansa namtaknangwu. Niiqe pay
songyawnen, "Pay nu' suyan
qatu," yan put aa'awnangwuniiqe
oovi pay haqawat qa hinwat
hintsanngwu, pay qa mashuruu-
tapnangwu. Pu' piw yaw hakiy
aasawve' pay yaw piw hakiy qa aw
hingqawngwu. Pay yan piw it pep
kivaape lavaytangwuniqw pay nu'
qa suukw pay aw yan tuqayiy'ta.

who spots him will naturally
maintain that the god truly exists.
People claim that he goes about
wrapped in a black blanket, which
is probably woven Hopi style.

They also say that he is tall in
stature. Since he reveals himself
unmasked, those who have seen
him state that his hair flows over
his shoulders in long tresses. Quite
a number of people have apparently caught a glimpse of him.
Revealing himself in this manner is
tantamount to him saying, "I
certainly live." For this reason he
does not harm the person who sees
him, nor does he frighten him
into a state of shock. Also, he
never speaks a word as he passes
by someone. Things like these
also used to be discussed there at
the kiva, and I have listened to
more than one person's narration
of this sort.

Kwan men play a crucial role during a *wuwtsimnatnga* or "Wuwtsim initiation." Reserved only for Hopi males, this most sacred of all Hopi rituals is referred to, by way of English circumlocution, as "Tribal Initiation" or "Manhood Initiation." Titiev, in his analysis of the cere-mony, lists three major objectives: "First, to confer manhood on boys; second, to establish co-ordination between living and dead members of the societies; and third, to renew the contacts between the populations of this world and the next" (1944:136). For this manhood initiation a candidate has the choice between four participating groups, the *kwaa-kwant, aa'alt, taatawkyam,* and *wuwtsimt.* Of these, the Kwan fraternity seems to have been the least desirable. It is followed, by degree of in-creasing popularity, by the Al, Taw, and Wuwtsim branches.

With Maasaw, god of death, as their patron deity, the mortuary associations of the *kwaakwant* are manifold. At one point in the course of the lengthy Wuwtsim ritual they stage a public dance which, in addition to the living Hopi, is said to be also observed by the Hopi dead.

TEXT 137

Noq pu' kyelmuyva natngay'- yungqw ep ima kwaakwant tuwat suutokihaq nöönöngangwu. Nen pu' puma pep kiisonve tiikivey'- yungngwu. Puma pangqw kivay angqw nöngakye' pu' puma paasat pangqw naanguy'kyaakyangw pu' hiita tawkyaakyangw pangso kiisonmi hoytiwisngwu. Noq naat pay pumuy kwaakwantuy qa nönakqw, ima aa'alt pumuy kwaakwantuy amungem naalöp kiisonve wupakotqatotangwu. Noq pu' puma kwaakwant aw ökiwisqw pu' puma aa'alt put ang uwimna- yaqw, pu' paasat pep kiisonve suyan taalawvangwu.

Noq pu' puma aw tiivantiwise' puma a'hohoytiwisngwu. Pansa puma aw hoytangwu. Niiqe pu' puma oovi kiskyangaqw aw kii- sonmi kuukuyvat pu' pay piw ahoy aqwhaqami tuutuwayat pu' piw ahoy angqaqwyangwu. Naa- nahoy puma pantsakwisngwu. Noq hakim teevep amumi maqaptsiy'- yungngwu. Pu' ason puma pangso yungye' paasat pu' puma haqe'wat oovi piw leetsiltingwu. Pu' puma kwaakwant pangso kiisonmi ökye' pu' puma pep tiivangwu. Nii- kyangw pu' puma piw suvaqhokya- tikyaakyangw pep tiivangwu. Noq pu' yaw yangqw tatkyaqw oongaqw imawat mongkivangaqw wuwtsimt

When a Wuwtsim initiation is held during the lunar month of Kyelmuya (approximately Novem- ber), the members of the Kwan society emerge from their kiva at midnight and then dance at the plaza. After leaving their kiva, they proceed toward the plaza holding one another's hands and chanting at the same time. Prior to the appearance of the Kwan society members, members of the Al society already have erected four stacks of wood for them within the plaza. As the Kwan members then near the plaza, the Al members set fire to these wood piles, brightly illuminating the plaza interior.

On their way to the plaza the dancing of the *Kwaakwant* or "Kwan members" typically involves both advancing and retreating movements. This is the only method by which they move to their destination. For example, they will appear from a covered alleyway, disappear back into it, only to reemerge a little later. There is a constant back and forth, and the spectators need to wait for them a long time. Once they have entered the plaza, they line up and then begin to dance. As they perform, they simultane- ously stick out the right leg bend- ing it at the knee to the beat of their song. Meanwhile, from a rooftop on the south side the Wuwtsim society members of the

yaw tuwat hiita taatawlalwangwu.
Noq pay pi as pam taawi'am
hiihinyungqw pay nu' put qa
hiitawat pas suyan taawi'ta.

Mong kiva sing various songs.
Since these songs are very intricate,
I do not know any of them by
heart.

Niikyangw oovi sinom paasat
taavangqwniikyangw pu' piw
hoopaqwsa tiitimayyangwu. Noq
oovi kwiningyaqw qa hak tiimay-
ngwu. Pangqw yaw ima mamsam
tuwat qeniy'yungngwuniiqe puma
yaw tuwat pangqwtiitimayyangwu.
Noq pay kay pi oovi ima mamsam
piw titimaysontningwuniiqe oovi
ep piw ökingwu.

Spectators at this time witness the
dance only from the west and east
sides of the plaza. No one watches
from the north side for this side is
said to be reserved for the dead
who observe the performance from
there. I guess, they crave to
watch a dance and therefore
show up at this occasion.

Prior to the actual *natnga* or "initiation," which takes place on the
night of Astotokya, "four of the Kwan men who had been inducted into
the society at the preceding Tribal Initiation are delegated, secretly, to
visit the local graveyard and to strip four recently interred corpses of
their burial garments. There the four Kwan members dress in the foul-
smelling grave-clothes, and soon after, they appear before the startled
neophytes in dimly-lighted kivas where they are readily mistaken by the
terror-stricken novices for the very dead men whose apparel they wear"
(Titiev 1944:136).

Many of the esoteric aspects of the actual initiation have never been
witnessed by cultural outsiders. While the above episode of the grave-
clothes stems from "a deposition made by a Christian Hopi who was
condemning the ceremony" (Titiev 1944:136), the following "practice,"
described by Titiev, constitutes an educated assumption on his part and
must be left to hypothetical speculation. "From the behavior of impersonators of Maasaw in other rituals, and from the well-known Hopi
belief that a touch from Maasaw's club causes death," he suggests "that
the Kwan chief appears at this time in the guise of Maasaw, god of
death, and simulates the killing of the tyros by touching them with the
club" (1944:126).

Text 138, which was volunteered to me, is a confirmation for the
presence of Maasaw during Astotokya.

TEXT 138

I' wuwtsim pi pay it maasawuy
himu'atniqw oovi wuwtsimnatngat
ep hintsatskyaqw i' maasaw pas
naap ep pitungwu. I' astotokya
nalöstalqat epningwu. Noq ep
puma wuwtsimt imuy kyekyelhoy-
muy hawiwmiq tsamye' pu' puma
pepeq pumuy hiita tuwitotoyna-
yangwu. Noq pay pi pangqaqwangwuniqw pay yaw piw pepeq
nuutsel'ewaytingwu. Hak yaw oovi
pas taaqanen yaw put ang ayo'
yamakngwu. Pu' pay yaw himuwa
piw tsako'nangwanen putakw piw
tsawne' pam yaw aapiy putakw
pas tuutuylawngwu.

The Wuwtsim ritual is the property of Maasaw; hence he is
personally in attendance during a
Wuwtsim initiation. Astotokya, the
night on which the "hair washing"
takes place, occurs on the fourth
day of the ceremony. At that time
the members of the Wuwtsim
society take their novices to the
Hawiwvi kiva where they reveal to
them the esoteric part of their
ritual. Those who have experienced
it relate that it is both a hideous and
terrifying ordeal. Therefore, one
needs to be extremely brave to
undergo and complete this rite.
If a person is timid and becomes
frightened, they say that this will
result in his constantly being ill.

Astotokya, "hair-washing or initiation night," has been termed an
"All Souls ceremony for the dead" (Tyler 1964:36). It is distinguished by
the belief that the dead, referred to as *mamsam* or *maamast*, which are
plural forms of *maasaw*, return to visit their home villages on this night.

TEXT 139

Noq pu' paasat tapkiwmaqw naat
pay puma qa hawiwmiqyaqw pu'
ima sinom hopkyaqe kiy'yungqam
paasat pay tuwat teevengewat
watkitangwu. Nen pu' puma
pangqe teevengeqe kiinawit waa-
tangaltingwu. Ima sinom pangsoq
watqe' pu' puma pangqe kiinawit
huur tangawtangwu. Panaptsava
puma huur utatotangwu. Pay pi
angqe' pi qa himu wiiqöhiningwu-
niqw oovi pep aasonve hihin

By the time evening approaches,
and still before the initiates have
been taken to Hawiwvi, all residents of the eastern section of the
village begin to flee to the west
side to seek refuge there within
the homes. Upon taking shelter
there, they remain indoors without
coming out. All the windows are
covered tightly, and since in the
old days kerosene lanterns had
not yet been introduced, there was

talngwu. Noq pu' hakim ep
tokninik hakim pangsoqwat
talvewisa qötöy'yungngwuniiqat
pangqaqwangwu.

Noq pu' hopkyaqe sinom kiikiy
ang it nöösiwqat imuy maamastuy
amungem tunösvongyaatotangwu.
Puma pay it tsaqaphoyat angqw it
öngavatnit pu' pay hiisa' piikit
enang tunösvongyaatotangwu. Pay
oovi puma piw qa pas hiita loma-
tsaqaphoyat ang put oyaatota-
ngwu. Pu' puma oovi pay piw
kiikiy qa ang utatotat pu' pang
put tunösvongya'iwtaqat maatatve-
ngwu.

Pu' paasat puma mamsam hisatniqw tuwat ökye' pu' puma pang
put tuwat noonovangwu. Pu'
puma mamsam put pay qa pas
suyan soswangwu. Puma pay put
nöösiwqat söviwangwuyat, hovala-
ngwuyat huttote' pay pan puma
tuwat put nöönösangwu.

hardly any light. When sleeping
on this night of Astotokya, people
are supposed to lie with their
heads pointed in the direction of
the rising sun.

Along the east side of the village,
which is now deserted, the people
prior to their leaving also spread
out food for the dead. They set
out small vessels containing boiled
beans along with some piiki.
Interesting in this connection is
that the bowls for the beans were
always quite shabby. The doors
to the houses are not shut and
the food is left sitting there.

The moment the dead arrive they
feast on the dishes provided for
them. However, they do not really
consume the food. They merely
inhale its steam and smell its
aroma. In this way the dead
partake of a meal.

Before the night ceremony gets underway, all access roads into the
village are barred except for the path to the northwest, the direction of
Maski, from which the dead spirits are expected. The task of closing and
guarding the access points falls to the Kwan society.

TEXT 140

Noq pu' pay naat pay qa pas
tapkiqw pu' ima kwaakwant ang
haqe' pangso kiimi pöhuniqw
puma pang put hoomay, mongkoy
akw utatotangwu. Puma pantote'
puma hoomay akw pang naalökye'
tutuwuutotangwu, qa hak hapi
sino pangso kiimi sasqaniqat oovi.

Before sundown the members of
the Kwan society seal off every
road leading into the village. This
is accomplished by drawing four
lines across a given trail with
sacred cornmeal. No person can
now enter the village. Once all
accessways are closed off, the

Puma put pang utatote' pu' puma put ang tunatyawyungngwu. Niikyangw puma suukw it pöhut taavangqwniiqat qa uutayangwu. Pangqw hapi yaw ima mamsam ahoy pangso kiimiyangwuniqw oovi pam pang pay pumuysa amungem hötsiwtangwu.

Kwaakwant keep an eye on them. Only one trail is not blocked, the one which leads into the village from the northwest. It is from this direction that the dead return to the village, and this path is kept open only for them.

In the course of Astotokya, members of both the Kwan and Al societies act as patrols. In the case of the Kwan men, their para-military policing functions seem to represent a direct tie to Maasaw's role as a war god. Also, of the two groups acting as sentries, the Kwan definitely appear the fiercer and more warlike. Titiev actually characterizes the society as "a warrior's group." To this effect the Kwan are found "painting themselves with typical warrior markings and carrying long lances as part of their equipment" (1944:135).

TEXT 141

Noq pu' paasat hisatniqw qa taalawvaqw pu' ima kwaakwant imuy aa'altuy amumum nöngakye' pu' puma kiinawit tuutuwalangwu, qa hak hapi ang waynumniqat oovi. Paasat pu' aw haykyal'iwmaqw pu' puma paasat pas nahalayvitote' puma paasat pas ang pisoqyaktangwu. Paasat yaw oovi hin töötöqngwu, tis ima aa'alt suulövaqw yöngösonay'yungngwuniqw oovi. Pu' ima kwaakwant piw eyokinpiy'numyangwu. Paasat yaw hin töötöqe' nuutsel'ewaytingwu. Hisatniqw pu' kya pi pas aw pituqw paasat pu' puma kwaakwantniqw aa'alt piw a'ni na'qalannumyakyangw pu' paasat piw pas ang yuyuttinumyangwu. Himuwa yaw haqam hiitawat aw pite' pu' yaw aw pangqawngwu,

As soon as night has fallen, the members of the Kwan and Al societies emerge from their kivas and mill about the village acting as sentries. No uninitiated person must be abroad. As the climax of the evening is nearing, they quicken their pace and rush around. At this time there is quite a din, caused primarily by the Al members, who wear tortoise-shell rattles on each leg, and the Kwan members, who carry their bells around. This cacaphony of sounds creates a dreadful atmosphere. At the hour of the initiation the members of the Kwan and Al societies go about shouting words of encouragement at each other. By this time they are actually running. As one en-

"Öqawmangwuy!" yaw aw kitangwu, niikyangw pas tönay anga'.
Yanhaqam yaw puma piw ep
hingqawnumyangwu. Pas pi yaw
oovi hin töötöqngwu.

counters another, he shouts, "Go
with strength!" at the top his voice.
This phrase they all go about
screaming on this occasion. There
is a pandemonium of eerie sounds.

The Hopi reasoning for the nightly patrols of the *kwaakwant* and
aa'lt are given in Text 142. The Kwan men are expected to deal more
viciously with an intruder than the Al men. They actually are privileged
to put him to death.

TEXT 142

Pay pi hopi hiita hintsakqw pay i'
himu nukpana pas son haqam piw
qe'ningwu. Noq pay pi son oovi
qa paniqw ima aa'altniqw pu'
puma kwaakwant ep astotokpe
mihikqw taltimi tuwalanyakta-
ngwu.

Pu' pay ephaqam himuwa piw
hiita pas hin naap yorikniqey
antangwu. Pay itam soosoyam
panyungwa. Niiqe oovi himuwa
pan hiita yorikniqey naawaknaqa
pam pi pay son haqam qa na'u-
yiy'tangwu. Pu' paasat hisatniqw
hin hiniwmaniqat aw pituqw, pu'
pam pangqw na'uyiy'kyangw pu'
pumuy amumi taytangwu. Niikyangw puma kwaakwantniqw pu'
aa'alt pay yaw pas son piw put
qa tutwangwu, naamahin pam
haqaqw huur na'uyiy'taqw. Noq
qa hak hapi pumuy amumi tayta-
niqw oovi puma paniqw pang
yaktangwu. Ispi pam hak pan
nana'uyvewat amumi taytaqa qa
wimkyaningwuniqw oovi. I' hapi
pas himuniqw oovi puma son
naap hakiy it aw maataknayani.

Whenever the Hopi conduct a
ceremony, evil forces are always
present. This must be the reason
for the Kwan and Al members to
act as guards until the morning
following the night of Astotokya.

In addition, people are curious
and feel like personally witnessing
an event. All of us have this
characteristic. The person wishing
to view such proceedings will
usually conceal himself at some
spot. From his hiding place he
will then watch the society members as the esoteric action takes
place. But the Kwan and Al men
are bound to discover such a
person even though he is well
hidden. They do not want anyone
to observe their ritual, hence the
reason for their patrolling the
area. As a rule, the person watch-
ing secretly is not a member of
these societies. The initiation is so
sacred that they will not reveal it
to just anyone. Consequently, they

Oovi puma piw put qa yu'a'atotangwu.

Pu' kur sen hak qa wimkya, qa
amumum put hintsakqa, pangqe'
waynumniniqw, pu' ima kwaakwant yaw put tutwe' puma yaw
put pay niinayat pu' put tutkitotat
pu' paasat put sikwiyat haqami
hom'oywisngwu. Niikyangw hiisavo
pi pas puma haqami nankwusat
pu' put hom'o'yat pu' angqw ahoy-
yangwu. Noq pay pi haqawat
pangqaqwangwuniqw ason yaw
pam kwaaniy'taqa pas haqami
maangu'e' pangso yaw pam paa-
savonit pu' put hom'oyt pu' angqw
ahoyningwu.

Noq pu' ima aa'alt kur mooti put
tutwe' puma yaw pay put qa
niinayat puma pay put yaw kivay
aqw wikye' pu' puma put pangsoq
panayangwu. Niikyangw puma
yaw put pangsoq pay pas tuuvayangwu. Noq pu' ima aa'ltniqw
pu' kwaakwant piw pep kiive hakiy
sungsaq tutwe' puma yaw put
hakiy oovi naanaqasyangwu. Qa
puma kwaakwant aw mooti öki-
niqat oovi puma aa'alt pas put
hakiy aw pisoqtotingwu.

also never talk about this in their
conversations.

When an uninitiated person or one
not participating in the ceremony
is around at that time, and spotted
by the members of the Kwan
society, they will slay him, cut his
corpse into pieces, and then take
his flesh someplace to dispose of
it along with some sacred cornmeal. How far they travel to rid
themselves of the corpse before
they return is not known. Some
believe a Kwan man will go as far
as his endurance will carry him.
At the place where he tires he will
deposit the pieces of flesh with the
cornmeal and then return.

In case the members of the Al
society first catch sight of the
trespasser, they do not kill him;
instead they take him to their kiva
and place him inside. They literally throw him in through the hatch
in the roof. Also, should the Aa'alt
and Kwaakwant discover a person
at the same time, they vie for him.
The Al members hurry to the
person as fast as they can so that
the Kwan members do not get to
him first.

The morning after the conclusion of Astotokya it becomes once
again the duty of the Kwan members to open the roads to the village.
The episode, in Text 143, shows Maasaw's respect for the ceremonial
closure of the roads by the men who serve him, and illustrates just how
intimate are their ties with the god of death.

Qavongvaqw pu' puma kwaakwant ang ahoy pöhut hötaatotanik puma pang pönawit ahoyye' paasat pu' puma mongkoy akw pang ahoy hötaatotangwu. Noq paasat pu' ima sinom ep tokinen teevenge watqaqam ahoy kiikiy angye' paasat pu' puma put ang tunösvongya'iwtaqat pu' tuwat put kwayngyavoq maspawisngwu.

Noq nu' hisat piw it navotq yaw ep puma kwaakwant put pöhut uutayaqw, yaw ep qavongvaqw pam yaw suukya kwaaniy'taqa haqe' pöhut uutsiwtaqw pangsoniiqe yaw aw pituqw, piw yaw naat pephaqam i' maasaw pööpamiq uutsiwtaqat aqw qatu. Pay pang hapi yaw naat pas uutsiwtaqw, pam yaw naamahin as a'ni himuniikyangw yaw put uutsiwtaqat kyaptsitaqe oovi qa pay naat paasat ang yamakt pay haak pep qatuptu. Pu' yaw pam kwaaniy'taqa pas put engem pang ahoy hötaqw, paasat pu' yaw pam maasaw tuwat haqami nakwsu.

The morning following Astotokya, when the Kwan initiates open the access roads to the village again, they go back to these trails and, using the *mongko* indicating their society affiliation, carry out this task. At this point the people, who on the previous evening took asylum on the west side, return to their homes. Then they gather up the food which had been laid out for the dead and go cast it out on the dumps along the outskirts of the village.

I once heard that on one such morning after the closing of the trails, one of the Kwan members found Maasaw sitting at the spot where the path had been sealed off. It was still unopened, and even though Maasaw is a powerful being, he respected the closure and instead of transgressing it, had squatted down to wait. It was only after the Kwan man had lifted the ceremonial blockade that Maasaw continued onward.

13

The Kachina Connection

In accordance with the Hopi view of things the *masawkatsina*,
"Masaw kachina," is held to be a very ancient kachina. Appearing in
both male and female forms, this kachina seems to represent certain
aspects of Maasaw. What these aspects are is not exactly certain, however. While the conceptual link with Maasaw as death personage is
clearly established on linguistic grounds, it is not so obvious that the
kachina embodies the essence of death. For this reason the kachina name
will not be rendered as "Death kachina" here, but in English translation
will simply be labeled "Maasaw kachina." All the while, that it is Maasaw's primary association with death which is represented, and not his

227

role as owner of the land, fire or crops, is evident from the many antithetical attributes and characteristics Masaw kachinas are endowed with.
Just as death is the opposite of life, so they do many things that are the
reverse of normal expectancy. Text 144 points to a number of these
antithetical traits. Most notable in this regard is the fact that *masawkatsinam* are the only Hopi kachinas that may appear any time of the
year. They appear even during the proscribed season.

TEXT 144

Ima peetu katsinam pay suyan
masawkatsinam yan maamatsiwya.
Noq puma pi son pi qa put pas
maasawuy tu'awiy'yungqe oovi. Pu'
hopiit pay pumuy katsintotaqe pu'
pay amumi hihin nukngwat,
lolmat yuwsinayaqw oovi puma qa
pas nuutsel'e'wayom. Noq hintiqw
pi oovi pam piw masawkatsina.
Pam hin masawkatsinaniwtiqw put
pay qa hak navotiy'ta. It pas
maasawuy pay qa hak pas suyan
yorikiy'taqe oovi hak put katsin-
taqa son pas put su'an soniwqat
yuku.

Pu' ima masawkatsinam, puma
pay qa mimuywatuy katsinmuy
pas suyan amunyungqe oovi puma
pay orayviy yepeq hopqöyvehaq
haqam pokkiveq kiy'yungwa.
Pepehaq haqam kya pi yaasay-
haqam aqw koroy'taqw pangqw
yaw puma kiy'yungwa, hiitu
masawkatsinam. Noq pay pi pepeq
son pi qa pan wuuyaq tuuwiy'taqw,
oovi puma pepehaq pang tuuwik
leetsiwkyangw tuwanlalwangwu,
pan ökininik. Pay hintiqw pi
oovi puma piw tuwat qa kivaape-
yangwu.

There are some kachinas who are
clearly known as *masawkatsinam*
or "Masaw kachinas." They most
certainly represent Maasaw, hence
their name. When made into
kachinas by the Hopi, they were
given costumes somewhat nicer
and better than the outfit worn
by the god. Therefore, they do not
look quite so grotesque. Why a
kachina symbolizing Maasaw
actually exists is anybody's guess.
No one knows how he came into
being. Since nobody is really
familiar with Maasaw's exact
appearance, the person who first
made him a kachina cannot have
portrayed him accurately.

The Masaw kachinas differ from
all other kachinas in that they
reside at Pokki, a shrine of their
own, on the east side of Orayvi.
There they live in a big hole in the
cliff. There must be a wide ledge
running along there which allows
them to line up and practice their
dance steps when they plan to
make an appearance, for they are
never seen rehearsing in a kiva. No
one knows why they do not re-
hearse in a kiva.

Pu' mimawat katsinam pi aye'
kiisiwuy, pu' nuvatukya'oviy,
sa'lakoy, weenimay, paavang puma
put ang haqe' kiy'yungwa. Noq
pu' ima katsinam paamuyve ökye'
puma pay yukiq nimaniwuy aqw
paasavo ökiwtangwu. Yangqe'
tala'kyamuyvahaqe' ima ninma-
niqam kuukuyvangwu. Pu' pumuy
ninmaqw hopi pangso katsinawuy
as hintsakngwu. Noq ep puma
ninme' puma katsinkimiq ninmangwu. Pu' ima momoyam pumuy
aqw piw kuuyiy'wise', puma yaw
pumuy tsöqa'asiyamuy akw tsöqa-
tote', pu' akw pumuy amumiq
uutayangwuqat pay hakimuy
amumi kitotangwu. Pu' pay hakimuy amumi pangqaqwangwu,
puma pumuy haqami tangatote'
pu' amumiq tukw'uutayangwuqat
kitotangwu. Noq kur puma hapi
pumuy putakw paahomyangwu-
niiqe oovi hakimuy tsaatsakwmuy-
niqw amumi pangqaqwangwu. Pay
pi himu naat qa wimkyat aw
tupkiwtangwuniqw oovi hakimuy
amumi pangqaqwangwu puma
pumuy aqw uutayaniqey.

Noq pu' i' nimaniwuy pas yukiltiqw paasat as pay qa himu
haqam katsinaningwu. Niikyangw
aapiy pantaqw pu' pay ima masawkatsinam ökininik puma pay
tuho'osvahaqe' ökingwu. Puma pay
naap hisat ökingwu, puma pi pay
qa mimuywatuy katsinmuy amunyungqe oovi. Puma pi pay maamastniiqe oovi hopi hin tuwiy'taqw
puma put qa an hintsatskya. Niiqe
puma pay oovi naap hisat ökingwu,
naamahin mimawat katsinam
soosoy pas kiikiy ang ahoyyaqw.

The other kachinas have their
homes in various places such as
Kiisiwu, Nuvatukya'ovi, Sa'lako,
and Weenima. They arrive in the
month of Paamuya (approximately
January) and then make frequent
appearances until the time of the
Niman ceremony, which is completed by the Home dancers in
summer during the month of
Kyaamuya (approximately July).
Upon their return home the
kachina season officially ends. The
destination of their journey home
at this time is the shrine Katsinki.
On this occasion, when the women
haul water to the shrine, they tell
people that they will seal up the
kachinas. They say they will do
this by making a mud mixture of
body paint and water, putting all
the kachinas in one place, and
sealing them off with a wall. In
reality the women simply go to the
shrine to give the dancers a bath,
but use this explanation for uninitiated children.

After the completion of the Niman
or "Homegoing" ceremony, no
kachinas are supposed to appear.
If, however, the Masaw kachinas
have a desire to come, they usually
do so in the fall, quite some time
after the Niman dance. Actually,
they can appear at any time since
they are unlike the other kachinas.
They represent the dead and
therefore do not conform to
established Hopi ways. For this
reason they may arrive at any
time, even though the other
kachinas have all returned home.

Pu' puma piw pay pas hiituniiqe oovi puma pay qa aasakis yaasangwuy ang haqam tiivangwu, pay ephaqamtiqwsa. Pu' puma pay piw katsinmuy su'amun tiivangwuniikyangw pu' puma pay piw pumuy amun naap tawvöy'yungwa. Pu' i' masawkatsina pay piw mimuywatuy katsinmuy su'amun putngaqwwat potsatsatangwuniiqe oovi pangqw yöngösontangwu.

Also, because they are powerful beings, they do not perform every year, only once in a great while. Their manner of dancing resembles that of other kachinas, but their song melodies are distinctly their own. Like the latter they also use their right feet in stomping their dance steps, and so they wear a turtle shell rattle on their right leg.

Masaw kachinas typically perform in the plaza during the daytime and in the late afternoon, but will also dance at night in kiva performances. Furthermore, the kachina may act as a *kipokkatsina* or "Fighting kachina" (Voth 1912a:1). Wright adds that the kachina may also appear during the Patsavu as a pair and participate with the *wawarkatsinam* or "Runner kachinas" as a racer (1973:254). None of my informants were able to confirm either of these assertions.

TEXT 145

Noq pu' pay kya pi puma ephaqam pas tiikivey'yungngwu, pu' ephaqam pay puma tatapkiqwyangwu. Pu' puma pay pas mihikqwsa mooti ökingwu. Pu' puma ahoy taalö' ökininik puma pay haqami katsinkimiqwat ninmangwu. Pu' puma pay qa ahoy ökininik puma pay ayoq pokkimiqwat ninmangwu. Noq oovi pumuy mihikqw ökiqw pumuy amumi tunatyaltotingwunen pu' haqamiwat ninmaqw pu' sinom suyan navotiy'yungngwu. Sen

Masaw kachina dances may be staged as all day performances or as late evening appearances. In the majority of cases, however, these kachinas arrive only at night. If they then intend to come back during the following day, they retire to Katsinki, the regular kachina resting place.[1] But if they do not intend to come back, they return home to Pokki. Therefore when the kachinas arrive at night, the people closely note the direction of their departure, for

[1] In a Masaw kachina dance, witnessed by Titiev, the kachinas "approached from the northwest because that is the direction where the home of the dead (Maski) is located" (1944:236).

Figure 15. — Masawkatsina dance formation. Photograph by Emry Kopta, 1915. Courtesy of Museum of the American Indian, Heye Foundation.

qaavo ökininiqw pu', "Katsinki-miqwat ninma," kitotangwu. Noq pu' puma qavongvaqw ökye' pu' paasat puma tiivangwu.

Noq pu' paamuyve puma masaw-katsinam pay ephaqam piw mimuywatuy katsinmuy su'amun kivanawit yungiwmangwu. Pu' pay ephaqam piw haqaqwwat ima soyohimkatsinamyaqw pay pam piw suukyahaqam pumuy amu-mumningwu. Noq puma soyohim-katsinam pi pay nana'löngkt hiihinyungqam katsinamyangwu-niqw oovi ephaqam pam pay suukyahaqam pumuy amumum-ningwu.

that is a sure clue to whether they intend to perform again. When the people realize there will be a performance the following day they say, "They went home towards Katsinki, the kachina shrine."

Occasionally, the Masaw kachinas will also go around and dance in the kivas just like the other kachi-nas do during a night dance in Paamuya (approximately Janu-ary). Then again, one Masaw kachina may be part of a kiva group performing a mixed kachina dance. Because *soyohimkatsinam* constitute a variety of different kachinas, a Masaw kachina can also be included in the group.

Songoopave masawkatsinam qa
hisat taalö' tiiva. Puma pay
mihikqwsa, angktiwqatsa ang
tiivangwu. Puma maamastniiqe
oovi maasawuy an mihikqw yak-
tangwuniiqe oovi puma qa hisat
pep taalö' tiiva.

At the village of Songoopavi,
Masaw kachinas never dance
during the daytime. There, they
only perform during the night
dances which follow the Powamuy
ceremony. Because they symbolize
the dead, according to Soongopavi
belief, they go about in the night
just as Maasaw does, and therefore
never dance during the day.

A detailed description of this kachina's appearance is given in Text
146.[2]

TEXT 146

I' masawkatsina pay qa hisat hiita
nukngwat hinta. Pay pi i' himu
maasaw tuwat okiwqatuuqe pay qa
hisat hiita nukngwat yuwsiy'ta.
Noq oovi i' masawkatsina pay put
tututskyaynaqe oovi pay piw put
an saskwit an'ewakw yuwsiy'tangwu. Pay pi pam put aw maa-
tsiwqe oovi son put qa antani.
Niiqe pam pay oovi okiw hiita
nukusyuwsiy'tangwu. Qa hiita pam
hisat nukngwat yewasvakiwta. Noq
pam hisat it sowitvuput kwasay'tangwu. Pay pi hisat pi pam naat
a'ni yuykiwngwuniqw oovi hopiit
put piw tavupuy'yungngwu. Noq
pu' pi pay pam himu sulawniqw
oovi pu' pi pay puma masawkatsinam hiita pivitamnit kwa-

The Masaw kachina never wears
anything attractive. After all,
Maasaw too lives in poverty, and
therefore is never garbed in anything pleasing to the eye. Since
the Masaw kachina is modeled
after the god's appearance, he
also wears tattered and worn
clothing. Because the kachina is
named after Maasaw, he must
appear like the latter, and is for
this reason so shabbily dressed.
Never is he seen attired in a nice
garment. In the past the kachina
wore a rabbit skin blanket in the
form of a dress.[3] In the days when
many of these blankets were still
being woven, the Hopi also used
them as covers while sleeping.

[2]Illustrations of the Masaw kachina can be found in the works of Stephen (1936:
317), Fewkes (1903: plate XIV), and Wright (1973: 154-55). The latter also features a
masawkatsinmana, the female companion to *masawkatsina*.

[3]The traditional rabbit-fur garment is said to represent "melon vines" (Titiev
1972: 140).

Figure 16.—Masawkatsina mask. Courtesy Heard Museum, Phoenix, AZ.

say'yungngwu. Pu' puma pay
ii'imuy hiituy totokotstuy, puuvumuy hiituy puukyayamuy nami-
tu'iilalwakyangw pay put yuuyuw-
siya.

Panhaqam pam kwasay'kyangw
pu' pam put atsva pay hin'ewakw
hisatmötsapngönkwewat kwee-
way'kyangw pu' piw hisathopi-
kwewat kwewtangwu. Pu' ephaqam
pay saskwit, kwaaya'iwtaqat pu'
pay sen pösngungrivut yuwsiy'tangwu. Noq pam pi pay masaw-
katsinaningwuniiqe oovi tuwat
yukiqwat suyvoqwat mötsapngön-
kwewtangwu.

Today these blankets are no
longer made, so the Masaw kachinas dress in robes pieced together
from bobcat pelts and the skins of
other animals.

The dress is girded about the
waist with an old ceremonial sash
and an old Hopi belt. At times
the kachina's costume will be
dilapidated and moth-eaten; it
may even have been chewed on by
mice. And of course, since the
kachina personifies Maasaw, his
sash falls from the left side of his
waist rather than the right, which
is the norm.

Panhaqam pam okiw yuwsiy'-
kyangw pu' it pitkunat ustangwu.
Pu' pam piw sawkototsiy'kyangw
pu' put atsva tsamimiy'tangwu.
Pu' pay pam piw qa lomatots-
kyangw qa tawapaproy'takyangw
pay panis yöngösonat hokyaasom-
tangwu.

Pu' pam piw pay suukw aalat pi
tukwapngöntangwu. Suukw aalat
tonit aw wiwakiwtaqat tukwap-
ngöntangwu. Noq it masaw-
katsinat qötöyat ang hiihinyungqat
kukwanat akw pey'yungngwu. Pam
pay nana'löngöt kuwanat pongom-
vut akw pang soosovik tsokom'iwtangwu, sikyangput, paalangput,
sakwawsat akwa'. Niikyangw puma
pi pay pas tutskwangaqwniiqatsa
it hiihiita kukwanat angqw yukiw-
taqat akw pang tsokomnayangwu.
Niikyangw pam it nana'löngöt
poshumit tu'awiy'ta.

Pu' pam pi yaasakwhaqam poo-
siy'tangwu. Maasawuy an wuko-
pongo'voy'tangwu. Pongo'voy'-
kyangw pu' piw supongmo'ay'tangwu. Niikyangw put poosi'atniqw
pu' mo'a'at pay it silaqvut ngöla-
'iwtaqat angqw yukiwtangwu. Noq
pam ngöla'iwtaqa pay tonit akw
toonaniwkyangw pu' paalangput
akw lewiwtangwu. Pu' pam pay
panis paykomuy tamay'tangwu,
atkyaqw suukwnit pu' oongaqw

Costumed in such a poor outfit,
the kachina further has a kilt
draped about his shoulders. His
brown-dyed moccasins have
fringed anklets and are quite
unattractive overall. Instead of a
string of dance bells, normally
attached below the left knee, he
only wears a turtle shell rattle on
the right leg.

For a necklace the kachina wears
a single horn hanging from a piece
of twine.[4] His whole head is
decorated with blotches of yellow,
red and blue pigments. These
pigments are produced entirely
from materials derived from the
earth, and represent the many
kinds of seeds in existence.[5]

The kachina's eyes are large and
round, just as Maasaw's are. His
mouth is also circular. Both his
eyes and mouth are fashioned
from dried corn husks woven into
hoops. These hoops are entwined
with string and painted red. The
mouth has only three teeth, one
which juts up from the bottom,
and two which stick downward

---

[4] According to one of Titiev's informants, the sheep horn necklace "stands for string beans" (1972: 140). Fewkes' picture of the Masaw kachina shows the figure with two dangling rings on the chest which are said to be "part of a necklace made of human bones" (1903: 90).

[5] Voth claims that the colored splotches on the mask "represent clouds" (1912a: 1).

lööqmuy. Pu' put tama'at pay it patangsivosit angqw yukiwyung-ngwu.

Pu' pam masawkatsina it pahoqekit riikokniy'tangwu, yangqw qötöy aakwayngyangaqwniikyangw pu' piw kwaatsakwa'at pay qötöyat aakwayngyangaqw aw somiw-tangwu. Noq mimawat peetu katsinam pi ephaqam lööqmuy kwasrut qötöy aakwayngyangaqw riikokniy'yungngwu. Noq put riikokni'at pay panis i' paaho paayom naalöyömhaqam put qötöyat aakwayngyangaqw oomiq iitsiwyungngwu. Pu' put paahot siwit angqw yukiwtaqat ang i' pöösöniqw pu' pay homasa haayiw-yungngwuniiqe oovi pay pam paahot an soniwngwu.

from the top. These teeth are made from squash seeds.

At the back of the kachina's head are sticks which point up-ward. Prayer feathers are tied to these sticks at intervals, and just above the nape of the neck and behind these sticks, a bunch of black eagle feathers is attached. While some of the regular kachinas normally have two eagle tail feathers jutting up from the back of their heads, the Masaw kachina features only three or four of these sticks. The sticks, consisting of dunebroom branches to which are attached wing feathers and very fine down feathers, very much resemble prayer sticks.

My informants were not in agreement as to what exactly decorates the rear of Masaw kachina's mask. While in Text 146 the mask is sur-mounted by twigs of *siwi* to which *nakwakwusi* or "prayer feathers" are affixed, Text 147 identifies the feather-studded attachments as a special kind of *paaho* that features several feathers in a row. This *paaho* is manufactured during the Soyal ceremony and generally termed *soyal-hotomni.*

TEXT 147

It soyalangwuy ep hakimuy it paahot huytotangwuniqw put hakim hom'o'yangwuniqw, ima masawkatsinam pay put aqw yukuwise' put puma tuwat na-kway'yungngwu. Puma put kwaa-tsiy aakwayngyangaqw aw somtote' put puma tuwat riikokniy'yung-ngwu. Pankyaakyangw pu' puma put kwaatsakwat aw somiy'yung-ngwu.

In the course of the Soyal cere-mony prayer sticks are distributed among the people. After they have been deposited, to the accompani-ment of sacred cornmeal and prayers, the Masaw kachinas go to fetch them in order to decorate their heads with them. They tie the long paaho rods to the backs of their masks in such a way that they stick upward. Attached to the rods are clusters of medium-sized eagle feathers.

Figure 17   Figure 18

Dolls of the Masawkatsina. Photographs for Figures 17, 18, and 20 by
E. Malotki; Figure 18 courtesy of Museum of Northern Arizona. Photograph
for Figure 19 courtesy of Museum für Völkerkunde, Berlin.

Arms and legs of the Masaw kachina are said to have been painted
white with kaolin. This information is corroborated by Stephen, who
indicates that they were "whitened" (1936:317). Fewkes, on the other
hand, reports that they were colored "red and spotted black" (1903:90).

TEXT 148

I' masawkatsina pi pay qa pas hin
yuwsiy'tangwuniikyangw pu' pam
piw oovi pay qa haqe' pas sus-

The Masaw kachina is not elaborately costumed and also does not
expose a great portion of his

mataq tokoy maatakniy'tangwu. Noq pay katsina pantaqa pam pay it tuumatsa akw pas tsöqa'asiy'- tangwu. Pam pay pante' pam pay panis maqtöynit pu' hokyaysa pas ang putakw naalelwingwu.

body. A kachina dressed in such a fashion usually paints himself only with kaolin. He then only daubs his hands and legs white.

None of my consultants had any recollection what the kachina used to hold in his hands. Stephen depicts the kachina in his rendition holding *sivaapi* or "rabbit brush," Fewkes' artist shows his figure carrying "a yucca whip in each hand." Voth, on the other hand, remarks that in regular kachina dances this kachina is equipped with a rattle in his right

Figure 19

Figure 20

hand and a pine branch in his left hand; he carries "a whip in both" when appearing as a *kipokkatsina* (1912a:1). According to Titiev, in place of spruce each dancer "carried in the left hand a sprig of cottonwood *teeve*" (1944:236). Note that *teeve* is wrongly identified by Titiev. It actually means "greasewood."

As Titiev has already pointed out, and as is confirmed by my informants below, "the outward structure of the Masaw kachina performance is an exact duplicate of the Hemis kachina" (1972:116). What is somewhat surprising in this context, however, is that the Hopi describe the Masaw kachinas as "funny." Indeed, their comic behavior was based in part on burlesquing other kachinas or aspects of other ceremonies.[6]

TEXT 149

Pu' it masawkatsinat taawi'at pay songyawnen qa put pas naap himu'atningwu. Pam pay soosok-muy hiituy katsinmuy taawiyamuy namikwapvut akw tuwat wunima-ngwu. Ephaqam pam pay koman-tsiwuukukiy'tangwu, pu' pay ephaqam pam piw mosayurwuu-kukiy'tangwu. Niiqe puma oovi pay hiihin taawiy'yungngwuniiqe pay put aa'an tiivangwu. Puma pay hiituywatuy katsinmuy tutu-tskyaynaye' pu' pay pumuy amun tiivangwu. Pu' puma ephaqam pay kunatawiy'yungwe' puma pumuy hiituy amun tiivaqw pay sinom pumuy amumi tsutsuyngwu. Hin pam taawi'am wuukukiy'taqw pay himuwa pi naap hin wukukuy-kungwuniqw oovi amumi tsutsuy-ngwu. Pu' piw kunatawiy'yungqw pu' sinom piw taawiyamuy aw pay tsuytingwu.

Pu' pam pay piw naap hin töötö-

The chants of the Masaw kachina cannot be said to be really his own. If anything, he dances to songs whose various parts may be assembled from the songs of other kachinas. Sometimes he uses the dance steps of the Comanche kachina, while at other times he may even follow the beat of a Buffalo song. Consequently, the Masaw kachinas may draw on a variety of songs, and they dance accordingly. Whenever they mimic some other kachinas, they dance exactly like them. Occasionally, when they sing funny songs and dance like other kachinas, people laugh at them. One kachina may not stomp his foot according to the beat of the song, and spectators will laugh at this.

The call or cry of the kachina is never the same. It may be that of

---

[6]Titiev witnessed a Butterfly burlesque and pantomiming of certain features pertaining to the Maraw and Lakon ceremonies (1944:238).

kiy'tangwu. Pam pay naap hiitawat katsinat an töötöqngwu. Ephaqam pay it kooyemsit ani', pu' pay piw hootet sen angaktsinat piiwu. Noq i' suukyawa masawkatsintawi tuwat it hemiskatsinat taawiyat anhaqam qatsngway'takyangw yanhaqam hinta:

Tutukyawyamu, tutukyawyamu
Sa'a'atota'a.
Amunkiwakw taavangqw
Suvuyoyangw, umuyoyangw
Hoyoyota pew'i.
Tukyaakiva mumuna.
Uni, uni, imöyhoya nukushoya
Tukya'ikwiwva.
Uni, uni, askwal yokva.
Aa'a'ahaa ahay'aa.
Aa'a'ahaa ahay'aa.
Aa'a haa ii'iyhii.

Pu' puma pay piw mimuy peetuy katsinmuy amun manmuy'yung-ngwuniqw puma pay kokopöl-manatuy anhaqam yuwsiy'yung-ngwu. Puma pay kwikwilhoyat usyungkyangw pu' piw kanel-kwasay'yungngwu. Pu' puma pay piw qa totsyungngwu. Pu' puma pi pay pan hemiskatsinwuukukiy'-taqat taawiy'yungngwuniqw oovi puma mamant pi pay piw ruukun-totangwu. Rukunpiy ang pay

any kachina. Thus it can sound like the cry of the Kooyemsi, the Hoote, or perhaps the Long-hair kachina. The following Masaw kachina song resembles the pattern of the Hemis kachina song and goes something like this:

Little prairie dogs, little prairie
    dogs
Are yelping out.
Threatening them from the
    west
Fine drizzling rain, thundering
    rain
Is approaching.
Into the prairie dog holes streams
    of water are flowing.
How nice, how nice, my grandson,
    the homely rascal,
Has brought home some prairie
    dogs on his back.
How wonderful, how wonderful,
    All this thanks to the rain.
Aa'a'ahaa ahay'aa.
Aa'a'ahaa ahay'aa.
Aa'a'haa ii'iyhii.

Like some of the other kachinas, the Masaw kachinas also have female companions. They are dressed similar to the Kokopol kachina girls, in that they have a young boy's blanket draped around their shoulders and wear a woolen woman's dress. In addition, they walk barefoot. Since Masaw kachinas usually chant songs following the dance pattern of the Hemis kachinas, the females also make rasping sounds by scraping a sheep scapula along a notched stick placed over a hollowed-out gourd. This rasping is carried out

katsinmamantuy su'amun piw
ruukuntotangwu.

in exactly the same manner as by
the *katsinmamant,* the female
companions of the Hemis kachinas.

Figure 21.—Doll of the Masawkatsinmana. Photograph by E. Malotki.
Courtesy of the Museum of Northern Arizona.

A hallmark of the Masaw kachina dance, still vividly remembered by
many elderly Hopi, was the distribution of ancient Hopi foods. This
eccentric trait of the kachina formerly engendered a great deal of merri-
ment, especially when a spectator was forced to consume in public a
particular food loathsome to him. Titiev remarks that "many of the
foods handed out are so archaic as to bring a laugh, and the manner of

gift distribution is frequently funny. A favorite trick is to have a kachina offer presents and then snatch them back (a comic device that resembles the ritual feint)" (1972:116).

TEXT 150

Masawkatsina an'ewakw noovat, hisatnovat, tuwat na'mangwuy'vangwu. Puma masawkatsinmamant kya pi tuwat pay hisathopinovatsa tuwiy'yungqw oovi puma masawkatsinam put sinmuy amungem kivayangwu. Hintiqw pi puma tuwat put hopinovatsa kivayangwu. Puma pay qa hisat pahanhiita kivaya. Sen pi puma masawkatsinam sinmuy, tsaatsakwmuy put hisatnovat as tuwiy'vayaniqat oovi put kivayangwu, pu' piw hintaqat hisatnovat akw hisatsinom yesngwuniqw. Noq put pi ima tsaatsayom qa tuwiy'yungqe puma oovi puuvut hiita qa kwangway'yungwa.

Pu' puma pumuy sinmuy amungem pan hiita kivaye' pu' puma ephaqam kiisonve hakimuy amungem put tunösvongyaatotangwu. Paasat pu' puma pangso hiihiita o'yangwu, tumkwivit, öngatokkwivit, puuvut hiihinyungqat nevenkwivit. Pu' it sakwapviqavikit, hurusukit, somivikit, koletvikit, pu'

The food presents brought by the Masaw kachinas consist of the old Hopi dishes and are not very appetizing. One must assume that the females of these kachinas are only familiar with old recipes, so perhaps this is the reason why they bring only these foods for the people. No one really knows for sure. In any event, they never come with any products of the White man. A possible reason behind the Masaw kachina's custom may be that they intend to familiarize the people, and especially youngsters, with the old types of food. Perhaps also they would like them to know what sort of dishes the old Hopi had to sustain themselves with. But since the younger people are no longer familiar with these foods, they do not enjoy the taste of them.

When bringing these various food presents for the spectators, the kachinas sometimes spread them out in the plaza. The kachinas may come with all sorts of dishes, such as the boiled wild greens of *tumkwivi* (beeweed) and *öngatoki* (saltbush) plants, as well as any of the following: *sakwapviqaviki* (small pancake-like dish made from batter of blue corn meal), *hurusuki* (very thick mush of blue corn meal), *somiviki* (boiled blue

it mumurpikit, pövölpikit enang.
Pu' piw kuluputsit, kopektukit,
wupölangvikit, paatupsukit,
tu'tsipvatupsukit, tsiliktukit,
qa'ötu'tsiphoy'anit, haahalvikit,
siitangu'vikit, sipaltsakwput,
öngavat, tu'tsipkwivit, sipongvikit.
Ii'it puma soosok hiita hisatnovat
tuwat makiway'yungqe oovi put

corn meal wrapped in corn husk
and tied with a yucca strip near
each end), *koletviki* (large egg-
shaped dumplings made from
coarse-ground blue corn meal),
mumurpiki (small egg-shaped
dumplings made of corn meal),
pövölpiki (sweetened or un-
sweetened marble-sized dumplings
made from blue corn meal). Also
included can be: *kuluputsi* (gruel
of fine-ground sweet corn), *kopek-
tuki* (corn kernels baked in a hole
in the ground by mixing them
with hot embers), *wupölangviki*
(very thick piiki made in much the
same way as regular rolled piiki;
may have zig-zagged designs
scratched on it), *paatupsuki*
(mixture of boiled corn and
beans), *tu'tsipvatupsuki* (stored-
away roasted dry corn whose
kernels are crushed and then
boiled), *tsiliktuki* (fried chili),
qa'ötu'tsiphoy'ani (stored-away
roasted dry corn which is boiled),
haahalviki (flat salty cakes baked,
layer by layer, between hot flat
sheets of rocks in a small pit
oven), *siitangu'viki* (a tamale-like
dish of coarse white cornmeal
mixed with rabbit intestines),
sipaltsakwpu (dehydrated peaches)
öngava (boiled beans), *tu'tsipkwivi*
(stored-away roasted fresh corn
which is boiled), *sipongviki* (blue
corn meal batter of medium
consistency mixed with lard,
stuffed into a squash blossom and
cooked in the same fashion as
haahalviki). Any of these old food
items can be brought by the
Masaw kachinas for they have

kivayangwu. Puuvut puma kiisonve
enang tunösvongyaatotaqw pu'
sinom put pep nöönösangwu.

Pu' hak piw hiita qa kwangway'-
taqw puma put hakiy aw navotiy'yungwe' pu' puma put hakiy
engem kwusivayangwu. Pu' puma
masawkatsinam oovi pep tiitso'e'
pu' puma kwatsmuy hepye' pu'
hiitawat hepnumyaqey put tutwe'
pu' puma put pangso kiisonmi
hawnayangwu. Pu' himuwa hakiy
kwaatsiy'taqa hakiy pas kiisonmi
wiikye' pu' pep put aw maqana-
ngwu. Paasat pu' pam masawkatsina put aw maqaptsiy'tangwu.
Pu' pam angqw sowaniqat aw yan
maasantangwu, pam masaw-
katsina. Pu' pam okiw nawus pep
put angqw tuumoytangwu.

Pu' hak pi tsaynen pay hiita qa
kwangway'tangwuniqw oovi puma
piw put hakiy engem kwusivayangwu. Noq pu' hak okiw pep
kiisonve sinsonve put sowaninik aw
ö'qalngwu. Pu' pay himuwa hakiy
ookwatuwe' pam pay hakiy angqw
amum tuumoytaqw pam suusu-
law'iwmangwu. Pay ephaqam
hakiy so'at, yu'at pay hak naat
hiisaq angqw sowaqw, pu' pam
haqawa hakiy awnen pu' pay hakiy
hiita maqayaqw, pam pay put ayo'
kimakyangw pu' piw hakiy pangqw
kiisonngaqw ayo' wikngwu.

been charged with producing
them. Once the kachinas set out
these foods in the plaza, the
people eat them right then and
there.

When a person has a strong dislike
for a certain food and the Masaw
kachinas learn of this, they will
make it a point to bring it to him.
After completing their dance
performance, the kachinas look for
their "friends;" that is, the people
their food gifts are meant for.
Upon finding the right person,
they have him come into the
plaza. The kachina who has a
particular gift recipient in mind
will lead him personally into the
plaza, present the dish to him,
and then remain there, waiting.
Usually, the kachina indicates by
gesture that he wants the person to
eat. The poor victim then has no
choice but to consume the dish.

Children especially, always hate
certain foods; consequently
kachinas come with these very
foods for them. The abhorred
dishes then must be eaten right
there in the plaza, in the midst of
all the people. Seeing a child's
distress, spectators may offer to
share its food, and the dish then
usually quickly disappears. At
times a grandmother or mother
will come to the child's rescue
when the child has only sampled
the dish, and will lead the child
out of the plaza, taking the food
along.

Maasaw kachinas also distribute *tithu*, "dolls." Fashioned in the style of the *putsqatihu* or "flat doll" which, as a rule, is reserved for the little baby girl, the *masawkatsintihu*, in keeping with the shabby appearance of its makers, is sloppily made. Normally representing a finger-painted "self-portrait" of the *masawkatsinmana* or "Masaw kachina girl," it is usually given to females who have long outgrown infanthood. Wright's statement that "the Hopi see nothing incongruous in giving the infant an effigy of the Deity of Death" (1979:14) is, consequently, not quite in line with Hopi cultural reality. Even though, once again the Masaw kachina displays antithetical behavior by bestowing these crude gifts.

TEXT 151

Ima masawkatsinam pay piw imuy nimankatsinmuy su'amun tithut kivayangwuniqw pumuy tihu'am pay okiw an'e'wayningwu. Puma it pas wuuwuyaq puuvutsit tihut kivayangwu. Noq pam pay nu'an tuumat' akw lewiwtangwu. Niiqe pam oovi qa hiita pas lolmat kuwanat akw enang pey'tangwu. Pay panis it sikyangputnit pu' piw tövumsit akw pam enang lewiwtangwu. Pu' puma katsinam piw oovi pay malatsiy akw put ang peenayangwuniqw oovi pam wuuwukoq akw ang pey'yungngwu. Pam pay oovi piw qa tuhisvey'tangwu.

Noq pay pi pangqaqwangwuniqw pam masawkatsina pay qa tuhisaningwuniiqe oovi put pan nukusvenangwuniikyangw pu' piw an'ewakw tihutangwu. Noq mimawat katsinam son hisat panhaqam nukustihut hakiy engem kwusivayani, pumuy himu'am qa masawkatsinmuy himuyamuy an yuykiwqw oovi. Pumuywatuy himu'am lolmatsa kukwanat akw lewiwyungngwu. Noq i' masawkatsina pay qa hisat hiita nukngwat kwusiva.

The Masaw kachinas bring dolls as gifts just like the Niman kachinas do during the Home dance, but their dolls are unattractive, flat, and quite wide. They are simply whitewashed with white kaolin and as a rule are not decorated with any colorful designs. The only colors used on them are yellow and charcoal black. In addition, the kachinas paint these dolls using their fingers, which accounts for their large and sloppily executed markings.

There is a consensus that the Masaw kachina in not very artistically inclined, and for this reason paints in this crude manner and produces dolls which are repulsive. The other kachinas would never bring unsightly dolls. Their dolls are painted only with brilliant hues. The Masaw kachina, on the other hand, never comes with anything that is pleasing and neat.

Pu' puma masawkatsinam pi
pay piw oovi hakiy engem sivap-
tsokit angqw qöhiknaye' pu' pay
sivaapit aw put tihut somiwtaqat
hakiy maqayangwu. Pu' puma pay
put wuyaqtihut soosokmuy amungem kivayangwu. Pu' puma put
niitiy'vaye' puma put imuy momoy-
muy, mamantuy, mamanhoymuy
huylalwangwu. Pu' pam masawkatsintihu pay put masawkatsin-
manat an soniwqa yukiwtangwu. Pu'
ephaqam pay qa pamniniqw pam
pay i' sikyaqöqlöningwu.

In presenting the dolls, the Masaw
kachinas take a sprig of rabbit
brush to which the gift is attached.
Their oversized dolls are for everyone. When they bring lots of
them, they hand them out to
married women, adolescent
females, and small girls. Generally,
the dolls resemble the appearance
of the Masaw kachina girl. Once
in a while, however, where they
do not represent their own image,
they have the features of
the Sikyaqöqlö.

Figure 22   Figure 23

Flat dolls of the kind distributed by the Masawkatsina. Figure 22 represents a Masawkatsinmana, Figure 23 a Sikyaqöqlö. Photographs by E. Malotki.

Elaborately carved figurines of *masawkatsina* are often identified simply as "Maasaw," both in museum collections and in the literature.[7] Such labeling is erroneous, for a Masaw kachina is not an effigy of the god Maasaw. This can easily be tested when, as a collector of *tihu*, one asks for a "Maasaw doll." Hopi reaction to such a request is usually one of horror. The request for a "Masaw kachina doll," on the other hand, elicits no such horrified response. Any representation of the god, be it in the form of a sculptured effigy or a drawing, is strictly tabooed. As may be gathered from Text 152, breaking the taboo would result in dire consequences.

TEXT 152

Pay pi maasaw pas himuniqw oovi son as put tihulawu. Hak antsa yaw pante' qa wuuyavo qatungwuniqw oovi hak put qa yuykungwu. Pu' son piw put penta. Pam hin pi pitsangway'tangwu. Hak yaw pante' mokngwuniqw oovi i' maqastutavoniqw oovi qa hak hisat haqam put peena. Pay imasa kookopngyam put wu'yay pasmakiway ep peeniy'yungwa.

Because Maasaw is such a sacred being, one should not carve a doll in his likeness. The person who attempts to do so will not live long. Also, one does not draw images of the god. No one knows what his face looks like. If someone should draw him, he would meet his death. Because of this taboo, no one has ever made a sketch of him. Only the Kookop people have Maasaw, who is their clan ancestor, depicted at the plot of land assigned to them [on a boundary marker].

[7]Two old-time carvings of the Masaw kachina can be seen in *The Goldwater Kachina Doll Collection,* p. 13. See listing in Bibliography. See also Wright (1977: 30), where the doll is identified as "Maasaw, Earth God."

The Changing God

Although endowed with greater than human powers and believed
to be larger in size than any mortal man, Maasaw, in his early mani-
festation, had the makings of an anthropomorphic god. But in spite of
his human attributes he was both feared and venerated by the Hopi and
he remained a viable force in their daily lives. All that was to change
following the historic confrontation between the god and the soldiers at
Orayvi, in 1891 (see Texts 101 and 102). Mocked as a ragtag mummer,
whose ritualistic threats failed to cow the hostile opponent, Maasaw was
deeply humiliated before the eyes of his very believers. So disastrous
was this loss of face that, inevitably, "if Maasaw and the ways for which

247

he stands were to survive under these new circumstances, the nature of the god would have to undergo changes" (Tyler 1964:36).

From all indications, Maasaw has succeeded splendidly in making his transition from anthropomorphic to a "larger size" of divinity. Today, as Tyler rightly points out, "he is firmly set as an omniscient and omnipresent supreme god" (1964:4). Obviously, this transformation of the god's image did not take place overnight. Nor was Maasaw ever hopelessly locked into the projections and expectations of a Pueblo farmer mentality. Indeed, it is his very role as tutelary god of the land and its inhabitants which may, ultimately, have assisted him in transcending his indigenous *genius loci* scope and in achieving the stature of a "Great Spirit" with a near-monotheistic aura.

The Hopis' changing attitudes toward Maasaw are, of course, reflected in the linguistic conceptualizations now surrounding the god. One finds not much reference any more to his associations with death, fertility, and fire. Rather, he is called *i' itananiqa* "the one who is supposed to be our father," *i' qataymataqniiqa*, "the one who is invisible," or *i' himu qataymataq qatuuqa,* "this being that lives unseen." Occasionally, the notion of invisibility is still linked with the god's name, for example, *i' qataymataq maasaw,* "this invisible Maasaw."[1] In addition, there exists a host of other periphrastic locutions, all of which attempt to capture various divine aspects of the deity: *i' hikwsit himuy'taqa,* "the one who has the breath," *i' hak tuuwaqatsit himuy'taqa,* "this unknown one who owns the earth," *i' hak itamuy tumalay'maqa,* "this unknown one who goes along taking care of us," and *pam hak itamumi tunatyawtaqa,* "the one that devotes his attention to us."

Furthermore, Maasaw has been elevated to the role of "creator." This is evidenced not only from such circumlocutions as *i' hak itamuy it hikwsit maqaaqa,* "the unknown being who gave us breath," but also from explicit Hopi statements to this extent. Text 153 is a typical example of such a statement.

TEXT 153

Pam maasaw yep it tuuwaqatsit yukukyangw pu' hiita pi akw yuku.

Maasaw created this world, but it is not known what he made it with.

[1]Shorris suggests that "to answer the plague of Christian and Mormon missionaries, they [the Hopis] have developed two descriptions of a purely spiritual being: 'the one who walks unseen' and 'the man without blood'" (1971: 152). While the first circumlocution is frequently attested in Hopi, none of my consultants had ever heard of the second one. It would scarcely characterize the Maasaw with his old mask.

The descriptive references to Maasaw, listed above, are so much in vogue today that they seem to be preferred by the Hopi over the god's actual name. The reasons for this noticeable tendency to suppress the god's original name may lie in the nature of the physical appearance still deeply associated with him. To facilitate the change, from earth and death spirit to supreme being, the god's physical presence has to be minimized and the image of a terrifying monster has to be discarded. To quote Tyler again: "If an impersonator of the god sprinkles the enemies of the race and they disappear, well and good, but if that medicine fails of its power, as under the circumstances it must, the physical presence of the deity becomes more of a handicap than a bene-fit. On the other hand, the power of an abstract god can remain an incalculable force" (1964:36).

Maasaw's changing image is nowhere better demonstrated than in the *Hopi Hearings*, which were conducted in all of the Hopi villages from July 15 through July 30, 1955, by a team appointed by the then Com-missioner of Indian Affairs. Representing a fascinating cross-section of traditional and progressive attitudes, of old and new philosophy, the testimonials of the many witnesses clearly attest to Maasaw's newly evolving image and underline the changes the god has undergone. While a number of speakers still call the god Maasaw, others refer to him in the binomial formula of the "Great Spirit Maasaw" (1955:1). Many Hopis identify him consistently as "Great Spirit" (1955:44), others again use such terms as "Supreme Being" (1955:31), "Executive Su-preme Being" (1955:242), "the Unseen God" (1955:212), even "God Almighty" and "the Holy One" (1955:212). In addition, Maasaw is referred to as "Purifier" and "Savior."

To be sure, the transformation of Maasaw cannot be attributed merely to the god's compromising debacle before the hostile soldiers in Orayvi. Obviously, a whole complex of forces must be considered to have been influential in this process. The initial shock resulting from culture clash and the gradual acculturation to a technologically oriented world; the loss of Hopi political autonomy; internal strife caused by pro- and anti-white sentiments; the undermining of indigenous beliefs through missionary proselytizing, and forced secular schooling away from home, are but a few of the factors which may have brought about the need for change in the Hopis' perception of the god.

Other reasons for Maasaw's transformation are rooted in the god himself, particularly in the prophecies which have sprouted up all about him. It is within the scope of these latter-day predictions that Maasaw transcends the confines of an earth-bound god of sedentary farmers. The prophecies are intimately linked with the stone tablets that formerly were given to the Hopi, by the god, as a solid reminder of his *pötskwani* or "life plan" for them, prior to their migrations (see Chapter 3). The following passage constitutes an excerpt from a Third Mesa emergence myth in which Maasaw, during his face-to-face encounter with the Hopi at Orayvi, delineated what they would have to expect in the future.

TEXT 154

Paasat pu' yaw maasaw amumi pangqawu, "Ta'ay, uma hapi sulaktutskwave yesvay. Niikyangw uma hapi pas kyahaktutskwave yesvay. Uma hapi pas it tuuwaqatsit hot'öqayat su'ep yesva. It tutskwat aatöqe himu nunukngwa tangawta. A'ni hiikyay'yungqasa pang himu tangawtaqw uma hapi pay put haak qa ipwantotaniy," yaw amumi kita. "Naat hapi yep paayis naaqöyiw kwuupukni. Noq pam naaqöyiw naat kwuupukiwtaqw, umuy put ang ipwayaqw, put hapi angqw hiihiita tunipit pas öqalat yuykuyakyangw pu' putakw sinmuy qöyantotani. Naap uma yantote' pay hapi uma qa antotini. Ason hapi powatiniwqat yukiltiqat epeq pu' uma ang hiita ipwayaqw, pepeq pu' hapi sinom akw mongvasyani. Pam hapi qa hakiy niinantaniqey, qa naaqöyiwuy aw awiwaniikyangw pang pantay. Niikyangoy, kur yep haqam pam naaqöyiw hisat kwuupukniqw uma hapi qa umuutunipiy ömaatotani. Uma hapi qa hakiy niinantotani. Taq uma haqaqw pew nankwusaqe'ey, haqaqw uma pew naakwiipaqe'ey, uma hapi hopit tungwniy'kyaakyangw pew ökiy. Uma hapi hopiitniiqe oovi qa hakiy niinantotani. Kur oovi yep haqam pam naaqöyiw kwuupukniqw uma hapi qa nuutum awyani," yan yaw amumi lavayti.

Maasaw said to them, "All right, you've settled in a desert, yet the land is filled with riches. You reside on the very backbone of the earth. All kinds of precious things are buried in this earth. There exists a storehouse of treasures underground but you must not dig them up yet," he instructed. "Three times big war will rage. Should you excavate these treasures while the killing is still taking place, powerful weapons will be forged from them and people will be slain by them. If you act on your own in this matter, you will do wrong. Not before the day of purification has been completed, may you unearth these things. At that time people will benefit from them. For those precious things do not exist for the purpose of killing or wars. However, if those wars ever take place here, don't pick up your weapons, and don't engage in the business of killing. After all, from where you started forth to this site and from where you transplanted yourselves here, you came bearing the name Hopi. Because you are Hopis, you must not kill anyone. Thus, if ever a war arises, do not join in with the rest." This is how Maasaw spoke to them.

Paasat pu' yaw atsve piw amumi pangqawu, "Ta'ay, niikyangw yankyango, hisat hapi i' naat qöötsat tokoy'taqa pituni. Pu' hapi yang oova piw pöötiwni. Yan oova pöötiwqw pu' hapi ang naanahoy sinom sasqayani," yaw pam maasaw amumi kita. "Pu' kookyangwso'wuutit wishövi'at hapi ang aqwhaqami tuuwaqatsit ang laanatotini," kita yaw amumi. Pam hapi yaw kur it talwipqöhit, yu'a'atapit sivatni'at yang laanatiniqat pangqawu.

"Paasat pu' hapi yaw i' wunasivu ngölay'taqa pituni. Pu' hapi himu aw somiwtani, put lölökintani. Pam hapi yaw paasat put angk pituni," pu' yaw kita amumi. "Pep pu' paasat i' angk hapini, i' himu kawayo'eway qa aw somiwtaqa. Pam hapi paasat pu' pitukyangw pu' yang warikiwnumni. Qa himu aw somiwtaqw pam warikiwnumqw uma kyaataayungwni aw'i," yan yaw amumi lavayti. Pep pu' paasat piw amumi pangqawu, "Naat hapi yankyangw pu' yang aqwhaqami i' pöhu naato talqasaltotini, pu' tis tsölöloykuqw'ö. Hak haqaminen aqw taymaqw aqwhaqami talqaqsalmantani. Pantaqat ang hapi uma yaktani. Pu' hapi piw naat ang palqekiwni."

Paasat pu' piw amumi pangqawu, "Paasat pu' hapi naat ima tutuhist naat piw son hapi qa muuyawuy haqawat aw wupnayaniy. Paasat pu' it taawat piw son aw naat qa pootayani. Niikyangw son hapi pangso himu pituni. Aw haykyale'e pay sonqa taqtini.

Then he continued and said, "Eventually a people with a light-colored skin will arrive. Also, there will be roads in the sky, and on them people will be traveling back and forth. Old Spider Woman's webs will be strung all over the earth." This was a reference by Maasaw to the power lines and the telephone wires which would crisscross the land.

"Then a wooden box on wheels will arrive. Something will be hitched to it and tow it along. That will come after the wires," Maasaw explained. "Next something will come to which no horses are hitched. That contraption will move about with nothing tied to it, thereby causing people to look upon it with awe. Then, one day in the future, all the roads will glisten, especially after a rainfall. As far as a traveler can look ahead, he will see the road glisten. On roads like these you will journey. These roads will also be plastered."

Again Maasaw added, "Then these light-skinned people with great talents will probably send someone up to the moon. Next they will also experiment with the sun. But nothing will reach it, for anything which comes close will burn up.

Put pay son hak aw pituni. Nii-
kyango, pay mukiyat sonqa angqw
hiita pay piw sokoptotani. Paasat
pu' hapi pam pay qa an mukini.
Paasat pu' hapi i' tal'angw pam
tsaap'iwmani. Haqaapiy uma qa
mukiitotimantani. Naamahin
wuko'uyispuva uma qa mukiitotimantani. Naat uma nuvalalwa-
mantani, wuko'uyistiqw'ö. Paasat
pu' uma nawus malatstukpuy'kyaakyangw pu' uma qastupoqviy'kyaakyangw uma uylalwamantani. Hak
uyte' ep ayo' nuvat kwekwtsit'a,
aqw qölötat aqw uymantani. It
hapi aqw pituni put uma hang-
waatotaqw'ö.

Pu' yang i' aqwhaqami soosoy
himu tuuwaqatsit ang i' tuusaqa,
putakw yang ima hiihiitu popkot
piw tuwat timuy wungwintotaqw,
pam hapi qa an wungwmantani.
Aqwhaqami puma timuy amumum
kyaananvotiwisni, it tuusaqat qa
tsiyakqw'ö. Haktonsa yokvaman-
tani. Muki qa antaqw son himu
hapi an wungwmantani.

Pu' yankyangw haqaapiy pu' hapi
umuy uu'uyaqw'ö pam paasat pay
panis talaakuyvayani. Paasat pay
soosoy himu sumvamantani. Pu'
piw umuy uu'uyyaqw'ö paasat pu'
pay panis puma pivikyawyam
angqw hihin kuukuyvakyangw pay
summantani. Pu' piw umuy uu'uyyaqw'ö paayistiqat ep pay hiisavo
wungwyakyangw pu' pay sumni.
Pu' naalöstiqat epeq pay pam
panis kuukuyvakyangw pay soosoy
sumni. Yuk hapi pu' uma it tso-
ngyat aqw ökini." It hapi yaw piw
pumuy aa'awna.

No one will be able to reach the
sun. But its heat will most likely
be exploited. Then the sun won't
be as hot anymore, and the
summer season will grow shorter
and shorter. One day the weather
will no longer get warm. You will
experience snowfall at the height
of planting time. Then you will
have to sow wearing gloves and
long underwear. To sow, the
farmer will have to push aside the
snow, dig a hole, and then plant
his seeds. It will come to this if
you extract those precious things
from the earth.

And all the grasses across the
land, which many different animals
feed on to raise their young, will
not grow as before. In the future
the animals will suffer great hardships when these grasses do not
sprout. There will be no point in
having rain, for when the warmth
is gone, nothing will grow as it
used to.

Gradually your corn plants will
only produce tassels and then
everything will freeze. And when
you replant, only tiny, stunted
ears will appear, and then they too
will freeze. The third time you
sow, the stalks will still be short
before the frost strikes. By the
fourth time the plants will barely
have pierced the earth before
freezing. At that time you will
come to a time of famine." All
these predictions Maasaw made to
the Hopi.

The motifs touched upon in the text above are echoed in numerous references throughout the *Hopi Hearings* and other published sources based on input from Hopi traditionalists. The Hopis believe that there are three looming wars and that the third is linked to the time of purification and to the return of "the lost white brother." The latter is generally referred to in Hopi as *itaanuutayi*, "our awaited one," or *itaaqötsapava*, "our older brother of white complexion."[2] "The Hopi only knows of three great wars to take place. The third war will be the one to take place at purification time upon this land. Therefore, the Hopi, knowing all this, did not consent to any of these wars anywhere. He was especially warned, never to allow himself to go to foreign countries to make wars upon other people, because this is our home land. Here we must stay and take care of it. Because we are still waiting for someone—a brother of the Hopi— who will come to prove this land for us. So we will continue to follow instructions of Maasaw and waiting for the time of our brother to come to prove this land. We have our stone tablet...which was given by him when we first came here. Our brother will come and look for this stone tablet, when placed side by side, which will show whoever comes to this land to purify this land for us and will be recognized as our true brother" (*Hopi Hearings* 1955:25).

While in the above citation the returning "white brother" is expected to assume the role of the *powataniqa*, "the one who will purify,"[3] occasionally it is Maasaw himself who is said to fulfill this function.

[2]According to Waters, *pahaana* is the lost White brother. Erroneously linked to *pasu* "salt water" [correctly *paaso* "water's end/seashore; the notion "salt water" does not exist in Hopi], *pahaana* designates the "White man" with the exception of the Spaniard. Maasaw is said to have elaborated on the role of *pahaana* at the time when he explained the markings of the *owatutuveni* or "stone tablet" to the Hopi (see also Chapter 4, Text 42): "The time would come after the people had migrated to their permanent home, he (Maasaw) said, when they would be overcome by a strange people. They would be forced to develop their land and live according to the dictates of a new ruler or they would be treated as criminals and punished. But they were not to resist, warned Maasaw. They were to wait for the person who would deliver them. This person was their lost white brother, Pahaana (from *pasu*—Salt Water), who would come with the people of the rising sun from across the great salt water with the missing corner of the sacred tablet, deliver them from their persecutors, and establish a new and universal brotherhood of man" (1969: 160).

[3]"Now we are awaiting our brother.... It is he, who, when he comes upon our land, will purify this land" (*Hopi Hearings* 1955: 261).

TEXT 155

Pam hapi hak yep itamuy tumalay'taqa, antsa yep itamumi tunatyawtaqa, hinwat itamuy öwihiniw-
totiqw pu' pam hapi yep itamumi
puutsemokye' pu' itamuy hinwat
yukunani.

The one who takes care of us and
really looks after us here will,
somehow, destroy us if we make
some gross mistake and he gets
disenchanted with us.

Maasaw will accomplish the task of purification of wicked mankind
by unleashing his dreaded *qöötsaptanga* or "jar of ashes," his ultimate
weapon. Ever since Hiroshima and Nagasaki the Hopi have interpreted
Maasaw's *qöötsaptanga* to stand for the atomic bomb.

TEXT 156

Pu' ima wuuwuyom piw lavaytangwuniqw naat yaw i' naaqöyiw
paayis kwuupukni. Paasat pu' put
nuutungkniiqat ep pu' pas qatu-
vostini. Imuy naatuwqamuy
amungaqw i' tunipi a'ni maskya'iwtani. Putakw pu' puma
namihepni. Niikyangw ep pu' i'
hak it itamuy hikwsit maqaaqa
pam pu' tuwat it qöötsaptangay
tuuvani, pam hapi itamumi paas
yaavatiniqe oovi. Pu' put aqw
pituniqw ep pu' itam pas soosoyam
sulawtini. Son hak hakiy pö'iy'tani.
Pay itam pangso yukiltini. Naamahin pam suukya qöötsaptanga
itamumi tuuviwkyangw pam
itamuy soosokmuy qöyani.

The elders also used to talk of a
time when three wars will arise.
During the third, things will really
become chaotic. On each opposing
side a myriad of weapons will be
prepared with which the two sides
will test each other's strength. At
that time the being who gave us
breath will, in turn, hurl his
container of ashes upon us. He will
do this out of frustration with
mankind. When that event occurs,
we will all be destroyed. No one
side will overpower the other. At
that time we will be annihilated.
Even though only one jar of ashes
will be dropped, it will kill us all.

In addition to the predictions of wars, the Hopis have been warned
that "blood will flow. Our hair and our clothing will be scattered over
the earth. Nature will speak to us with its mighty breath of wind. There
will be earthquakes and floods causing great disasters, changes in the
seasons, and in the weather, disappearance of wildlife and famine in

different forms. There will be gradual corruption and cunfusion among the leaders and the people all over the world" (Katchongva 1975:13).

Similar dire warnings though less specific than hindsight and contemporary news media can provide, were already recorded by Wallis from a Songoopavi informant in 1912. They are attributed to Maasaw at the occasion of handing over to the Hopi the stone tablets with his inscribed instructions. "When this story is forgotten, something disastrous will happen. Perhaps the stars will fall down into the ocean, and the ocean will become oil. Then the sun will set fire to it, and the conflagration will consume everyone. Perhaps there will be an earthquake that will kill everyone" (1936:16-17).

Central to many of Maasaw's prophecies is the god's concern to leave the land undisturbed, especially the treasures underground. Mining the earth will result in terrible consequences, as may be gathered from the subsequent statement:

TEXT 157

Pu' kur yang it itamutpikyaqe himu tangawtaqat put ang ipwanvayaqw pu' put qö'angw'at ang yanmakyangw oomi höltini. Noq pam pay qa lolmani. Pantaqat itam hiikwistotani. Pu' pam put enang yokvakyangw pu' yang paanawit patuphava yeevayakyangw pu' pam put ang itsehe'tani. Pu' itam pantaqat hiihikwyani. Pu' akw itam tuutuylalwakyangw pu' pay itam so'iwmani.

Pu' yaw haqam wuuti nö'yiwtaqa pam yaw pantaqat itsehe't hiikwistamantani, pantaqat itsehe't yaw pam hiihikwmantni. Pu' yaw pam aasonveq tsayhoya pay qa lomahintimantani. Pu' sen yaw pay as pam yamaknikyangw pay kya yaw pam qa taykyangw yamakmantani. Pu' pay piw sen as yaw yamaknikyangw sen yaw sutsngaqwwat ngasta may'tani, sen

When people begin to unearth the treasures buried underground, dust from this operation will rise into the sky. That will be dangerous because we will inhale this dust. Mixed with the rain it will eventually fall into springs and lakes and contaminate them. We will be drinking polluted water then. Polluted water, in turn, will be the cause for illness and disease, from which death will result.

It is said that a pregnant woman who breathes of this foul air and drinks this impure water will develop a fetus which is malformed. The infant may be delivered, but it will be stillborn. Or the mother may give birth to the baby, but one of its arms or legs will be missing. Or other parts

yaw sutsngaqwwat ngasta hokyay'-
tani. Sen yaw tokoyat ep himu
sulawmantani. Ispi yaw itam
pantaqat itsehe't hiihikwyakyangw
pu' pantaqat itam yaw hiikwistotani. Yan it hapi enang tutaplalwangwu. Meh, it hapi aqw itam
oovi pu' naa'ökiniy'yungwa. Angqe'
hapi put ipwantotaqw pay aqw
angqe' sinom qa lomahinwisa.
Akw himuwa hinkyangw tiitiw-
ngwu. Akw pay pu' sinom tutuy-
kiva tangawta. Yantini hapi. Noq
oovi itam put hapi haak as qa
ipwantotani.

Yan hapi it tutaplalwangwu. I'
hapi pas put maasawuy tutavoyat
angqö, put pötskwaniyat angqö.
Noq oovi yan itam haqawat it
qataymataq qatuuqat, it maasawuy, angqw it tutavoyat naat
u'niy'yungwa. Naat itam peetu
put maasawuy tutavoyat hapi ang
hinwisa. It hapi itam qa haqam
alöngtota.

of its body may be lacking. All
of this will be the outcome of our
consuming tainted water and
breathing polluted air. All these
things are included in the teachings
of our elders. And look, we have
already maneuvered ourselves into
this state of affairs. In areas
where mining is going on, people
are contracting maladies. Children
are born sick and people fill up
the hospitals. This was bound to
happen for we were not yet supposed to mine the earth.

These are the elders' instructions.
They are derived directly from the
teachings and the life plan of
Maasaw. Here and there one of us
still remembers the words of
Maasaw, the god who lives unseen.
A few of us actually still follow his
directives. We have not strayed
from them.

Most frightening of all Hopi prophecies is Maasaw's expected use of
the *qöötsaptanga* or "jar of ashes." In addition to Text 156, the two
following statements underscore this deep-rooted and wide-spread belief
on the part of the Hopi.[4]

TEXT 158

Naat yaw itam it hakiy itamuy it
hikwsit tuuhuytaqat tutavoyat
angqw ayo' lasyakyangw pu' itam
it itaawimiy aw qa tunatyaltoti-

They say that if in the future we
deviate from the teachings given to
us by the one who gave us the
breath of life, and if we ignore our

---

[4] "A gourd of ashes would be dropped from a carriage in the sky that would destroy
everything within sight—all life and vegetation" (Brinkerhoff 1971: 71).

kyangw pu' itam it koyaanisqatsit
piw ahoy aqw ökiqw paasat pu'
yaw pam itananiqa it hiita qöötsaptangay itamumi tuuvaqw aw
pu' yaw itam soosoyam sulawtini.
Pu' pam put pan tuuvaqw ep hapi
yaw i' tutskwa soosoy uwikni. Pu'
i' paatuwaqatsi soosoy kwalalay-
kuni. Aw pu' pay i' qatsi so'tini.

religious beliefs, thereby bringing
ourselves to *koyaanisqatsi* or "a life
of turmoil," at that time our
father will cast down upon us a jar
of ashes as a result of which we
will all perish. Thereupon the
entire earth will go up in flames
and all the seas will boil.[5] At
that point life will cease to exist.

TEXT 159

Pay pi pam son it hakiy yep
tuuwaqatsit qa himuy'taqat tutavo'atniqw oovi itaawuwuyom
pangqaqwangwu, put akw hapi
yaw naat i' yep itaaqatsi so'tini kur
itamuy pas qa nanaptaqw, it
qöötsaptangat akwa'. Pam i' hak
itamuy it qatsit huytaqa pam yaw
put tuuvaqw, itam pangso paasavo
yesniqat pay ima wuuwuyom yan it
yu'a'atotangwu. Noq put ang i'
himu pas a'ni öqalasa tangawta-
niqw oovi son hak yaw yep akw-
singwni pam put tuuvaqw. Pu' i'
yep tuuwaqatsi hin yukiwtaqey pas
soosoy sakwitini.

Our elders maintain that, according to an instruction from the one
who owns this world, our existence
will cease by means of a jar of
ashes, if we are unable to control
ourselves. They also claim that he
who gave us life will throw this jar,
whereupon our lives will terminate.
Since the jar contains nothing
but extremely potent materials,
no one will survive when he tosses
it at us. And the shape of this
earth as we know it will be totally
destroyed.

The concept of Maasaw as a "purifier" really involves two separate
aspects. As a destroyer or punisher he will eradicate all evil in the world;
as a savior and redeemer he will lead those who stood by his teachings
into eternal life. With this apocalyptic prospect, which transpires from
Text 160, the god assumes the dimension of a Supreme Being or Great
Spirit.

---

[5] This prophetic warning is one of the three prophecies, chanted in Hopi, in Godfrey
Reggio's movie *Koyaanisqatsi.*

Noq ep yaw puma nankwusani-
niqw pam yaw talvew nakwsuniqey
pangqawu. Niikyangw pay yaw
naato ahoy pituniqey pangqawt
pu' yaw pam naatupkya.

Noq oovi wuuwuyom it yu'a'atota-
ngwuniiqe pangqaqwangwu yaw
put hisat ahoy pituqw, pepeq pu'
yaw it nuutungk talöngvaqat aw
pituni. Noq pay yaw son hak put
hisatniqat pas suyan navotiy'tani.
Noq oovi ima itaakwam, itanam
pangqaqwangwu, "Sen itaatimuy
qatsiyamuy epni, sen umuutimuy
timuyatuy qatsiyamuy epni. Hakiy
pi yaw qatsiyat ep pam hakiy
itanay tiingaviyat, tokilayat aw
pituni. Pepeq yaw itam as powa-
tiwni, nuutungk talöngvaqat epeq.
Niikyangw son yaw hak suyan
hisatniqat put navotiy'tani. Pas
pamsa naala put navotiy'ta. Yan it
puma wuuwuyom yu'a'atotangwu.
Niiqe puma oovi it soosok hiita
ang itamuy u'nantoyniy'wisa. Pu'
pay antsa pi sonqa panta. Niiqe
oovi itam soosoyam yaw haqami
tokilay'kyaakyangw yep itaaqatsiy
kwilalatota. Itam yaw put maasawuy tutavoyat u'niy'yungwni. Pu'
yaw itam put tutavoyatnit pu' piw
put pötskwaniyat angye' pu' yaw
itam paapiy put hakiy amum
sutsepyesni. Ep nuutungk talöngvaqat ep pu' yaw pam hakiy aw
hin navotiy'te' pu' pangqawman-

At the time the Hopi were about
to embark on their migration,
Maasaw stated that he would
journey towards the rising sun.
After making this statement, he
removed himself from their sight,
but not before promising that he
would return someday in the
future.

When the elders talk about this
promise by Maasaw, they claim
that his return would mark the last
day of this world. Of course, no
one knows for certain when that
day will be. Therefore, our grand-
fathers and fathers say, "Maybe
it will happen during the lives of
our children, maybe in the genera-
tion of your children." During
whose lifetime this date or dead-
line set by our father Maasaw will
occur, is simply not known. On
that last day we are to be purified.
But no one can say with certainty
when this purification will take
place. Maasaw alone knows the
exact date. This is what the elders
foretell. For this reason they constantly remind us of all these
things. They are most probably
true. Hence, each and everyone of
us has an appointed time at which
he is to meet his fate. Therefore,
we are to remember Maasaw's
words. If we follow his instructions
and the plan of life which he laid
out for us, we will dwell with him
from that last day on forever. On
that day he will reveal how he
appraises a person. He may either

tani. Sen hakiy engem lavaytimantani, sen hakiy nukpanayat suu-
putsnamantani. Pu' pay yaw
himuwa hakiy aw hiita lomahintaqat navotiy'te' pu' yaw pam
hakiy engem lavaytimantani. "Ura
nuy suushaqam put kiiyataqwniqw
pam nuy paas tavit pu' piw nuy
paas nopna." Pu' sen haqawa piw
pangqawmantani, "Ura nu' paa-
naqmokiwnumqe put aw kuytuving-
taqw pam nuy angqw kuynaqw
nu' hiiko." Naamahin yaw i' himu
yaasayhoya pepeq pas himuniwti-
niqw oovi yaw hak sinot paasni-
ngwu. Paasat pu' hak hinwat hak
makiway'taqw pam aw aniwtiman-
tani. Kur yaw hak qa hiita akw
hovariwkyangw pangsoq pituqw
paasat pu' yaw hak pay qeniva-
mantani. Pu' itam pepeq nahoy'oyiltini. Nuunukpant sutsvo-
watyaqw pu' pay pumuy amungem
i' qa lomahintaqa pi paas pasiw-
taqw, puma pay oovi pangso
yukiltotini. Niiqe itam naavaasyani
asa'. Naavaasye' itam soosoyam
sinom it tutskwat ang mongvasye'
pay itam hiita akw nayesniy'yungwni.

Noq oovi pay as pam naat sonqa
qatukyangw pay naat itamumi
maqaptsiy'ta. Ason itam yanwis-
kyaakyangw haqami pas paapu
hisat qatsit, pötskwanit, wiimit,
puuvut hiita aw qa tunatyaltotiqw
pangsoq hapi i' qatsi yukiltini.

speak up in his behalf or simply
divulge his evil side. Other people
who are familiar with a person's
good deeds can then also speak up
for that person. "I recall that once
when I went to his home
he welcomed me and fed me."
Someone else might say, "I remember when I was thirsty and
asked this person for water, he
gave it to me, and I was able to
drink." Even such insignificant
acts will become quite important
at that time, hence one should
always be kind to people. Whatever fate is in store for a person
will become a reality on that day.
If one's character is not blemished
in any way upon reaching that
day, one will be in the clear. Then
we will be segregated there. Those
who are evil will be placed to one
side, and in accordance with the
punishment devised for them, they
will be done away with. We should
therefore care for one another. If
we treat one another with kind-
ness, all of us will reap the benefits
from this land and be able to
sustain ourselves.

Maasaw probably still exists and is
just waiting for us. If at one
point as we progress through time,
we disregard all respect for life,
the instructions according to which
we are to live, the religious beliefs,
and things of this nature, then life
will truly come to an end.

In light of the above, Maasaw has indeed become the beginning and end of Hopi life. He even says of himself, before leaving the Hopi to their migrations across the land:

TEXT 161

Pay pi as nu' mootiy'makyangw   I'm the first but I'm also going to
pay nu' piw naat nuutungktato.   be the last.

While Maasaw's image, due to the influence of new Hopi traditionalists, has definitely changed in the direction of a supreme deity, there are also forces at work in Hopi society that are trying to undermine the god's continual rise. Outspoken among these counterforces are Hopi Baptists who connect Maasaw with the Christian "devil." Statements to this effect are found in the *Hopi Hearings*: "We have learned from the Bible this Maasaw is Lucifer, Satan, or the Devil... He has deceived the first two human beings which God had created in his own image from the dust of the earth....Maasaw, Devil, had evil mind being in the presence of god in heaven so he was thrown out from heaven down to earth. There he came to Adam and Eve in form of a snake to tempt them to eat of a tree of knowledge....Maasaw, Devil, is the deceiver of the world, yet some Hopis choose to follow his life plan. He will not have eternal life for his followers, but will lead them straight to everlasting fire, burning with brimstone, where his followers will suffer for ever and ever" (1955: 267-8).

Passages of this kind are rather ephemeral, however, and are unlikely to seriously check Maasaw's rise. While testimonials of this sort seem extraneous to the Hopi mainstream of religious thought they, nevertheless, reveal the fact that Maasaw has been "shaping up" in competition with Judeo-Christian monotheism.

While the above quotes were recorded some thirty years ago, the subsequent prayer to Maasaw with which I want to end this book, was published in the traditional Hopi newsletter *Techqua Ikachi*.[6]

---

[6]The full title of the newsletter is *"Techqua Ikachi*: Land and Life—the Traditional Viewpoint from the Hopi Nation." No. 25. No date. Its editor considers it a voice from "the traditional village of Hotevilla in the Hopi Independent Nation."

PRAYER TO MAASAW THE GREAT SPIRIT

Here I am asking you
You who own the world
There are two of you.
It is you with the simple way of life
Which is everlasting
That we follow.
You have the whole universe.
We do not follow the materialistic god.
We ask you, with your strength,
To speak through us.
With the prayers of all the people here
We shall reclaim the land for you.

Bibliography

Beaglehole, Ernest, and Pearl Beaglehole
    1935   "Hopi of the Second Mesa." *American Anthropological Association, Memoirs* 44: 5-65.

Beaglehole, Ernest
    1936   "Hopi Hunting and Hunting Ritual." *Yale University Publications in Anthropology* 4: 3-26.
    1937   "Notes on Hopi Economic Life." *Yale University Publications in Anthropology* 15: 1-88.

Bradfield, Richard Maitland
    1973   *A Natural History of Associations: A Study in the Meaning of Community*. London, Duckworth.
    1974   "Birds of the Hopi Region, Their Hopi Names, and Notes on Their Ecology." *Museum of Northern Arizona Bulletin* 48.

Brinkerhoff, Zula C.
    1971   *God's Chosen People of America*. Salt Lake City, Publishers Press.

Carr, Pat
    1979   *Mimbres Mythology*. Southwestern Studies, Monograph no. 56. University of Texas, El Paso, Texas Western Press.

Courlander, Harold
  1972   *The Fourth World of the Hopis.* Greenwich, Conn., Fawcett
         Publications.
  1982   *Hopi Voices.* Albuquerque, University of New Mexico Press.

Crane, Leo
  1926   *Indians of the Enchanted Desert.* 2nd ed. Boston: Little,
         Brown, and Co.

Curtis, Edward S.
  1922   *The Hopi.* Vol. 12 of *The North American Indian.* New
         York and London: Johnson Reprint Corporation, 1970.

Cushing, Frank Hamilton
  1923   "Origin Myth from Oraibi." *Journal of American Folk-Lore*
         36: 163-170.

Fewkes, Jesse Walter
  1895   "The Tusayan New Fire Ceremony." *Boston Society of
         Natural History, Proceedings* 26: 422-58.
  1900   "The New-Fire Ceremony at Walpi." *American Anthro-
         pologist* 2: 80-138.
  1902a "Sky-God Personations in Hopi Worship." *Journal of Ameri-
         can Folk-Lore* 15: 14-32.
  1902b "Minor Hopi Festivals." *American Anthropologist* 4: 482-511.
  1903   "Hopi Katcinas Drawn by Native Artists." *Bureau of Amer-
         ican Ethnology, Annual Report* 21: 3-126.
  1917   "A Religious Ceremony of the Hopi Indians. An Initiation
         at Hano in Hopiland, Arizona." *Scientific American* 83:
         226-7.
  1920   "Fire Worship of the Hopi Indians." *Smithsonian Institution,
         Annual Report* 1920: 589-610.

Fewkes, Jesse Walter, and Alexander Stephen
  1892   "The Na-ac-nai-ya. A Tusayan Initiation Ceremony." *Journal
         of American Folk-Lore* 5: 189-221.

Forde, C. Daryll
  1931   "Hopi Agriculture and Land Ownership." *Journal of the
         Royal Anthropological Institute* 61: 357-405.

Hopi Hearings, July 15-30, 1955. Keams Canyon, Arizona, U.S. Depart-
1955   ment of the Interior, Bureau of Indian Affairs, Phoenix Area
       Office, Hopi Agency.

Geertz, Armin W.
1984   "A Reed Pierced the Sky: Hopi Indian Cosmography on
       Third Mesa, Arizona." *Numen* 31: 216-41.

The Goldwater Kachina Doll Collection. Tempe, Az.: Arizona Histor-
1969   ical Foundation.

Hargrave, Lyndon Lane
1930   "Shungopovi." *Museum Notes, Museum of Northern Arizona*
       2: 1-4.

Hartmann, Horst
1976   "Wesensart und Bild des Hopi-Gottes Sootukwnangwu."
       Baessler-Archiv, new series 24: 333-63.
1978   *Kachina-Figuren der Hopi-Indianer.* Berlin, Museum für
       Völkerkunde.

Hermequaftewa, Andrew
1954   "The Hopi Way of Life Is the Way of Peace." No place.
       No publisher.

James, Harry Clebourne
1974   *Pages from Hopi History.* Tucson, University of Arizona
       Press.

Katchongva, Dan
1975   *Hopi. A Message for All People.* Ithaca, New York, Glad
       Day Press, 2nd printing.

Lowie, Robert H.
1929   "Notes on Hopi Clans." *American Museum of Natural
       History, Anthropological Papers* 30, pt. 6: 303-360.

Malotki, Ekkehart
1978   *Hopitutuwutsi. Hopi Tales.* Flagstaff, Museum of Northern
       Arizona Press.
1983   *Hopi Time. A Linguistic Analysis of the Temporal Concepts
       in the Hopi Language.* Trends in Linguistics. Studies and
       Monographs, vol. 20. Edited by Werner Winter. Berlin, New
       York, Amsterdam: Mouton Publishers.

Miller, Wick R.
   1967   "Uto-Aztecan Cognate Sets." *University of California Publications in Linguistics* 48: 1-83.

Mindeleff, Cosmos
   1887   "Traditional History of Tusayan." In "A Study of Pueblo Architecture: Tusayan and Cibola" by Victor Mindeleff. *Bureau of Ethnology, Annual Report* 8 (1886-7): 3-228.

Nequatewa, Edmund
   1936   "Truth of a Hopi: Stories Relating to the Origin, Myths and Clan Histories of the Hopi." *Museum of Northern Arizona Bulletin* 8. Reprint. Flagstaff: Northland Press, 1973.
   1946   "How the Hopi Respect the Game Animals." *Plateau* 18: 61-2.

Parsons, Elsie Clews
   1922   "Oraibi in 1920." In "Contributions to Hopi History" by J.W. Fewkes. *American Anthropologist* (1922): 253-98.
   1923   "The Hopi Wöwöchim Ceremony in 1920." *American Anthropologist* 25: 156-87.
   1926   *Tewa Tales.* New York, American Folk-Lore Society.
   1939   *Pueblo Indian Religion.* Chicago, University of Chicago Press.

Powell, John Wesley
   1972   *The Hopi Villages: The Ancient Province of Tusayan.* Palmer Lake, Colorado: Filter Press.

Shorris, Earl
   1971   *The Death of the Great Spirit: An Elegy for the American Indian.* New York: Simon and Schuster.

Simpson, Ruth DeEtte
   1953   *The Hopi Indians.* Los Angeles, Southwest Museum.

Stephen, Alexander M.
   1929   "Hopi Tales." Edited by Elsie Clews Parsons. *Journal of American Folk-Lore* 42: 1-72.
   1936   "Hopi Journal." Edited by Elsie Clews Parsons. *Columbia University Contributions to Anthropology* 23 (2 vols.).

1939 "Hopi Indians of Arizona." *Masterkey* 13: 197-204.
1940 "Hopi Indians of Arizona-III." *Masterkey* 14: 102-09.

Talayesva, Don C.
1942 *Sun Chief: The Autobiography of a Hopi Indian.* Edited by Leo. W. Simmons. New Haven, Yale University Press.

Titiev, Mischa
1937 "A Hopi Salt Expedition." *American Anthropologist* 39: 244-58.
1939 "Hopi Racing Customs at Oraibi, Arizona." *Papers of the Michigan Academy of Science, Arts, and Letters* 24: 33-43.
1944 "Old Oraibi. A Study of the Hopi Indians of Third Mesa." *Papers of the Peabody Museum of American Archaeology and Ethnology* 22 (1).

Tyler, Hamilton A.
1964 *Pueblo Gods and Myths.* Norman, University of Oklahoma Press.

Voth, Henry R.
1905a "The Traditions of the Hopi." *Field Columbian Museum Publications* 96. Chicago.
1905b "Hopi Proper Names." *Field Columbian Museum Publications* 100: 65-113.
1912a *The Henry R. Voth Hopi Indian Collection at Grand Canyon.* Prepared for the Fred Harvey Company, 40 pages. Reprint. Phoenix: Arequipa Press, 1967.
1912b "The Oraibi New Year Ceremony." In "Brief Miscellaneous Hopi Papers." *Field Columbian Museum Publications* 157: 89-149.
no date "Hopi Vocabulary." Manuscript no. 203-3. Museum of Northern Arizona Library. Typed version by Robert P. Sies. Museum of Northern Arizona Library, Manuscript no. 149-3,

Wade, Edwin L., and Lea S. McChesney
1980 *America's Great Lost Expedition: The Thomas Keam Collection of Hopi Pottery from the Second Hemenway Expedition, 1890-1894.* Phoenix, The Heard Museum.

Wallis, W.D.
1936 "Folk Tales from Shumopavi, Second Mesa." *Journal of American Folk-Lore* 49: 1-68.

Waters, Frank
    1963   *Book of the Hopi*. New York, The Viking Press.
    1969   *Pumpkin Seed Point*. Chicago, Sage Books.

Whiting, Alfred
    1939   "Ethnobotany of the Hopi." *Museum of Northern Arizona Bulletin* 15. Reprint. Flagstaff: Northland Press, 1966.

Wright, Barton
    1973   *Kachinas: A Hopi Artist's Documentary*. Flagstaff, Northland Press.
    1977   *The Complete Guide to Collecting Kachina Dolls*. Flagstaff, Northland Press.
    1979   *Hopi Material Culture: Artifacts Gathered by H.R. Voth in the Fred Harvey Collection*. Flagstaff: Northland Press and The Heard Museum.

Yava, Albert
    1978   *Big Falling Snow: A Tewa-Hopi Indian's Life and Times and the History and Traditions of his People*. Edited by Harold Courlander. New York, Crown Publishers.

THE HOPI ALPHABET

Ekkehart Malotki

Hopi, an American Indian language spoken in northeastern Arizona, is a branch of the large Uto-Aztecan family of languages, which covers vast portions of the western United States and Mexico. It is related to such languages as Papago, Paiute, Shoshone, Tarahumara, Yaqui, and Nahuatl, the language of the Aztecs, to mention only a few. Navajo, Apache, Havasupai, Zuni, Tewa, and many other languages in the American Southwest are completely unrelated to it, however. At least three regional Hopi dialects, whose differences in terms of pronunciation, grammar, and vocabulary are relatively minimal, can be distinguished. No prestige dialect exists.

While traditionally the Hopi, like most Amerindian groups, never developed a writing system of their own, there today exists a standardized —yet unofficial—orthography for the Hopi language. Langacker has presented a "simple and linguistically sound writing system" (Milo Kalectaca, *Lessons in Hopi,* edited by Ronald W. Langacker, Tucson,

1978) for the Second Mesa dialect of Shungopavi (Songoopavi). My own generalized Hopi orthography is equally phonemic in nature and is based on the dialect habits of speakers from the Third Mesa communities of Hotevilla (Hotvela), Bakabi (Paaqavi), Oraibi (Orayvi), Kykotsmovi (Kiqötsmovi), and Moenkopi (Munqapi), who comprise the majority of Hopis. Speakers from the First Mesa villages of Walpi and Sichomovi (Sitsom'ovi) as well as from the communities of Shungopavi (Songoopavi), Mishongnovi (Musangnuvi), and Shipaulovi (Supawlavi) simply need to impose their idiosyncratic pronunciation on the written "image" of the preponderant dialect, much as a member of the Brooklyn speech community applies his brand of pronunciation to such words as "bird" or "work."

Hopi standardized orthography is thus truly pan-Hopi; it is characterized by a close fit between phonemically functional sound and corresponding symbol. Unusual graphemes are avoided. For example, the digraph *ng* stands for the same phoneme that *ng* represents in English si*ng*. Symbols like *ṅ*, as the translator of the New Testament into Hopi elected to do, or *ŋ*, which is suggested in the symbol inventory of the International Phonetic Alphabet, are not employed. In all, twenty-one letters are sufficient to write Hopi, of which only the umlauted *ö* is not part of the English alphabet. For the glottal stop, one of the Hopi consonants, the apostrophe is used.

Hopi distinguishes the six vowels *a, e, i, o, ö,* and *u*, the last of which represents the international phonetic symbol *ɨ*. Their long counterparts are written by doubling the letter for the corresponding short vowel: *aa, ee, ii, oo, öö,* and *uu*. The short vowels are found in combination with both the *y*- and *w*-glide to form the following diphthongs: *ay, ey, iy, oy, öy, uy* and *aw, ew, iw, öw, uw*. Only the diphthong *ow* does not occur. The inventory of consonants contains a number of sounds which have to be represented as digraphs of trigraphs (two or three letter combinations): *p, t, ky, k, kw, q, qw, ', m, n, ngy, ng, ngw, ts, v, r, s, l*. The two semi-vowels are the glides *w* and *y*. Notably absent are the sounds b, d, and g, to mention only one prominent difference between the Hopi and English sound inventories. Because Hopi *p, t,* and *k* are pronounced without aspiration, speakers of English tend to hear them as *b, d,* and *g*. This accounts for many wrong spellings of Hopi words in the past.

The following table lists all the functional Hopi sounds, with the exception of those characterized by a falling tone — a phonetic feature not shared by First and Second Mesa speakers. Each phoneme is illustrated by a Hopi example and accompanied by phonetic approximations drawn from various Indo-European languages.

PHONEME	SAMPLE WORD		SOUND APPROXIMATIONS

1. Vowels:

    (a) short vowels

a	pas	very	E cut F patte
e	pep	there	E met F herbe
i	siihu	flower	E hit G mit
o	momi	forward	F col G soll
ö	qötö	head	F neuf G Löffel
u	tuwa	he found it/saw it	R BbiTb E just (when unstressed)

    (b) long vowels

aa	paas	carefully/completely	F pâte G Staat
ee	peep	almost	F être G Mähne
ii	siihu	intestines	F rire G wie
oo	moomi	he is pigeon-toed	F rose G Boot
öö	qöötö	suds	F feu G Töne
uu	tuuwa	sand	G Bühne (but lips spread without producing an [i] sound)

2. Diphthongs:

    (a) with y-glide

ay	tsay	small/young	E fly G Kleider
ey	eykita	he groans	E may
iy	yaapiy	from here on	E flea
oy	ahoy	back to	E toy G heute
öy	höykita	he growls	F oeil
uy	uyto	he goes planting	G pfui (but with lips spread instead of rounded)

    (b) with w-glide

aw	awta	bow	E fowl G Maus
ew	pew	here (to me)	E met + E wet
iw	piw	again	E hit + E wet
ow	nonexisting		
öw	ngölöwta	it is crooked	G Löffel + E wet
uw	puwmoki	he got sleepy	R BbiTb + E wet

3. Consonants:

  (a) stops

p	*p*aahu	water/spring	F *p*ain
t	*t*upko	younger brother	F *t*able
ky	*k*yaaro	parrot	E *c*ure
k	*k*oho	wood/stick	F *c*ar
kw	*kw*ala	it boiled	E *qu*it
q	*q*ööha	he built a fire	G *K*raut (but *k* articulated further back in mouth)
qw	yang*qw*	from here	E *w*et, added to pronunciation of *q*
	pu'	now/today	G Ver'ein

  (b) nasals

m	*m*alatsi	finger	E *m*e
n	*n*aama	both/together	E *n*ut
ngy	yu*ng*ya	they entered	E ki*ng* + E *y*es E si*ng*ular (casually pronounced)
ng	*ng*öla	wheel	E ki*ng* G fa*ng*en
ngw	kookya*ngw*	spider	E ki*ng* + E *w*et E pe*ng*uin (casually pronounced)

  (c) affricate

ts	*ts*uku	point/clown	E hi*ts* G Zunge

  (d) fricatives

v	*v*otoona	coin/button	E *v*eal G *W*inter
r	*r*oya	it turned	syllable initial position: E lei*s*ure (with tongue tip curled toward palate)
r	hin'u*r*	very (female speaking)	syllable final position: E *sh*ip F *ch*arme
s	*s*akuna	squirrel	E *s*ong
h	*h*o'apu	carrying basket	E *h*elp

  (e) lateral

l	*l*aho	bucket	E *l*ot

4. Glides:

  (a) preceding a vowel

w	*w*aala	gap/notch	E *w*et, ho*w*
y	*y*uutu	they ran	E *y*es, ha*y*

  (b) succeeding a vowel
    see diphthongs